RELIGION

An Anthropological View

RELIGION

An Anthropological View

by

ANTHONY F. C. WALLACE

UNIVERSITY OF PENNSYLVANIA AND
EASTERN PENNSYLVANIA PSYCHIATRIC INSTITUTE

NEW YORK

2 4 6 8 B 9 7 5 3

 Published in New York by Random House, Inc. and in Toronto, Canada, by Random House of Canada Limited
Library of Congress Catalog Card Number: 66-15811
Manufactured in the United States of America

DESIGN BY *Jaime Davidovich*

Preface

LIKE MOST HUMAN BEINGS, I was raised in a religious household. In the small college town where I grew up, there were a number of churches: the college church, supported by a small Protestant denomination where, more or less regularly, and more or less reluctantly, I attended Sunday School and Sunday Services until early in my teens; a Lutheran church, across the street from the college church; a Church of the Brethren, near our house, attended by "plain people" of Pennsylvania Dutch heritage; a Catholic chapel; a Holy Roller meeting place of some Baptist or Fundamentalist persuasion; and no doubt others that I do not now recall. Among my parents' kinfolk were at least three men of the cloth; my relatives by marriage include both Catholics and Jehovah's Witnesses.

Many of the townspeople still believed in magic and witchcraft, and one of my early memories is of interviewing my schoolmates in the primary grades about witchcraft. My father was collecting Pennsylvania Dutch folklore and I served as a sort of field worker and interviewer, collecting tales for him about such local events as the alleged wounding of a woman on Main Street by a silver bullet (she became lame and bedridden the day after a farmer shot at a black cat in his garden). This happened when I was about nine years old. And there was at least one "pow-wow doctor" who lived in the hills above the town and for a small fee removed the warts of college students and farmers alike by prayer and the prescription of amulets.

When I was in my teens, I visited the Iroquois reservation at

Grand River in Ontario with my father, who was interested in the leaders of the Handsome Lake religion and in the League of the Iroquois. That experience, together with early studies of Teedyuscung, an eighteenth-century Delaware Indian convert to the Moravian faith, led me to the study of the Handsome Lake religion, from which my more general interests grew. Thus, although my associations for many years have been principally with people who have lost whatever allegiance they may have had to the traditional religious institutions of their own society, and although my own confidence has been given to science rather than to religion, I retain a sympathetic respect and even admiration for religious people and religious behavior.

Thus this book is not, I think, motivated by a need to destroy, by dissection, a way of thinking and acting that many educated people feel is of little use, or is even disadvantageous, in a world increasingly committed to the search for scientific and technological solutions of human problems. Rather, I aim to preserve a friendly detachment in the asking of fundamental scientific questions about religion.

In the accomplishment of this task, I believe that it is necessary to bring together under the rubric of religion both primitive and civilized faiths, both supernatural superstition and human wisdom, both the magical and the spiritual. In so recognizing certain common features, I do not demean the differences between present-day liberal theologies and ancient cults. But my point of view is naturalistic. Religion is a fact in nature and, to be understood, must be seen as a product of the same laws of nature that determine other natural phenomena. It is a nearly ubiquitous form of human behavior, culturally established in complex elaborations, but absolutely useless, from a crudely technological standpoint, in the accomplishment of the primary economic, domestic, and political tasks of mankind. Furthermore, religion is based on supernaturalistic beliefs about the nature of the world which are not only inconsistent with scientific knowledge but also difficult to relate even to naive human experience. Magic does not make the rains come. The gods do not win battles at man's request, and witches do not make the cattle barren. Yet this "useless" behavior persists—presumably because it is not really useless, but is either gratifying in itself or is an important part of one or more processes by which major human wants are gratified.

This book, although it attempts a broad and inclusive treatment of religion, and in that sense is a text, can best be regarded as a statement of the issues which I think are most salient in the vast literature on religion. My own personal feeling is that sociological viewpoints (including much of social anthropology) tend to focus on the scaffolding and milieu of religion rather than on religion itself and that religion can be best understood from a combination of psychological and cultural points of view. Accordingly, the program of the book develops the psychological and cultural approach in five chapters. The first briefly outlines some of the traditional anthropological theories of religion. The second undertakes to analyze the categories under which religion is described and to make a rough and ready classification of religious institutions and culture areas. The third states the major goals of religious ritual and the ritual devices for achieving these goals. The fourth reviews some of the currently available information on the functions of religion, both in the sense of religion as a product of other cultural and social conditions, and in the sense of religion as a cause of other social and cultural circumstances. In this review emphasis is placed on "hard" data and particularly on statistical cross-cultural studies, rather than on the multitude of more or less plausible, and generally argumentative, inferences about the real social functions of religion in individual societies. And finally, in the fifth chapter, considerations of processes of long-term historical and evolutionary change in religion are presented, in conjunction with a statement of a theory of the ritual process. The statement of this theory of ritual is put in the last chapter partly because it can be best understood after the presentation of the materials of the first four chapters and some of the historical data as well, and partly because it is immediately relevant to any thoughtful speculation about the future of religion.

Scientific efforts to learn just what are the forms and functions of religion have not been few; it is the purpose of this book to review some of them and to synthesize the suggestions and findings in a general formulation. In this program I have been helped, over the years, by many people, to only a few of whom can I make specific acknowledgment here. I am particularly indebted to Mrs. Sheila Steen, who worked for several years as my research assistant and who contributed much to my thinking on the subject of revitalization movements. I also wish to thank other staff assistants whose comments and suggestions, as well as technical services, have been indispensable: Robert Ackerman, Fred Adelman, Josephine Dixon, Helen Dow, Raymond Fogelson, Arlene Fonaroff, Ruth Goodenough, Robert Smith, and Herbert Williams. Faculty colleagues and students too numerous to name have given valuable thoughts and information, but I am particularly grateful to Beate Salz for her thoughtful reading of the manuscript. To the University of Pennsylvania and the Eastern Pennsylvania Psychiatric Institute I am grateful for long-continued institutional support. I am also grateful to several fund-granting agencies for financial aid: initially to the Social Science Research Council for a Faculty Research Fellowship, and subsequently to the National Institute of Mental Health and the American Philosophical Society for research grants. To the following individuals and organizations I express thanks for permission to quote from various publications:

Aldine Publishing Co. and Yehudi Cohen for material from *The Transition from Childhood to Adolescence*;

American Journal of Sociology for material from "The Function of Male Initiation Ceremonies: A Cross-Cultural Test of an Alternative Hypothesis" by Frank W. Young;

Ralph Burhoe of the Institute on Religion in an Age of Science for permission to incorporate sections of "Religious Revitalization" in Chapter I;

Thomas Y. Crowell Co. and Methuen & Co. Ltd. for selections from *King Solomon's Ring* by Konrad Z. Lorenz;

E. P. Dutton & Co., Inc. and Methuen & Co. Ltd. for selections from *Mysticism: A Study in the Nature and Development of Man's Spiritual Consciousness* by Evelyn Underhill;

Ethnology and Robert A. LeVine for material from "Witchcraft and Co-Wife Proximity in Southwestern Kenya";

Harper & Row, Publishers, Inc. for material from *The World of Man* by John J. Honigmann;
Alfred A. Knopf, Inc. for selections from *The Myth of the Birth of the Hero* by Otto Rank;
W. W. Norton & Co., Inc. for selections from *Totem and Taboo* by Sigmund Freud;
Philosophical Library, Inc. for selections from *The Trickster* by Paul Radin;
Psychiatry and John Gillin for selections from "Magical Fright";
The University of Michigan Press for material from *The Birth of the Gods* by Guy Swanson;
Vanguard Press, Inc. for selections from *Divine Horsemen: The Living Gods of Haiti* by Maya Deren;
Viking Fund Publications, Wenner-Gren Foundation for Anthropological Research for material from *Paiute Society* by Beatrice Whiting.

Of course, no such text as this can claim either to represent fully all points of view or to be the final word on a subject. If this book encourages further empirical research into the critical issues on religious behavior, it will have served its most important function.

A.F.C.W.

Philadelphia, Pennsylvania
February, 1966

Contents

RELIGION

An Anthropological View

I

Introduction:

Some General Theories of Religion

NEW RELIGIONS are constantly being born. From the most ancient of archaeological records, from the history of the most recent past, and from the millennia in between, rises a ceaseless clamor of new faiths. Every year, about the globe, dozens of new cults add their voices to the cry. They are rarely faiths unique in doctrine and ritual; almost invariably they are composed for the most part of pieces and patterns of older, more routinized, more conservative religions. Their newness resides in an attitude of their membership: their members—few or many—are once-disillusioned, newly inspired people who have forsaken the ways of the world about them, and have banded together to build what they believe will be better selves and a better world. Rarely indulged by the old religions, the new are variously ignored, sneered at, or violently suppressed; a few survive, grow, and become old religions. But all old religions were new religions once.

How many religions has mankind produced? If we say that one religion, as an entity, is distinct from another when its pantheon, its ritual, its ethical commitments, and its mythology are sufficiently different for its adherents to consider that the adherents of other religions are, in a general sense, "unorthodox" or "pagans" or "nonbelievers," then we must conclude that mankind has produced on the order of 100,000 different religions. This figure is based on several assumptions: first, that religion began with the Neanderthals, who about 100,000 years ago were carefully burying their dead with grave goods and building small altars of bear bones in caves; second, that there have been at all times since the

Neanderthals a thousand or more culturally distinct human communities, each with its own religion; and third, that in any cultural tradition, religions change into ethnographically distinct entities at least every thousand years. Religion is a universal aspect of human culture. Furthermore, for every religion which has survived and been routinized, either as a small community faith or a "great religion" such as Christianity or Islam, there are dozens of abortive efforts by untimely prophets, victims of paranoid mental disorders, or cranks which are ignored or suppressed by the community.

If we understood the process by which new religions come into being, we should be close to understanding other basic processes of human life. New religions have been the inexhaustible fountains from which, for thousands of years, have flowed, in turbulent variety of form and color, the waters which make up the sea of faith. That sea has nourished much of man's still-infant culture—not merely his theological belief and sacred ritual, but his values, his principles of social organization, even his technology. And it is man's capacity to create new religions that in large measure has made all chronicles of individual and social behavior chronicles of cyclical decline and renaissance. For new religions are, above all else, movements toward the revitalization of man and society. Periodically, new religions reverse the course of decline by supplying the energy and direction for a new, and often higher, climax of development. Once a plateau has been reached, of course, religion functions as a kind of governor for society, stabilizing its members and correcting the tendency of institutions to wobble or drift. And even when a religion becomes old and crabbily conservative, it will still, despite the reluctance of its priesthood, provide the cultural building blocks for the next religion. Old religions do not die; they live on in the new religions which follow them.

The Abiding Interest of Anthropology in the Study of Religion

Before going on to suggest what may be the essential nature of the religious process, let us consider the development of anthropological opinion about religion. In this review we shall ignore the extremes of fundamentalist piety and anticlerical iconoclasm. Thus, for us, religion will be neither a path of truth nor a thicket of superstition, but simply a kind of human behavior: specifically that kind of behavior which can be classified as belief and ritual concerned with supernatural beings, powers, and forces.

Anthropology has maintained a tempestuous relationship with religion for over a hundred years; it is still too early to say whether or not this union will ripen into mutual understanding—let alone love. Religion, which should have played the role of the submissive bride, has been enigmatic and shrewish; and anthropology, which fancies itself an irresistible penetrator of mysteries, has not infrequently been locked out, or even rudely assaulted.

The early anthropologists placed religion in the center of the stage of culture. E. B. Tylor devoted the major part of *Primitive Culture* (1871) to the subject of religion, suggesting a still-respectable minimum definition of religion as animism or the "belief in spiritual beings" and developing a useful repertoire of taxonomic concepts and psychological hypotheses. Current anthropological interest has, however—in part, I think, because of the subject's recalcitrance—shifted from religion to other matters, such as kinship, function, and culture and personality, and the style of anthropological discourse has moved generally in the direction of abstraction. "Religion" is not even consistently to be found now as a chapter heading in elementary texts; not infrequently the topic must be pursued piecemeal among discussions of social organization, ethos, folklore, medical practice, economic behavior, psychopathology, structural–functional analysis, and so forth.

Only the ethnographers and historians have kept snapping snapshots of the whole lady in her various costumes, and it is to them that we owe the present availability of detailed descriptions of shamans, pantheons, ceremonial calendars, states of possession, cargo cults, world views, and a host of other interesting phenomena. This body of material today makes possible a sensitive anthropological appreciation of religion as a unitary process rather than as a conglomeration of arbitrary forms and functions and thus should help the two parties to our marriage along the path toward sympathetic understanding.

Evolutionary Theories: Religion as an Expression of Stages in Man's Cognitive Development

One major theme in anthropological studies of religion, particularly during the nineteenth century, has been the development of evolutionary theories. These theories are grounded in the idea of progress, which holds it as axiomatic that improvement comes with age. According to evolutionary theories various religious beliefs—cosmology, theology, and even ethics—are generally to be regarded as primitive, prescientific efforts to explain and predict natural events. The events of concern may be physical phenomena; they may be animal and human behavior. In this view, the problem is an intellectual one, and religion is seen as providing one sort of rational solution. Man, facing the unknown, must, in order to reduce cognitive discomfort (sometimes referred to as "anxiety"), generate a formula which yields a satisfying sense of understanding. Although this approach has been roundly criticized for avoiding the emotional aspects of religion and for failing to recognize religion's dynamic, functional role in society, it has merit, for religious beliefs are cognitive products and deserve evaluation as such. Even primitive peoples ask questions, experience curiosity, and attempt to make order out of the apparent disorder of human experience.

E. B. Tylor best represents the nineteenth-century evolutionist's theories of religion. The feature of religion to be explained was belief rather than ritual. In *Primitive Culture* (1871), he advanced an interesting hypothesis for the origin of religious belief. Early man, he suggested, postulated the existence of the soul as an explanation for two universally observed human phenomena: dreaming, in which the self seems to leave the body during sleep; and death, in which some vital principle, associated with the breath, appears to abandon the body. Tylor also worked out a rough sequence for the evolution of religion: first, a belief in souls; then animism, a belief in many spiritual beings, including souls and various deities; and finally, the consolidation of animistic doctrines into pantheons containing powerful deities, culminating of course in monotheism.

Although Tylor's suggestion concerning the origin of belief in souls has remained respectable, the evolutionary sequence he worked out was quickly criticized and supplemented by his contemporaries. Marett (1909) suggested that even earlier than the belief in souls came a stage of "animatism." Impressed by descriptions of the concept of *mana* (that is, impersonal supernatural power) among peoples of Oceania and of analogous concepts among tribal peoples in other parts of the world, Marett suggested that a logically simpler belief preceded animism. This was the belief that there existed in the world an intangible, invisible, impersonal power (one might think of it as comparable to electricity) which, if incautiously handled, was dangerous, but which could, by one means or another, be controlled by man and used for good or ill. Andrew Lang (1898), on the other hand, pointed out that some very primitive peoples believed in the existence of a high god and were, in this sense, virtually monotheistic. As we shall see, a school of Catholic anthropologists later pursued Lang's insight intensively. Thus Tylor's seemingly clear vision into the origins and evolution of religion was clouded by uncertainties as to the actual chronology of events.

Tylor's greatest disciple, Sir James Frazer, carried on the tradition of psycho-evolutionary theory in still another direction. In his celebrated *The Golden Bough* (1911–1915) and in other works, Frazer developed a clear and precise thesis to explain the evolutionary relationship between magic, religion, and science. Magic, he explained, was of two kinds: imitative and contagious, the former working by a principle of similarity in form or process, the latter by physical contact. In early times, man had no science; instead, he depended upon magic to explain, predict, and control the forces of nature. As time went on, magicians became specialists, performing ritual for the community. In order to explain their powers, ordinary men attributed to them extraordinary spiritual powers and revered their departed souls as deities. On earth the magician gradually became divine king; eventually he became priest.

The problem with all such detailed evolutionary theories, of course, lies in the impossibility of their verification. Tylor, Lang, Marett, Frazer, and others could assert plausible—and differing—schemes for the evolution of religious thought among preliterate peoples, but there was no way of proving whose theory was the most valid.

In order to avoid these embarrassments, others have attempted to define the intellectual characteristics of primitive religious beliefs in a nonevolutionary tradition—or, at least, with less detailed evolutionary models. These attempts are directed toward answering the question of whether there is a categorical qualitative difference between "primitive" and "civilized" mentality, a difference of thought process rooted in a totally different world view. To those best acquainted personally with contemporary primitive peoples there seems to be little significant difference between their mentalities and those of more sophisticated folk. To be sure, primitive people by definition "know" less than civilized people about the world, in a scientific sense, and perhaps in consequence seek supernatural explanations for events which are given naturalistic explanations by Western science. But the intellectual goals and the logical procedures are the same for both groups. Thus Malinowski (1925), after close acquaintance with primitive folk in Melanesia, agreed with Frazer in calling the magic of living primitives a "pseudoscience," a set of pragmatically intended and rationally calculated ritual procedures based falsely on a belief in the impersonal power, *mana*. "Religion," which he distinguished from magic, was directed toward the inculcation of socially desirable sentiments or values. "Science," considered as a set of valid conclusions from experience, he felt was not the exclusive property of Western civilization, but to the contrary was a mode of thought employed in varying measure by all human beings. Malinowski, in other words, saw both the practical knowledge and the magico-religious beliefs and rituals of primitive peoples as growing from the same mental characteristics as the religion and science of civilized man. Paul Radin, writing in the tradition of American cultural relativism, likewise insisted that primitive man does not employ a different and inferior order of mentality but on the contrary is as logical and sophisticated in his ways of thought as Western man. Radin quoted extensively from "primitive" religious and philosophical texts to demonstrate, in *Primitive Man as Philosopher* (1927), that primitive peoples do not have an inferior mentality.

But there is the contrary view: that primitive man, who is admittedly "different" in the content of his beliefs, including religion, is also characteristically different in his method of mental operation. It is not just that primitive peoples tend to have—as Redfield (1952) pointed out—a different "world view," in which they perceive man's relation to his environment as an intimate participation rather than a manipulative transformation. Rather, in this view, primitive peoples have an inferior mentality. Thus Lévy-Bruhl, in his work *Primitive Mentality* (1910), asserts that primitive man cannot distinguish between subject and object, cannot form abstractions, perceives nature in the course of a *participation mystique.* Cassirer (1946) conceives of a type of "prelogical mentality" which would naturally generate mythic and supernatural constructs from the data of experience. Arieti (1956), a psychiatrist, conceives of primitive man as employing a certain specific logical principle which, he feels, is in civilized societies characteristic only of children and of psychotic mental patients. According to this rule—the so-called "principle of Von Domarus" —the thinker inverts the syllogism and concludes that because two things share an attribute, they are one and the same.

In all these rationalistic exercises, the explanation for the observable differences between ancient or non-Western religious belief and Western scientific knowledge is sought in some cognitive process. The difference, in the opinion of the evolutionists, is merely a difference in content of knowledge, in what has been learned. Undoubtedly the evolutionist's position, however faulty it may be in method and historical detail and however naively ethnocentric, is more nearly consonant with the contemporary view that differences in innate mental characteristics are not likely to explain cultural differences than the view that sees the difference between primitive and civilized belief as an unbridgeable gulf. The latter, however ecstatic its authors may wax over the childlike beauty of primitive perception, is far more ethnocentric, far more prejudiced, and far less appreciative of the continuities between savage and civilized ways of life—including the continuities between savage and civilized religions.

Devolutionary Theories: Religion as an Expression of Stages of Degeneration from Primitive Revelation

Less sanguine views of religious evolution have been entertained by worthy scholars. The emergence of a nonprogressivist position is hardly surprising; we need only remind ourselves that before the fifteenth century, the very idea of progress was alien to European thought (*vide* Bury [1921]). Western historical philosophy, based on ancient and widespread cosmological beliefs of the Mediterranean world, had for centuries conceived of the universe as a great hourglass whose sands were running out. Primitive Christianity was, in Christ's time, a millennial movement which anticipated an imminent and apocalyptic end of things, and although the millennium was permitted by theologians to recede gradually into the indefinite future, the doctrine remained that the world was inexorably becoming, not better and better, but worse and worse, and would sooner or later come to an end. The trees were growing shorter, animals and men were living briefer and more corrupt lives, wisdom and art were less noble—in sum, the world was running downhill toward the ultimate catastrophe. The Christian, intent on saving his own soul and that of his neighbor, might anticipate a personal translation to a higher realm, or even a general *Kairos*—an irruption of the City of God into the time of man. But the world itself was not destined to survive.

In this somber view, Christian theologians were merely reiterating, in truncated form, the theory of secular cycles, widespread throughout the Mediterranean world in the millennia before Christ. According to this theory—epitomized in the Greek myth of the Gold, Silver, Bronze, and Iron ages—man's spiritual evolution proceeded in inverse relation to his social and technical sophistication. In the beginning, man was morally pure and lived a simple, happy life. As he became increasingly practiced in the arts of civilization, however, his spiritual qualities declined; and his further course was a continuous fall into the depths of urban wickedness until the world itself came to an end and the cycle began anew. This theme of spiritual decline is clearly recognizable not only in the ancient myth of the Garden of Eden but also in the idealization of the primitive by more recent ethnological philosophers like Lafitau, Rousseau, and—more importantly for our purposes—some of the German students of the history of religion.

One of the first religious-degeneration theorists was Max Müller (1892). He suggested, as early as 1856, that religion as it was practiced by his contemporaries was the result of a "disease of language." In the beginning, he argued, primitive peoples—particularly the ancestral Indo-European peoples—had been awed and impressed by the powers of nature, as found in lightning, thunder, raging torrents, roaring winds, and so forth, and had referred to these forces by descriptive appellations. Gradually, this descriptive terminology for awesome events came to be understood as a nomenclature for deities responsible for these events; ultimately, fanciful myths were invented to account for the actions of these increasingly anthropomorphic nature gods. In this sense, modern religion had come into existence as the result of a long, degenerative series of errors in semantics.

The degenerative view was more solidly developed in the early twentieth century by the school of Jesuit ethnologists known as the *Kulturkreislehre* (*vide* Schmidt [1931]; Kluckhohn [1936]) and more recently by their legatees in "the German historical school" (*vide* Jensen [1951]; Heine-Geldern [1964]). In regard to religion (which was not, by the way, its only concern), the *Kulturkreis* group addressed itself to the problems of the origin of religion and of the relation of both ancient and modern non-Christian religions to Christianity itself. This group of well-informed and well-trained clerical scientists, recognizing the fact of biological evolution, asked: At what point did God grant to early man a soul? And what religious inspiration did He vouchsafe to this early soul?

A theologically acceptable hypothesis—and, as it turned out, an ethnologically defensible one, too—was that God revealed Himself directly to early man, communicating the fundamental monotheistic theology and the natural moral law. Thereafter, however, mankind was on his own until the advent of Christ, and during the eons of spiritual independence, slid more and more away from the aboriginal revelation. Thus, it was argued, it should be found by field investigation that the *most* primitive peoples of the earth were followers of a high god and of a simple, natural moral code. The most primitive religions, therefore, would be construed as relatively uncontaminated relics of the primeval revelation. The more sophisticated the culture, the more degenerate would be the faith, overlaid by animistic and polytheistic paganisms. Only with the second great revelation, the coming of Christ, did God make Himself manifest again.

Although the theological preconceptions of these writers are manifest, their work had considerable merit. There is, first of all, no a priori reason to suppose that, historically, cultural forms may not degenerate; and furthermore, it is a matter of fact, as Andrew Lang pointed out, that some primitive peoples do conceive of a high god. Not only this: the *Kulturkreis* and German historical viewpoint is actually far more respectful of, and far less flippantly amused by, pagan superstition than is, at times, the positivistic and progressivist Anglo-Saxon tradition. The Catholic school sees primitives as, first of all, men like ourselves, with fundamentally similar appetites and faculties; they see no categorical dichotomy between civilized and primitive religion. Secure in their own religious faith, they can appreciate that of their fellow men, whether they wear business suits or loincloths, and can accept differences in form of expression without denying the essential community of intent. Thus, while the religiously uncommitted scientist may wish to dispense with the notion of savage revelation and barbarian degeneration, he may also find that the field reports and comparative studies of the German historical school have, because of that school's lack of preoccupation with the notion of primitive inferiority, a refreshing objective quality.

Similar in doctrine, but not in spirit, are the works of those English and American scholars who profess to see, in the ruins of ancient Egypt or Greece or Babylon, the source of analogous and now defunct monumental religions in other parts of the world. The more adventurous members of the heliocentric school, for example Perry (1923) and Raglan (1949), locate the origin of religion at approximately Latitude 30° North, Longitude 30° East and attribute the diversity of recorded religions around the world to the combined effects of continued progress at the point of origin, diffusion from this center, and degeneration in alien circumstances. Raglan's work, indeed, is of considerable value in other aspects, particularly when he is analyzing the relationship between myth and ritual. But diffusionist speculations of this kind merge without boundary into fantasies about the global voyages of Alexander's fleet and the lost, primeval empires of Atlantis and Mu.

Religion as a Projection of, and Therapy for, Emotional Problems

Psychoanalytic and Anxiety-reduction Theories: Religion as Symptomatic

Psychoanalytic theory, as it was developed by Freud and his associates in the early twentieth century, seized upon and elaborated a home truth that had been appreciated by religionists in many societies for centuries, if not millennia: that for at least some individuals, various aspects of belief or ritual can serve as prime generators, apt expressions, or more or less expedient symptomatic solutions of emotional problems. Anthropological study of the relationship between religion and personality dynamics has been much influenced by psychoanalytic theory and, as a consequence, has taken a different course from that it might have followed if William James's *The Varieties of Religious Experience* (1902) had provided the inspiration, for example.

Freud's philosophical position on religion was essentially evolutionary. This evolutionary attitude represented itself in two assertions: first, that religious doctrines, myths, and rituals are inherited (Freud was not entirely clear as to whether the inheritance was biogenetic or cultural or both) symptom formations expressing in symbolic form a neurotic compromise between Oedipal wishes and super-ego commands; and second, that the fantastic repressions, denials, displacements, reaction formations, and other defensive maneuvers institutionalized by religion are a necessary but painful discipline imposed on an immature humanity incapable, for the time being, of rational ego control of sexual and aggressive instincts.

Although many anthropologists have been rather critical of Freud's publications on religion (1907, 1911, 1913, 1928, 1939), a few psychoanalytically trained anthropologists—Roheim (1943), in particular—have developed, and modified in a measure, the original argument. Perhaps the most persuasive effort to incorporate these ideas into the mainstream of anthropological thought was that of Kardiner and Linton (1939, 1945), who developed the concept of religion as a "projective system." A projective system is a body of beliefs and rituals which ventilate and more or less adequately resolve those tensions of the typical individual that his society, particularly by its child-rearing methods, has built into him during the process of enculturation. As Roheim once acidly observed, this formulation solves the chicken-and-the-egg problem by claiming that half a chicken lays an egg which then hatches out the other half of the chicken.

The special psychoanalytic conclusions about religion, however, contribute less to an understanding of religious behavior, both normal and pathological, than do the basic concepts of psychoanalysis. The basic assumption of psychoanalytic theory is that all emotionally significant mental content is automatically (and for the most part unconsciously) coded by the brain under a few elementary categories. These categories are derived from the organism's early experience of the world. Human beings are coded as fathers, mothers, brothers, and sisters; and other objects and body parts are coded as breasts, mouths, genital organs, and organs of elimination. Interactions with other human beings, with social institutions, with the material culture, and even with nature are coded as elementary interpersonal transactions: sucking, biting, swallowing, expelling, striking, having sexual intercourse. This is not at all to say that objects and relationships are never "realistically" perceived and rationally thought about, but only that, at a certain level of mental activity, largely unconscious but powerful feelings of sexual love and destructive hate are applied to representations of reality coded in primitive form. Furthermore, the dynamic structure of this internal world is determined by the stages of biological maturation and by the vicissitudes of the organism's experiences, both satisfying and unsatisfying. The pattern of these experiences tends to fixate the emotional attention of the individual on certain primitive objects and relationships. Individuals differ because their experiential patterns differ. Thus one child may be fixated, as the psychoanalyst might say, at the "oral sucking stage," and will thereafter tend throughout his life to react to people, objects, and situations as if they were motherly breasts from whom sustenance could be sucked in an infantile, irresponsible way. Another child, fixated at the "anal retentive stage," will tend throughout his life to clamp down tightly on people and things, to scrimp and save, to be meticulously clean, and to let nothing get away.

Needless to say, such a primitive and indiscriminate process of thought must constantly plunge the person into conflict with his environment and with his own values. Furthermore, many motives and beliefs arising from these primary processes are likely to be mutually contradictory; consequently, much of this material has to be kept out of consciousness, lest its dissonance with other primary strivings and with reality prove to be too uncomfortable and too inconvenient. But this work of rejection cannot be total because the inner strivings are too powerful; complete denial would virtually destroy the human being by cutting him off from the possibility of satisfying many of his most compelling desires. Therefore, for every person, there must exist a system of temporary compromises between opposing internal demands. These compromises, *in toto,* are the "neurosis" of the individual. This neurosis is expressed in dreams and in the work of the defense mechanisms which select compromise behaviors that will satisfy primitive inner needs without unduly risking catastrophe in the real world; sometimes it is expressed in the more extreme compromises of clinically neurotic symptomatology. When, however, these compromises fail and growth does not occur, the great catastrophe of narcissistic neurosis (i.e., psychosis) may overtake the victim; he retreats in despair to a private world of fantasy or of crude, impulsive interaction with his environment, behaving according to the dictates of the primary process.

Now the application of these views to religion is not difficult. Much of religious behavior is reminiscent of dream experience, of neurotic ritual, even of psychotic fantasy, in the sense that the meaning of the behavior and the satisfaction it brings to the participant cannot be found in a rational, realistic, scientific definition or manipulation of the actual world. This is not to say that religion *is* neurotic or psychotic in any clinical or pejorative sense, but only that analysis of religious behavior as a symptom—as a compromise among primary inner promptings and the demands of reality as rationally perceived by the subject—will yield understanding of many religious phenomena.

The idea of religion as projection of and therapy for emotional problems has, in fact, been applied very widely to an understanding of myth and ritual. The widely distributed Indo-European myth of the birth of the hero, for instance, has been interpreted psychoanalytically. This myth has the following general features, according to Otto Rank, an early disciple of Freud's:

> The hero is the child of most distinguished parents, usually the son of a king. His origin is preceded by difficulties, such as continence, or prolonged barrenness, or secret intercourse of the parents due to external prohibition or obstacles. During or before the pregnancy, there is a prophecy, in the form of a dream or oracle, cautioning against his birth, and usually threatening danger to the father (or his representative). As a rule, he is surrendered to the water, in a box. He is then saved by animals, or by lowly people (shepherds), and is suckled by a female animal or by an humble woman. After he has grown up, he finds his distinguished parents, in a highly versatile fashion. He takes revenge on his father, on the one hand, and is acknowledged, on the other. Finally he achieves rank and honors. [Rank, 1914, p. 61.]

Freud offered a simple, clear, and plausible analytic interpretation of such myths:

The source and the tendency of such myths are familiar to us through Rank's work. I need only refer to his conclusions with a few short hints. A hero is a man who stands up manfully against his father and in the end victoriously overcomes him. The myth in question traces this struggle back to the very dawn of the hero's life, by having him born against his father's will and saved in spite of his father's evil intentions. The exposure in the basket is clearly a symbolical representation of birth; the basket is the womb, the stream the water at birth. In innumerable dreams the relation of the child to the parents is represented by drawing or saving from the water. When the imagination of a people attaches this myth to a famous personage it is to indicate that he is recognized as a hero, that his life has conformed to the typical plan. The inner source of the myth is the so-called "family romance" of the child, in which the son reacts to the change in his inner relationship to his parents, especially that to his father. The child's first years are governed by grandiose over-estimation of his father; kings and queens in dreams and fairy tales always represent, accordingly, the parents. Later on, under the influence of rivalry and real disappointments, the release from the parents and a critical attitude towards the father set in. The two families of the myth, the noble as well as the humble one, are therefore both images of his own family as they appear to the child in successive periods of his life. [Freud, 1939, pp. 9–10.]

The psychoanalytic explanation for the myth's wide distribution thus is that the myth celebrates a universal psychic theme; there is no need to invoke a process of diffusion of the story through the early Mediterranean world from a single origin point in Egypt or Mesopotamia. Whether the myth was in fact independently invented many times or was spread by diffusion from one center, the psychodynamic interpretation would still remain the same. In dreamlike language, a mature man is depicted as satisfying a primitive urge to kill his father and seize his mother for himself; it is, in analytic terms, an Oedipal fantasy.

Rituals, likewise, are susceptible of analytic interpretations. Freud himself wrote a celebrated treatise entitled *Totem and Taboo* (1913) which has excited strongly adverse comment from anthropologists, principally because in it Freud offered some incautious remarks on the historical origins of totemism. Freud's analysis of the possible meaning of totemism (or at least of certain of its varieties) to its contemporary practitioners has interest, however. Among Australian aborigines, for instance, a certain animal species will be held sacred by a particular tribe. The members of the tribe assert that they are descended from this animal. They do not normally hunt or eat its flesh; they paint themselves at ceremonial occasions to resemble it; and—on one occasion during the year—they do eat this animal. Freud's explanation of the ritual of eating the totem animal was, in effect, that this animal represented the father, whom each person came both to hate jealously and to love and identify with. The desire to kill and eat the animal was, thus, the desire to kill (destroy) and eat (identify with) the father. But these desires are guilt-provoking; therefore it must be taboo, not only to kill and eat real fathers, but also to kill and eat even the totem animal since it has come to represent the father. At certain specific occasions, however, when brotherly group solidarity and the promise of future abstinence make the cannibalistic feast upon the flesh of the totem animal temporarily tolerable to the conscience, that animal can be devoured. Freud described how, he thought, totemism had begun:

> One day the brothers who had been driven out came together, killed and devoured their father and so made an end of the patriarchal horde. United, they had the courage to do and succeeded in doing what would have been impossible for them individually. (Some cultural advance, perhaps, command over some new weapon, had given them a sense of superior strength.) Cannibal savages as they were, it goes without saying that they devoured their victim as well as killing him. The violent primal father had doubtless been the feared and envied model of each one of the company of brothers: and in the act of devouring him they accomplished their identification with him, and each one of them acquired a portion of his strength. The totem meal, which is perhaps mankind's earliest festival, would thus be a repetition and a commemoration of this memorable and criminal deed, which was the beginning of so many things—of social organization, of moral restrictions and of religion.

In order that these latter consequences may seem plausible, leaving their premises on one side, we need only suppose that the tumultuous mob of brothers were filled with the same contradictory feelings which we can see at work in the ambivalent father-complexes of our children and of our neurotic patients. They hated their father, who presented such a formidable obstacle to their craving for power and their sexual desires; but they loved and admired him too. After they had got rid of him, had satisfied their hatred and had put into effect their wish to identify themselves with him, the affection which had all this time been pushed under was bound to make itself felt. It did so in the form of remorse. A sense of guilt made its appearance, which in this instance coincided with the remorse felt by the whole group. The dead father became stronger than the living one had been—for events took the course we so often see them follow in human affairs to this day. What had up to then been prevented by his actual existence was thenceforward prohibited by the sons themselves, in accordance with the psychological procedure so familiar to us in psycho-analyses under the name of "deferred obedience." They revoked their deed by forbidding the killing of the totem, the substitute for the father; and they renounced its fruits by resigning their claim to the women who had now been set free. They thus created out of their filial sense of guilt the two fundamental taboos of totemism, which for that very reason inevitably corresponded to the two repressed wishes of the Œdipus complex. Whoever contravened those taboos became guilty of the only two crimes with which primitive society concerned itself. [Freud, 1913, pp. 141–143.]

In a similar vein, Theodor Reik (1931) explains the ritual of couvade (the father's simulation of pregnancy during the terminal phase of his wife's actual pregnancy and parturition) as a compromise formation. The father is torn between jealous rage against his new child (whom he perceives as a sibling competing for his wife's attention) and conscientious concern for the welfare of the child and its mother. By taking to his bed and observing various taboos, such as not handling weapons, he protects the child from the overt expression of these hostile impulses. And Bettelheim (1954) interprets the Australian male puberty ritual of sub-incision as a "symbolic wound" which satisfies the unconscious male desire to give birth to new life by providing the male with a vagina. The penis, slit lengthwise on the underside deep to the urethra, displays in its gaping wound visible evidence of the maternal strivings of the male, and permits the proud initiate to flaunt his identification (albeit an unconscious one) with the mother, whose procreative powers he envies.

In the area of morality, again, the classic psychoanalytic approach treats religion as a system of defense mechanisms which relieves man of guilt and anxiety by simultaneously satisfying, in part, and in part diverting from consciousness, strong but irrational or disallowed desires. By discovering what it is that the moral code most stringently prohibits, one discovers precisely what is secretly most desired; by looking at the ritual activity, one finds a return of the repressed. Thus the ardent pacifist may be suspected of harboring strong hostile impulses, and his angry castigation of the warlike is itself easily seen as a satisfaction of his own repressed combative feelings. The psychoanalytic formulations about the origins of myth and ritual arouse distrust, however, because they generalize very specific ideational content over all mankind—and, it sometimes appears to the uninitiated, by a rather arbitrary interpretation of symbols. In partial response to this distrust, there have developed alternative theories of religious psychodynamics which, while equally general in reference and not necessarily opposed to the psychoanalytic theses, are much less specific in content. These are the anxiety-generation and anxiety-reduction formulations offered by such writers as Kluckhohn (1942), Homans (1941), and Malinowski (1925). They do not assume any particular, universal source of anxiety, such as Oedipal conflict, but rather work with the premise that anxiety may spring from diverse roots, such as "rational" economic uncertainty (for example, fear that the rains may fail), "irrational" economic uncertainty (for example, worry about food, springing from oral frustrations in infancy), a realistic fear of death, or the pseudo-realistic fear of witch-caused illness, always depending of course on the local cultural situation. In this view, religion offers a body of belief and ritual which both expresses and works to relieve those chronic anxieties, arising from whatever source, which are apt to plague the members of a given society.

The most elegant formulation of this position has been offered by Spiro (1952). Under the rubric of "teleological functionalism" he delineates the plausible thesis that society, for its very survival, must provide outlets for the unconscious infantile strivings of its population, lest the anxiety prompted by their frustration lead to socially destructive behavior. Using as an example the culture of Ifaluk, a small Micronesian atoll, Spiro points out that in a small, isolated community of a few hundred people, maximal social co-operation is required. Quarrels, feuds, and alienation would seriously threaten a community living so close to the margin of food resources. Yet such irritations as are produced by close living constantly do threaten to arouse anger so intense that it can be relieved only by mayhem or murder. The cultural solution is religious: the people of Ifaluk believe that their ills—hunger, disease, accident, and other misfortunes—are brought by evil spirits, the *alus*, among their ancestors. It is upon the *alus*, rather than upon each other, that the people of Ifaluk vent their spite. This displacement of venom has as its happy, if not intentionally calculated, function the voiding of interpersonal conflicts. The people freely and openly hate the *alus* rather than each other and thus are relieved both of anxiety and of the real evils which interpersonal conflict would bring upon a small island community. A control case of sorts is presented by the ill-fated colony of *Bounty* mutineers on Pitcairn Island, where the Englishmen—not equipped with the island-adapted religious apparatus of either the Micronesians or the Polynesians—dwindled to a population of one English survivor as a result, in large part, of murderous brawls and intrigues.

Jungian Theory: Religion as Therapeutic

Neither the formally psychoanalytic nor the anxiety-reduction formulations present religion in a very favorable light. It is viewed as at best a kind of cultural patching-plaster, or as a superficial reaction-formation against obtrusive hatreds and lusts, or at worst as the effective cause of the very anxieties it professes to relieve. A more positive approach is that of William James (1902), who presented a considerable body of biographical material in support of the thesis that religious experience cures sick souls; but James has had little influence on anthropology. Nor has Erich Fromm, who has supported a similar view of religious experience as a type of therapeutic integration of experience and of religious doctrine as a rationalization of social forms (in this latter approach depending somewhat on Bachofen's evaluation of religion as "myth" in the sense of a mystical rationale for social forms) (*vide* Bachofen [1861]; Fromm [1950, 1951]).

Carl Gustav Jung (1938) and his followers in "analytic psychology" have viewed religion both as a cultural product and as an experience which at once integrates the personality and unites the individual with society and its traditional values. This line of work, perhaps as much because of a mystical and dogmatic tendency which offends empiricists as because of the contempt visited upon Jung's work by orthodox analysts, has had less influence on the mainstream of anthropological thought than the importance of its central premise—that the religious experience is positively therapeutic or constructive—would justify. Nevertheless, a more or less Jungian approach has inspired work by Radin (1956) and others. It will be worth our while to consider Jung's ideas more carefully.

Jung was, at first, a disciple of Freud, and his work adheres to the basic psychoanalytic principle, namely, the reduction of the phenomenological complexity of conscious, everyday affective experience to a simplified, coded set of elementary and more-or-less unconscious processes. But Jung increasingly diverged from Freud's position in his application of this principle. Whereas Freud, who was primarily interested in hysteria as a clinical problem, looked upon overt behavior (including religious behavior) primarily as symptomatic of unconscious conflict, Jung, who was principally concerned with schizophrenia, looked upon behavior (and *especially* religious behavior) as instrumental in the striving of the personality to grow, mature, and achieve integration. Jung felt that the self was, in general, always divided between the *persona*, or mask, which was presented to the world and to the ego, and the *anima*, or real and often unconscious personality. For instance, one aspect of the self might be feminine in orientation, and the other masculine. In the normal course of development, the two aspects would fuse; maturation by synthesis of opposing forces was, accordingly, the proper course of growth. But, by reason of various vicissitudes, this happy resolution often did not occur. And herein lay the need for religion, which provided encouragement and a stock of symbolic models for the synthesis of opposing complexes in the psychic life.

From this point of view, then, religion was seen not merely as an institutionalized, quasi-pathological symptom of human neuroses, destined to be outgrown in some future utopia, but rather as a mechanism by which men transcend the limitations imposed by infantile fixations. Hence, in the work of Jung and his followers, there is intense interest in the themes of rebirth, the magic journey of the hero, transformations from base into higher forms. The Winnebago Trickster myth, for instance, has been analyzed from this point of view by Paul Radin (who perhaps more than any other American anthropologist was influenced by Jung) and by Jung himself and his associate Karl Kerenyi (Radin [1956]).

Trickster (who, under one name or another—such as Raven, Hare, Br'er Rabbit—is known in most cultures) undergoes various harrowing adventures and misadventures. He was once, for instance, possessed of a very long penis—perhaps a hundred feet long, according to some of the episodes—of which he was extraordinarily proud, but which he used for all sorts of vain and foolish activities. He carried his penis, which he called his younger brother, coiled in a box or pack. One day he was teased by a chipmunk, who, when Trickster threatened to kill him, fled into a hollow tree. Trickster probed the tree with his penis but, although he uncoiled the whole length of it, he could not find the chipmunk.

> Then he kicked the log to pieces. There he found the chipmunk and flattened him out, and there, too, to his horror he discovered his penis all gnawed up. "Oh, my, of what a wonderful organ he has deprived me! But why do I speak thus? I will make objects out of the pieces for human beings to use." Then he took the end of his penis, the part that has no foreskin, and declared, "This is what human beings will call lily-of-the-lake." This he threw in a lake near by. Then he took the other pieces declaring in turn: "This the people will call potatoes; this the people will call turnips; this the people will call artichokes; this the people will call ground-beans; this the people will call dog-teeth; this

the people will call sharp-claws; this the people will call rice." All these pieces he threw into the water. Finally he took the end of his penis and declared, "This the people will call pond-lily." He was referring to the square part of the end of his penis.

What was left of his penis was not very long. When, at last, he started off again, he left behind him the box in which he had until then kept his penis coiled up.

And this is the reason our penis has its present shape. It is because of these happenings that the penis is short. Had the chipmunk not gnawed off Trickster's penis our penis would have the appearance that Trickster's had first had. It was so large that he had to carry it on his back. Now it would not have been good had our penis remained like that and the chipmunk was created for the precise purpose of performing this particular act. Thus it is said. [Radin, 1956, pp. 39–40.]

Now the proper road to interpretation of this catastrophe is not, according to Radin and Jung, merely the Freudian path of recognizing such motives as Oedipal urges and castration anxiety. There is a story being told. This story is the life history of a primordial infantile nature gradually achieving a socialized awareness of himself and the world around him. In a word, it is the story of growing up, told in that primitive language of the unconscious which both Freud and Jung sought to understand. In the whole Trickster cycle, composed of dozens of Rabelaisian episodes, the stages of normal psychosexual development are depicted, humorously but with very serious moral intent, as Trickster gradually integrates his experience into a reasonable, mature human personality. The myth, then, serves the audiences as a literary model of how to grow. Jung's approach to religion thus does not deny the validity of symptomatic interpretation, but goes beyond it, asserting that the emotional conflicts expressed in religious behavior are visible there because religion is working to resolve them. Just as the hospital is the scene of much suffering precisely because it aims at and often succeeds in helping the sufferer, so religion is the site of much neurotic symptomatology precisely because it is one of the aims of religion to assist in growth, in the resolution of conflict, and in the treatment of emotional ills.

The Functions of Religion in Sociocultural Systems

It is impossible to discuss anthropological interest in the sociocultural functions of religion without introducing the names of three scholars who are conventionally regarded as sociologists: Émile Durkheim, Max Weber, and Talcott Parsons. All have contributed importantly to the literature anthropologists read, and all have directly influenced the thinking of anthropologists about religion. Durkheim's formulations (1912) underlie much of the work of Radcliffe-Brown (1933) and other "social anthropologists"; and Weber, through his influence on Talcott Parsons, has come particularly to the attention of those anthropologists at Harvard who have participated in the work of the Department of Social Relations. In this connection should be mentioned Goode's treatise on *Religion in Primitive Society* (1951), which undertakes to formulate systematically the functions of religion in relation to economic, kinship, and political institutions, and which with respect to values leans heavily on the thinking of Parsons, Kluckhohn, and others.

The primary functional thesis is a simple one: that the religious institutions of a society represent, and elicit acceptance of, certain central values whose internalization by members of the society is necessary for the adequate integration of that society's various parts. This simple melody can be played in innumerable arrangements but, however it is played, the normative function of religion with respect to the whole sociocultural system remains the leitmotif. Such a theme, indeed, can offer to religion a degree of primacy in culture change beyond what most anthropologists, until a few years ago, would have been willing to accept. Thus Max Weber was able to discover in the Protestant ethic a new value system which was uniquely suited to the nourishment of capitalism in post-Renaissance Europe, and he demonstrated convincingly that the special capitalistic ethic could be rationally derived from the more general Protestant ethic (Weber [1904]). Durkheim, who was searching for the origins of religion, proposed that the true object of religious veneration was not a god but a society itself and that the mission of religion was to inculcate those sentiments necessary to society's survival (Durkheim [1912]). As someone has observed, the function of religion is to make people want to do what they have to do anyway.

From the postulate of religion as the inculcator of social values, and from the known diversity of values among various cultures, it can readily be deduced that religion should vary from one society to another and from one group to another within a society, depending on the values necessary for that society's and that group's integration and survival. If a group has strong need for commerce, then among the values to be supported by its religion must be fidelity to contract, payment of debts, honest measure, and the like. If the group is a tribe of hunters, then such values as strength to endure cold and fatigue and loneliness, and loyalty to the hungry family back at camp must be celebrated in ritual and rationalized in myth. Other values than these can be recognized as obviously instrumental in ensuring the smooth operation of the group. Such values may perhaps be lumped as identity values; included among them are such group-related aspects of identity as patriotism and ethnocentrism. To the extent that religion supports the individual's identification with his in-group—whether it be a class, a tribe, or a nation—it must define (however loosely and broadly) the boundaries of loyalty, assert that outsiders are outsiders, and insist upon the distinctive virtues of one's own kind. Thus to the differences among religions based upon the different instrumental values required by their different cultures must be added the different identity values group solidarity requires. It is not surprising, therefore, to find that religion is frequently a way of asserting an ethnic or class or racial identity in a situation of intergroup conflict, and resistance to change in religion may be based more on grounds of identity than on reluctance to adopt instrumental values more appropriate to the new circumstances of the society.

Among the Plains Indians, for instance, the annual Sun Dance was an occasion on which the values of physical endurance and fortitude under pain were publicly celebrated. The Sun Dancer, tied to a pole by a long cord which was passed through his torn flesh, walked around the pole, tugging at the restraint, until he collapsed or until the skin ripped and he was freed. Whatever else was intended by this ritual, it served as a dramatic reminder of the respect accorded to men who were able to carry on in spite of pain, hunger, thirst, and fatigue. Furthermore, fortitude was not only useful in hunting and warfare but was a criterion of masculine adequacy in the marital role, in council, in all of the important transactions of life. Thus the ritual emphasis on the value of fortitude animated a part of the moral code to which all social behavior was referred and without which the intricate system of rights and duties would (presumably, at least) have operated far less reliably.

Inherent in the value thesis is the assumption that a culture is normally well integrated, in the sense that it implies no major internal contradictions in the values presented to individuals at any one time. The ordinary person, in the course of an ordinary life, does indeed at certain stages in his career need to abandon some values and accept others, to learn new priorities for behavior, to recognize the different occasions on which one value or another should be involved. In American society, for instance, there is an ethic of nonviolence ("Thou shalt not kill") and also an ethic of violence in self-defense and of responsibility to others (including patriotic duty) which may involve killing to defend one's family or friends or one's country from attack. These apparently conflicting values are, however, generally rationalized by statement of the conditions of their separate application: nonviolence must be the ethic under ordinary circumstances, but if self or group is physically attacked, violence is one's duty. The two values are not contradictory, and do not arise from an internal structural contradiction in the culture, but rather are complementary, each value being appropriate to separate occasions for which separate "structural poses" (Gearing [1958]) are well established.

There can, however, be internal structural contradictions in the society which *do* plunge ordinary people in the course of ordinary lives into continual uncertainty over the choice of ethic. Here, it has been suggested, religion often plays a further role. It is necessary not merely to support and inculcate values, but also to devise some means for resolving the conflicts, or at least for providing a vent for the relief of tensions which a society's structural contradictions generate. The discussion of the meaning of the Oedipus myth—a religious theme given dramatic expression by Sophocles—provides an excellent illustration of how religion can help to resolve value conflicts.

In the Oedipus myth the infant prince Oedipus is abandoned by his mother to die; he is rescued and raised by a shepherd and, not knowing his true identity, grows up to kill his father Laius, the king of Thebes, and to marry his mother Jocasta, the widowed queen. In expiation for this unwitting parricide and incest, to which he was destined by fate, he blinds himself. Freud treated this myth as the classic, symptomatic expression of the neurotic problem that he felt was universal in men. But Erich Fromm regards the myth as a symbolic expression of a structural contradiction in Greek society:

> An analysis of the whole Oedipus trilogy will show that the struggle against paternal authority is its main theme and that the roots of this struggle go far back into the ancient fight between the patriarchal and matriarchal systems of society. Oedipus, as well as Haemon and Antigone, is representative of the matriarchal principle; they all attack a social and religious order based on the powers and privileges of the father, represented by Laius and Creon. [Fromm, 1951, pp. 204–205.]

Fromm quotes the early anthropologist Bachofen as his authority for an historical reconstruction that sees Greek society as still in turmoil from its recent change from "the matriarchal system" to "the patriarchal system." Now, while we may not agree with this reconstruction of Greek history nor with this interpretation of the Oedipus myth, we can recognize the utility of the principle of interpretation that Fromm is introducing. He is saying that the Greeks recognized the strong attachment they still felt to the ancient matriarchal system but were concerned to point out to themselves that when there was a clear confrontation between patriarchal values and matriarchal values, the patriarchal values were to be given priority.

In an anthropologically more sophisticated way, Lévi-Strauss

(1955) has suggested a similar function for myths and folk tales. They are symbolic expressions and symbolic formulas for the resolution of the value conflicts implicit in societies containing structural contradictions which place in moral quandary ordinary people living ordinary lives. Just as Jung saw myth as suggesting the path of psychological maturation to people faced by the problems of growing up in society, which demands conformity, so Lévi-Strauss regards myth as depicting the course of resolution of value conflicts intrinsic to the social structure of each society—even stable societies. Myth permits the society to maintain the partial advantages of its own contradictory segments by relieving in a symbolic, ritualized, mythic system of behavior the tensions it produces.

One is reminded here of the implications (proceeding from somewhat different data and assumptions) of the theory of cognitive dissonance (Festinger [1957]; Festinger, Riecken, and Schachter [1956]). Where mutually contradictory cognitions (including perceptions, knowledge, motives, values, and hopes) are entertained, the individual must act to reduce the dissonance. While, theoretically, he can do this by changing the real world in some respect, so as to modify the data coming in, he may also achieve the same effect by modifying his perceptions of self and of the real world in such a way that one horn of the dilemma is no longer recognized. This sort of autoplastic modification of experience may be a part of the work of religion and would seem to be particularly likely where the problem is a conflict of values arising from social contradictions. It may be far easier to reinterpret values than to reorganize society. In a negative sense, of course, such a view of religion could lead to the antireligious dictum that religion is an "opiate for the masses" provided by a cynical Establishment which realizes that the discrepancy between promise and fulfillment can be obscured by assurances of "pie in the sky." But, in a less cynical way, religion can be seen as general rationalizer for all those inescapable contradictions of expectation and experience with which even the best of all possible worlds must confront its most trusting traveler.

Religion as a Revitalization Process

But, it would seem, religion at times is unable to patch up the dissonant cognitions of members of societies structurally riven by internal strain. Societies are not, after all, forever stable; political revolutions and civil wars tear them apart, culture changes turn them over, invasion and acculturation undermine them. Reformative religious movements often occur in disorganized societies; these new religions, far from being conservative, are often radically destructive of existing institutions, aiming to resolve conflict not by manipulation of the self but by manipulation of the real world.

Anthropologists in particular have traditionally been interested in those enthusiastic religious movements which seem to develop so frequently among primitive peoples after contact with European civilization. Such movements have been called cargo, nativistic, and messianic cults; sociologists and historians writing of similar events have used other terms. Interest in these events has been increasing of late and, in order to provide a more general vocabulary, the writer has suggested the term "revitalization movements" to denote any conscious, organized effort by members of a society to construct a more satisfying culture. Since many revitalization movements are religious, the concept of revitalization becomes central to the analysis of the development of new religions, new denominations, new sects, new cults. Furthermore, it is attractive to speculate that all religions and religious productions, such as myths and rituals, come into existence as parts of the program or code of religious revitalization movements (Wallace [1956]). Such a line of thought leads to the view that religious belief and practice always originate in situations of social and cultural stress and are, in fact, an effort on the part of the stress-laden to construct systems of dogma, myth, and ritual which are internally coherent as well as true descriptions of a world system and which thus will serve as guides to efficient action. It is too early to say what will develop from this approach, although interesting contributions are being made by Mead (1956), Schwartz (1957), Voget (1956), and others. There are now, also, a number of compendia of descriptions of such movements containing descriptions of variant types: cargo cults have been summarized by Worsley (1957), messiahs by Wallis (1943), millenarian movements by a number of authors writing under Thrupp's editorship (1962), nativistic movements around the world by Lanternari (1960).

Revitalization Movements among the Iroquois

Examples of revitalization movements are easy to find. In 1799, for instance, the Iroquois Indians of New York State produced a new religion (Deardorff [1951]; Parker [1913]). These Indians had never numbered more than about 15,000 souls. They were, technologically, a simple people, residing in small villages and depending for marginal existence on crops of corn, squash, and beans, eked out by the products of the chase. They lived in long houses built of wood and bark.

The prophet of the new religion was Handsome Lake, a Seneca chief who had fallen upon evil days and become a drunkard. Handsome Lake's personal difficulties mirrored the tribulations of Iroquois society. In two generations the Iroquois had fallen from high estate to low. With the British victory in the French and Indian War they had lost the respect of the two groups of white men between whom they had for years been able to hold a balance of power. They had seen their towns burned, their people dispersed, and, after the American Revolution, their statesmen and warriors made to seem contemptible because they had supported the losing side. They had lost their lands and were confined to a sprinkling of tiny reservations, slums in the wilderness, lonely islands of aboriginal tradition scattered among burgeoning white settlements. They faced a moral crisis: they wanted still to be men and women of dignity, but they knew only the old ways, which no longer led to honor but only to poverty and despair; to abandon these old ways meant undertaking customs that were strange, in some matters repugnant, and in any case uncertain of success. And so the Iroquois stagnated, bartering their self-respect for trivial concessions from the Americans, drinking heavily when they had the chance, and quarreling among themselves.

Into this moral chaos, Handsome Lake's revelations of the word of God sped like a golden arrow, dispelling darkness and gloom. Heavenly messengers, he said, had told him that unless he and his fellows became new men, they were doomed to be destroyed in an apocalyptic world destruction. They must cease drinking, quarreling, and witchcraft, and henceforth lead pure and upright lives. Handsome Lake went on, in detailed vision after vision, to describe the sins that afflicted the Iroquois of 1799 and to prescribe the new way of life that would avert the fiery judgment. Some of his instructions were directed toward theological and ritual matters, but the bulk of his code was directed toward the resolution of moral issues presented by the new social and economic situation of the reservation Iroquois. He told the Iroquois to adopt the white man's mode of agriculture, which included a man's working the fields (hitherto a woman's role); he advised that some learn to read and write English; he counseled them to emphasize the integrity of the married couple and its household, rather than the old maternal lineage. In sum, his code was a blueprint of a culture that would be socially and technologically more effective in the new circumstances of reservation life than the old culture could ever have been.

The Code of Handsome Lake met with astounding success. The Iroquois became widely known for their sobriety; the new pattern of agricultural living, with its associated emphasis on the farm family, rapidly became the norm rather than the exception; and the code itself became the bible of a church which, as the reforms initiated by Handsome Lake prevailed, gradually became a conservative force to maintain the successes of the period of enthusiasm. The Handsome Lake religion is still followed by hundreds of Iroquois on reservations in New York and Ontario.

Now the Handsome Lake movement is relatively recent and we have excellent reports of it, written by Quaker missionaries who were in the village when Handsome Lake recited his first visions (Deardorff [1951]), and by literate Indians who committed his code to paper within three generations of his death (Parker [1913]). It is as if we had found authentic scrolls written by a scribe who personally followed Jesus about the Holy Land, day by day writing down His words and noting the daily events in the communities He visited. But there was another revitalization movement in Iroquois history which occurred before white men ever arrived in their part of the New World, and which is known only through the semimythological accounts of its occurrence. This earlier movement (Wallace [1958a]) was the founding of the celebrated League of the Iroquois, by Hiawatha and Dekanawidah, about 1450. We know less in detail about this earlier movement because it is necessary to reconstruct from the myth what probably occurred in historical reality, but it is instructive for the light it sheds on the origin of culture-hero myths generally.

According to the Dekanawidah myth, there was a time when the five Iroquois tribes were not united in a league. They constantly warred and feuded among themselves and were continually being warred upon by neighboring tribes, so that no man, woman, or child was safe. At last a man named Hiawatha, depressed by the death of his wife and family, fled into the surrounding forests, where he lived as a cannibal, waylaying and devouring luckless travelers. One day the god Dekanawidah, who had come across the lakes in a white stone canoe, found Hiawatha's cabin in the forest. Climbing on the roof, he gazed down through the smoke hole. Now at this moment Hiawatha within was staring into a pot of water and he saw the face of the god reflected from its surface. He thought that it was the image of his own face that he saw and he said to himself, "That is not the face of a cannibal." This was the moment of moral regeneration. Dekanawidah now entered the cabin and revealed himself and his mission to Hiawatha.

Dekanawidah's mission—and, thereafter, Hiawatha's—was to persuade the Iroquois to unite in a confederacy which would prohibit the usages of the blood feud among the five tribes, substituting in cases of homicide an obligatory payment of wergild. Hiawatha now became Dekanawidah's spokesman, for the god had an impediment in his speech which prevented his ever addressing an audience (and some say he was never seen by any man but Hiawatha). With tribe after tribe, Hiawatha's eloquence persuaded the people and the chiefs to lay aside the blood feud and unite. At last, having combed the snakes out of the shaman Atotarho's hair, he was able to bring sachems from all the tribes together into the

Great Council at Onondaga. The formation of this council, and the institution of the Condolence Ritual, which precluded the blood feud on the occasion of the death of any of the forty-nine sachems, were apparently effective in materially reducing the frequency of internecine blood feuds among the Iroquois. In fact, they had as an unintended consequence the development of a political institution which enabled the Iroquois to bring to bear, in the seventeenth and eighteenth centuries, economic and military force superior to that which could be mobilized by any of their Indian neighbors.

By the twentieth century, when well-trained ethnographers were able to record the Dekanawidah myth, the origin of the League was remote by five centuries. But, if we view its origin as a revitalization movement and consider Dekanawidah as a god who spoke to Hiawatha in a dream, rather than a god incarnate, then we may discern the lineaments of very much the same process as that invoked by Handsome Lake three centuries later. In the case of Hiawatha, as in the case of Handsome Lake, the prophet probably claimed only to have spoken with deity in visions of revelation. As the story passed from teller to teller, however, the distinction between a god seen in a vision and a god seen in the flesh was lost, and so the final form of the myth has Dekanawidah born on earth of a virgin mother and presenting himself physically to his prophet (albeit with a speech difficulty which prevented him from simply taking over the prophet's role directly).

THE SIGNIFICANCE OF REVITALIZATION FOR THE INDIVIDUAL AND FOR SOCIETY

The revitalization theory depends partly on psychological and partly on sociocultural considerations. Psychologically, it recognizes the integrative power of religious experience for the distraught and disillusioned individual in search of salvation. In the earlier discussion of the psychoanalytic views, we observed that the classic Freudian approach to religious myth and ritual was symptomatic rather than dynamic, claiming only that the stable and institutionalized forms of religious behavior were often able to hold in balance the conflicting emotional forces. Jung, on the other hand, was able to see in myth and ritual positive models of maturation and spiritual renewal. But the recitation of myth and the performance of ritual are conventional and repetitive acts. The kind of religious experience which is of particular interest in the context of revitalization theory is that usually labeled "ecstatic" or "enthusiastic."

Among non-psychiatric scientists, the significance of these experiences has perhaps been more fully recognized by psychologists than by anthropologists and sociologists. William James, in his classic *The Varieties of Religious Experience* (1902), drew attention to the importance of ecstatic religious experience, and especially of religious revelations, not only in the effective introduction of new content into the religious and cultural repertoire of mankind, but also in the rehabilitation of shattered souls. Boisen (1936), in a somewhat similar vein, documented the role of religious revelation in the reintegration of the emotionally disturbed; his statements are of additional interest in that they were written by a clergyman who had experienced a psychotic breakdown and whose emergence from the mental hospital was apparently facilitated by an intense religious experience. Erich Fromm (1951), likewise, has suggested that dreams, and particularly prophetic dreams, should be regarded as efforts at the creative solution of real personal or social conflicts, not just as neurotic compromises concocted to preserve the dreamer's sleep from the disturbance which an awareness of his real desires would bring. Freud, of course, in a clinical vein, was not unaware of the ecstatic phenomenon; he dealt with it under the rubric of paranoid processes, however, and devoted a paper to his analysis of the case of Schreber, a religious paranoid schizophrenic who received divine revelations (Schreber [1903]; Freud [1911]). The psychoanalytic view of such religious revelations is that, as with paranoid systems generally, they are a "restitution syndrome." In the schizophrenic process, the victim increasingly withdraws affective interest from the world outside himself and may eventually, in attempting to understand this distressing experience of withdrawal, come to believe that the real world is threatened or has actually been destroyed. The "revelation" that the world can be saved by the dedicated efforts of the schizophrenic himself, according to a program laid down by his divine leader, is thus an effort at recovery by reinvesting the world —albeit in a distorted way—with emotional significance. To what extent, then, the process of spiritual rebirth of the individual prophet or convert is to be regarded as a healthy, therapeutic experience, and to what extent it is to be viewed as a distorted, emotionally crippled struggle to achieve a plateau of adjustment on the way up from psychosis, is an important issue. Perhaps, as Boisen suggests (1936), it is best to evaluate the prophet and his prophecy separately. As he put it, "It is not the fact of hearing voices, but what the voices say, that is the important thing."

Paralleling the spiritual regeneration of individual prophets and converts, there may also occur a real change in the society, and even if this aim of social and cultural reform is not achieved, it is nevertheless believed by the devout to be possible. If the new religion is successful in establishing its new rituals and new morality and in institutionalizing to some degree its novel way of life, then it produces, in effect, a new conservatism. Thus, in the revitalization model, the religious institutions of a society are seen as passing more or less regularly, over the generations, through a cycle of revitalization, stabilization, and decline. The rituals and myths of the new religion during the revitalization phase are closely and consciously relevant to the real functional needs of the society as these are perceived by the reformers. As the new religion passes through the period of stability, however, and on into the era of decline, the function of its practices and beliefs changes. Where they once were needed to establish and support the values deemed necessary to the new order, they are now increasingly directed toward the maintenance of values no longer necessary, or even deleterious. Although the rituals and myths of the now-old religion may be reinterpreted so as to apply more closely to the changed circumstances of the society, they gradually lose their appeal and eventually function only as a conservative influence, a symbol of group identity and more or less out of touch with real needs.

This process of cyclical change, to the extent that it occurs, will tend to make the sort of functional analysis described in the preceding section difficult unless, as is rarely done (except by members of the historical school like Jensen [1951]), the stage of religious development is taken into account. If the rituals and myths of "old" religions are the relics of earlier revitalization movements, then functional interpretation needs to be re-examined.

Many religionists will gladly confess—indeed, they may claim—that unless men do accept the values that they teach, society will crumble. Yet it is commonly observed that the efficiency with which religion internalizes its values is not overly impressive, that religious values may be mutually inconsistent, that they may conflict with values inculcated by other institutions. The functional type of analysis of religion generally depends rather too heavily on the superficial plausibility of its assertions of relationship; under critical analysis, the asserted relationships sometimes tend to disintegrate. Thus, for example, Goode suggests in his functional analysis of Manus religion that because "the occasion and need for political action on a large scale [were] not frequent," Manus religion did not sanction any elaborate political structure, but that because the economic life of the Manus involved trading, and trading demands the performance of contract, the Manus Sir Ghost did offer supernatural sanctions in support of strict probity in commercial dealings (Goode [1951], pp. 155–159). Recently, however, the Manus have come under the influence of a revitalization movement led by Paliau which emphasizes that political action on a large scale is essential to the Manus and that collective rather than individual commerce is desirable. The new religion promptly dispensed with Sir Ghost (Mead [1956]). Now what happened was that the opinion *of the Manus* about the prerequisite values for the successful functioning of Manus society changed as soon as their image of the ideal society was modified by the influence of the war years and of the prophet Paliau's teachings. As the ideal image changed, so did other formal institutional patterns. This suggests the formulation that a religious institution is more demonstrably functional with respect to a specific image of the ideal society than with respect to an existing system of events, and that the organizational "needs" which functional analysis must postulate are "needs" chiefly with respect to a particular ideal image. Whether or not the Manus society "needed" major political institutions ten years before the advent of Paliau is a meaningful question only in the context of somebody's image of what Manus society "should" be like.

This line of argument suggests that it is a matter of importance to the ethnographer interested in the functions of religion to investigate not only what the sociocultural system *is* and what members of the society *think* it is, but also what the members of the society—and particularly the devotees of a religion—think it *should* be. It also suggests that the functional thesis—and related notions of pattern, ethos, and national character—require considerable conceptual working over before they can be used confidently by the social sciences. Such a working over as Ernest Nagel provides, in his critique of Robert Merton's essay (Merton [1949], pp. 21–81), is an example of what has to be done (Nagel [1952], pp. 247–248).

From the revitalization viewpoint, therefore, it would appear that the essential theme of the religious event is the dialectic of disorganization and organization (*vide* Wallace [1961b]). On the one hand, men universally observe the increase of entropy (disorganization) in familiar systems: metals rust and corrode, woods and fabrics rot, people sicken and die, personalities disintegrate, social groups splinter and disband. On the other hand, men universally experience the contrary process of organization: much energy is spent preventing rust, corrosion, decay, rot, sickness, death, and dissolution, and indeed, at least locally, there may be an absolute gain of organization, a real growth or revitalization. This dialectic, the "struggle" (to use an easy metaphor) between entropy and organization, is what religion is all about. The most diverse creeds unite in the attempt to solve the Sphinx-riddle of the relationship between life and death, between organization and disorganization; the ideas of the soul, of gods, of world cycles, of Nirvana, of spiritual salvation and rebirth, of progress—all are formal solutions to this problem, which is indeed felt intimately by all men.

But religion does not offer just any solution: characteristically, it offers a solution that assures the believer that life and organization will win, that death and disorganization will lose, in their struggle to become the characteristic condition of self and cosmos. And religion further attempts to elucidate and describe the organization of self and cosmos. Religion, then, may be said to be a process of maximizing the quantity of organization in the matrix of perceived human experience. Religion maximizes it, perhaps, beyond what rational use of the data of this experience would justify, but in so doing it satisfies a primary drive. We must, I think, postulate an organization "instinct"—an "instinct" to increase the organization of cognition and perception. Religion and science, from this point of view, would seem to be direct expressions of this organizational "instinct."

Conclusion: Progress, Utility, and Evolution in Theories of Religion

Many of the really interesting ideas of scientists are not the product of original field or laboratory research. They are, rather, the application of powerful concepts derived from other fields of knowledge or from the general intellectual milieu of the time to an already defined issue.

The most interesting theorists about religion—men such as Tylor, Freud, Jung, Schmidt, Durkheim, Linton—have all responded to the implications of the ideas of progress and of natural selection, attempting to explain why progress (or degeneration) takes place by invoking the idea of functional utility. But no more conspicuous example of this process can be found than Charles Darwin himself, whose application of the idea of functional utility to the idea of organic progress was to inspire students of religion so profoundly. Inasmuch as Darwin's writings on organic evolution have influenced not only students of religion, but theologians themselves, and have been the basis for proposals for new, "scientific" religions, it may be worthwhile to discuss the relation between Charles Darwin and the idea of progress.

The idea of social progress was not new in England when Charles Darwin was writing *The Origin of Species* (1859). It had been well entrenched since the seventeenth century and by Darwin's time was more than a theory: it was a doctrine, a dogma, an article of faith. The doctrine of progress was simply that, despite temporary lapses, absolute improvement in man's worldly and moral well-being was possible; that such improvement had occurred in the past and might confidently be expected in the future. Nineteenth-century England was permeated by the idea of progress: it was the basis of political, economic, and social theory, and the very atmosphere of intellectual life.

Darwin grew up in a circle of family and friends to whom the idea of progress was the ultimate rationale of human values (Litchfield [1915]; Barlow [1945]; *Dictionary of National Biography*). His father, Dr. Robert Darwin, was a well-to-do physician, a reformer in education (after Rousseau's principles), and an ardent Whig. Young Charles inherited a comfortable estate, and married a first cousin, Emma Wedgwood, who was a woman of parts: she had taken piano lessons from Chopin and had read widely in French, Italian, and German, as well as English. The Wedgwood family had connections with the most prominent people of the day and were important in their own right. Emma's grandfather, Josiah Wedgwood (1730–1795), had been a potter. He had introduced the factory system into English pottery-making and had in consequence become a very wealthy man. In 1762 he was made "Queen's potter." He built a model village for his workers, called Etruria, and left his heirs, in addition to the pottery business, a fortune of £500,000. His interests and ambitions expanded to keep pace with his income: he made not only utilitarian ware of superior quality, but also ornamental ware modeled after recently discovered Etruscan pottery. He became a member of the Royal Society in 1783 and a fellow of the Society of Antiquaries in 1786. He concerned himself with improvements in roads and schools, and influenced Parliament on canal-building. Emma's uncle, the younger Josiah Wedgwood, continued the business of pottery. "Uncle Jos," as Darwin called him, made his mansion at Maer a base for operations in the social as well as the business world. Uncle Josiah was an intimate friend of a son of James Watt; he knew Coleridge; he read, in his "philosophical days," Godwin and Rousseau, although he disagreed with Godwin's ideas on free love. His family were intimate with the Whig politicos, with Mme. de

Staël, with Byron and the historian Hallam. Agricultural experimenters visited his home. He was very active in the (liberal) antislavery agitation. The rest of the family were similarly progressive. The younger Josiah's brother Thomas helped give Coleridge an annuity of £150 beginning in 1798 to let the poet write without the necessity of taking a Unitarian chapel. This brother was also a friend of Wordsworth, Sydney Smith, Sir Humphry Davy, Thomas Poole, and Sir James Mackintosh. Emma's brother, Hensleigh Wedgwood, was a philologist and mathematician who developed an onomatopoeic theory of the origin of language and opposed Max Müller's theory of ultimate intellectualistic roots. Still another of Emma's uncles was the founder of the reformist Horticultural Society.

Charles Darwin was deeply impressed by the Wedgwoods. He "revered" his "Uncle Jos" (who sometimes deigned to speak openly to Charles, and then "with the clearest judgment"). With the well-heeled and well-connected Wedgwoods surrounding him, Darwin moved as he wished in a glittering society of nobility, politicians, and literati who held more or less radical (for the times) views on everything from politics, economics, and history, to religion and ethics. Darwin had been a good antislavery Whig at Cambridge; he was enthusiastically for the Reform Bill of 1832, when he learned of it aboard the *Beagle*, and contemplated the abolition of the monarchy. When he returned to England, and married Emma, his opinions jelled. Observed his son in later years, "He was an ardent Liberal, and had a very great admiration for John Stuart Mill and Mr. Gladstone."

Darwin's Whig views were derived, somewhat diluted by the exigencies of politics, from the stern utilitarianism of Hume and Bentham. The Whigs were earnest reformers who aimed at the progressive improvement of mankind by abolishing slavery, reducing the power of the landed gentry (in favor of the manufacturing and commercial interests), extending the suffrage, and evaluating the worth of social institutions, not by their antiquity, but by their usefulness to the greatest number of people. Sir James Mackintosh, the Whig philosopher, whom Darwin regarded as "the very first" of all the good talkers he had known, wanted to "promote peace, increase knowledge, extend commerce, diminish crime, and encourage industry; whatever could exalt human character, and could enlarge human understanding . . . ." [Litchfield, 1915, I, p. 3.]

Darwin was not exposed to the progress theory only through the agency of his political, social, and economic alliances, however. "Progress" was the banner that flew at the masthead of every enterprise, including the sprawling young science of anthropology, with whose major discoveries Darwin was well acquainted. He was, for example (probably through his connection with Hensleigh Wedgwood and Sir Charles Lyell), aware of the efforts of the philologists to trace the genetic relationships of languages and to express those relationships as a progressive differentiation from parental forms. He knew of the early archaeological discoveries of the century: the uncovering of the classical civilizations of Italy, Greece, and Egypt; the lake-dwellings in Switzerland; the forest-covered religious monuments of the New World. He had read James Cowles Prichard's *Researches into the Physical History of Mankind* in its third edition (1836 and 1837). He was acquainted with the startling discoveries in paleolithic archaeology by Schmerling and Boucher de Perthes in Europe, and Lund and Clausen in Brazil; these latter researches he regarded as suggesting a vast antiquity of man in South America (Darwin [1846], 2: 133). By 1846 he had done a lot of reading in comparative ethnography—such as it was in those days: Mungo Park, Purchas, Drake, Vancouver, Cook, Humboldt, Bougainville, Molina, Azara, Ellis, Kotzebue. Of the "social evolutionist" Sir John Lubbock he wrote in 1846, "Mr. Lubbock is my neighbor, and I have known him since he was a little boy; he is in every way a thoroughly good man."

Knowing his background, therefore, it is not surprising to discover that long before he articulated his evolution theories, Darwin, like most other educated Englishmen, was firmly convinced that the savages of today represented a cultural stage through which his own ancestors had once passed. In 1846, after he had been to Tierra del Fuego, he wrote dramatically about "the first sight in his native haunt of a barbarian—of man in his lowest and most savage state." He remarked, "One's mind hurries back over past centuries, and then asks, could our progenitors have been men like these?" (Darwin [1846], 2: 309). Of the Australian aborigines he remarked, "On the whole, they appear to me to stand some few degrees higher in the scale of civilization than the Fuegians" (Darwin [1846], 2: 218). Throughout his letters written aboard the *Beagle*, and in his popular 1846 book describing his adventures, he spoke of "the progress of civilization," of what happens when "civilization has arrived at a certain point," of "savages of the lowest grade," of how "advanced in culture" the Fuegians were or were not. It is plain that Darwin, by 1832, was not only a believer in the theory of progress, but had accepted the early formulations of what later anthropologists called "cultural evolution."

It would be a mistake to suppose that the infusion of the idea of progress into the biological sciences was the accomplishment of Charles Darwin. By 1833, when Lyell published *The Principles of Geology*, few European scholars held to the classical notion of the Great Chain of Being, which affirmed that, even though its species could be classified, as Linnaeus had seen, in terms of gradually increasing complexity, the organic world had been created at one stroke by God and had remained fixed, without extinction, ever since. Popular and scientific writers alike now viewed the fossils accumulating in studies and libraries as evidence that forms of life *had* become extinct, and that the more complex organisms had appeared *later* in geological time than the simpler ones. The fourth edition of Robert Chambers' successful *Vestiges of the Natural History of Creation* (1845) cited Cuvier's researches, which showed that various types of organisms had become extinct. Chambers spoke of "a clear progress throughout, from humble to superior types of being." He even noted that the successive forms of life were specifically adapted to their particular environments: for example, "the huge saurians appear to have been precisely adapted to the low muddy coasts and sea margins of the time." Chambers assumed that this "progress" (he did not call it evolution) was guided by "laws" (undescribed) established in the beginning by God, and thereafter left to operate without His interference. The only essential difference between Chambers' theory of progress and Darwin's was the absence of the idea of selection.

Charles Lyell, whose *Principles of Geology* made Darwin finally accept the fact of progressive organic change through time, as revealed in the successive rock strata, likewise couched his statements in terms of "progress." In 1832 he showed that (as he described his own work later)

> there must be a perpetual dying out of animals and plants, not suddenly and by whole groups at once, but one after another. I contended that this succession of species was now going on, and always had been; that there was a constant struggle for existence, as De Candolle had pointed out, and that in the battle for life some were always increasing their number at the expense of others, some advancing, others becoming exterminated. But while I taught that as often as certain forms of animals and plants disappeared, for reasons quite intelligible to us, others took their place by virtue of a causation which was beyond our comprehension; it remained for Darwin to accumulate proof that there is no break between the incoming and the outgoing species, that they are the work of evolution, and not of special creation. [Lyell, 1881, 2: 436.]

Darwin knew Lyell personally as well as through his books. After his return from the *Beagle* adventure, Darwin described Lyell's home at 16 Hart Street, London, as his "morning house of calls." Later he wrote, "I saw more of Lyell than of any other man, both before and after my marriage. . . . His delight in science was ardent, and he felt the keenest interest in the future progress of mankind." As Darwin here suggests, Lyell's interest was not confined to rocks. He was a cosmopolitan gentleman-scholar, a polymath, and also something of a socialite. He held enthusiastic views on liberal politics not only in England, but also on the Continent and in America; and on education, new steam engines, Catholic Emancipation, and the "progress" of "Truth." It seems to be no accidental association that those who were preoccupied with social progress saw the data of geology and paleontology and geographical distribution in a structure of organic improvement.

So much for the general background of Darwin's thought—a society which saw all phenomena, including the organic world, in terms of progress. Let us now glance at the particular way in which

Darwin expressed his own views. Darwin's work was not aimed at proving "evolution" in the sense of an historical series of nicely graded organisms: that had been done well enough by geologists. We have already seen that he accepted the notion of organic progress as a fact, certainly no later than about 1835, when he read Lyell, and presumably earlier. It was the mechanism of that progress which now intrigued Darwin, as it had intrigued others before him—notably Lamarck. It is very difficult to use Darwin's own acknowledgments here as a guide. Although he had read practically everything relevant to his study, he was very offhand in his tributes to earlier theoretical writers and carefully avoided giving any impression that his thought depended on earlier work (*vide* Eiseley [1959]). Chambers, for instance, had noted that the production of new varieties was the source of new stocks; that the organism, to survive, had to be "adapted" to its environment; and that the relation between environment and structure could transmute a species. Chambers argued the transmutation hypothesis from the data of embryology and vestigial organs; he spoke of "advances," "progress," "higher and lower," and "development"; he drew the classic parallel between linguistic differentiation and evolutionary radiation. Yet Darwin was very tardy in acknowledging that he had read Chambers. Lamarck had emphasized the transmutation hypothesis, which had by 1859 become a widely discussed idea, and had drawn up a phylogenetic family tree; he had used the inheritance of acquired characteristics as a mechanism—a mechanism which, though it has no verification in experimental genetics, is still used by implication in the writings of paleontologists. Darwin denied his debt to Lamarck, yet himself constantly treated cultural traits as both hereditary and acquirable, and as being material of evolution. (For instance, in 1846 he wrote, "Nature, by making habit omnipotent, and its effects hereditary, has fitted the Fuegian to the climate and productions of his miserable country" [p. 278]). In *The Descent of Man* (1863) a large proportion of the development (evolution) of humanity is described in terms of culture traits, particularly ethical and social systems, which Darwin firmly regarded as being acquired through learning, since he was a lifelong subscriber to various missionary enterprises which had for their object the civilization of native peoples.

It seems that Darwin first approached the problem of the *processes* of progress by accepting the general doctrine of transmutation, which had been discussed for a generation by such men as Lamarck, Geoffroy Saint-Hilaire, Rafinesque, Chambers, and Herbert Spencer. He next proceeded to take note of the effects of domestication in producing new varieties. This in itself is testimony to his dependence upon the idea of progress to provide him with the mold for his data. For many years British gentlemen-farmers (including the younger Josiah Wedgwood) had been interested in plant and animal breeding, the object of which was to improve the agricultural yield by improving species. The success of these agricultural experiments has been dignified by historians with the term "Agricultural Revolution," as a parallel to the Industrial Revolution (in which old Josiah Wedgwood had progressed from potter to capitalist). One of the facets in the worldly progress of British society was the variation, and selection by man, of domesticated plant and animal species. The phenomenon of variation appeared to Darwin, as it did to all practical breeders, to be of cardinal importance. If he had not been interested in the progress of commercial agriculture, if that industry had not existed, it seems unlikely that his study of the mechanisms of evolution would ever have taken the direction it did.

The concept of "survival of the fittest" (though not the phrase) had been implicit in Chambers' work (and of course also in Spencer's, who had coined the slogan), and in the work of Edward Blyth (Eiseley [1959]). It was also the cornerstone of Darwin's theory of natural selection. As Schurman (1888) has pointed out, the "survival of the fittest" principle was a projection into biology of one of the tenets of "the national ethics"—utilitarianism. Survival of the fittest was the implicit principle of laissez-faire economics in both its internal and international aspects. Utility was the criterion of social value; to Darwin it was also the determinant of survival. Variations, to survive, had to be useful (if only to themselves), and Darwin continually spoke in terms such as "profitable to itself," "useful," "the good of each," "direct or indirect use," and so forth. As Schurman remarked, "No one uninfluenced by the ethics of the school of Hume and Bentham would have ventured to interpret the evolution of life as a continuous realization of utilities" (p. 117). Even Darwin's recognition of the struggle for existence, which selected for survival (in a state of nature) those variations which were most useful, did not arise from observations of plant and animal communities. As Darwin himself records it, his realization of this struggle came from reading Malthus on population. Darwin was not reading Malthus for scientific enlightenment but for spiritual edification, for, like Darwin, Malthus was a Whig. In the words of Leslie Stephen (1900), Malthus was "one of the leading prophets, if not the leading prophet, of the Utilitarians. Belief in the Malthusian theory of population was the most essential article of their faith" (Vol. 2, p. 138). And, as we might suspect, Malthus' book (1798) is predicated on the idea of progress. The opening phrase is, "In an enquiry concerning the improvement of society. . . ." The book is dedicated to an investigation of certain factors which have impeded "the progress of mankind towards happiness," and to a consideration of whether or not these factors will be removed in the future.

But probably the most convincing evidence of the influence of prior ideas of progress and function comes from *The Origin of Species* itself. Here Darwin unconsciously reveals how his thought is constantly guided by the idea of progress. He repeatedly compares organisms as "lower" and "higher"; he speaks of the emergence of the "perfect and complex" out of the "imperfect and simple"; he sees natural selection as working for "perfection." He brings in, in wild profusion, parallels and analogies from linguistics, archaeology, and history. And he sums it all up as demonstrating "one general law leading to the advancement of all organic beings,—namely, multiply, vary, let the strongest live and the weakest die" (p. 208). That statement, indeed, seems to show the structure of his thinking in transparent clarity: he accepted progress, including the history of organic change, as the law of life; and in searching for a theory to explain the process by which this law of progress worked, he made use of principles explicit in the doctrines of social progress of his day.

As many people have pointed out, the success of the Darwinian hypothesis was due to its being congenial with the spirit of the times. But it rapidly acquired such *éclat* that its humble origin in the ideas of progress and utilitarianism (functionalism) was forgotten, and scientist and layman alike have sometimes preferred to see these ideas as originating with Darwin. This curious delusion has been actively fostered by anthropologists who, blinded by the great light of 1859, have claimed that their theories of progress are based on Darwin's work. "Evolution" is a respected word, and it sounds much grander to speak of "cultural evolution" than humbly to mumble something about "cultural progress" or "utility." And yet, the fact remains that anthropological theories of cultural evolution—including the evolutionary and functional theories of religion—are derived, not from Darwin, but from eighteenth-century ideas of progress and utility. Darwin himself built his theoretical edifice of organic evolution on that older plan.

The progressivist and functionalist theories have been least effective, however, in the presence of the ecstatic, the quasipathological, the mystical. As Robert Lowie once remarked, in defending himself against Goldenweiser's criticism that his book on *Primitive Religion* (1924) said nothing about the "core" of religion (". . . a stirring subjective event, in which the whole personality is for the time being submerged. . . ." [p. v]):

> Writing a scientific work, not a devotional tract, I treat the mystic experience as a datum of objective reality; but since it is by definition ineffable, a lengthy discussion would be a waste of effort. . . . What is communicated about such experiences is summed up in the statement that they are incommunicable. [Lowie, 1924, p. v.]

Methodological dilemmas, here as in other areas of scientific interest, obviously impede the development of knowledge.

In the work on cognitive processes by the early evolutionists, and in the psychiatrically inspired reflections of the analysts, the so-called "comparative method" was used. This involved identifying similar myths and customs in cultures widely scattered in place and in time, and reconstructing from these bits and pieces not only ancient institutions, but also the "meaning" of contemporary

(contemporary primitive or contemporary civilized or both) beliefs and rituals. Although this method has certain values, it has been properly criticized as begging historical and psychological facts which can be adequately demonstrated only by specific evidence. The "historical" (as opposed to "evolutionary") schools have not so much abandoned the comparative method as improved it, by paying close attention to the distributional evidence for diffusion and to the criteria of form and style from which can reasonably be inferred the historical connection of customs now widely separated. But despite the apparent hardness of their data, the historical evolutionists are very much committed to the study of what Lowie regarded as the "ineffable": affective states of awe and holy terror; prelogical mentalities; primitive revelations; strange concepts of souls, forces, and causality; universal but unconscious symbols, and so on. One might regard the historico-evolutionists as asking the right questions but as seeking answers in the wrong places with the wrong tools.

Lowie and his friend and colleague Paul Radin are somewhat transitional figures, bridging—in different ways—the gap between the older, historico-evolutionist traditions and the modern ethnographic, functional, and culture-and-personality oriented schools. Although these schools of thought diverge in various ways, they unite on the methodological doctrine that the anthropological "truth" about religion is not to be found in museums, libraries, and ancient tombs, but in the field—that is, in communities populated by living people. When Malinowski invited the reader "to step outside the closed study of the theorist into the open air of the Anthropological field," he was voicing the sentiments of a new generation of scholars. Instead of comfortably reclining in a leather chair to read about strange ceremonies, or standing, chin in hand, before museum glass to ponder the meaning of the jeweled skulls of the dead, the new breed of anthropologists were, like Malinowski among his Trobriand Islanders, "paddling on the lagoon, watching the natives under the blazing sun at their garden work, following them through the patches of jungle . . ." (Malinowski [1926], p. 17).

Two kinds of new approaches to religion (at least for anthropologists) emerged from these field enterprises: functional, in the sociological sense, and psychological, in a more directly empirical sense than heretofore had been the case. Functional interpretations of religion sought to reveal the intimate connections between religious ritual and belief and other institutions of the society—kinship, economic, political. They commonly employed the concept of "values" (or "sentiments," "needs," and so on) as a kind of logical glue to hold together disparate propositions. One main problem with functional interpretations, however, has been their provincialism. After one or two years (or more) in the field, and steeped in the lore of his own tribe, the returning field worker commonly has little time or energy—and sometimes no talent—for comparative study and the validation of generalizations. Functional interpretations, based on experience with one or two communities (usually all in the same general culture area), depend on the authority of their authors and on their a priori plausibility for proof of local validity; only the most banal principles are safe to extrapolate beyond the single island or reservation or whatever where the field work was done. Furthermore, in their professional anxiety to claim a unique contribution to knowledge, many functionalists desperately avoid the appearance of being psychological. Like Lowie, they prefer to leave the ineffable alone.

On the other hand, the culture-and-personality people, who have *not* feared to use the concepts of Freud, and who *are* willing to approach the ineffable monster of religious experience in its lair, also suffer from provincialism. They have frequently been heavily committed to their own locality and can only with difficulty see the rest of the world as more than a variant form of their own little tribe.

With all these major difficulties, it is possible, nonetheless, to see progress. There exists, by now, a substantial archive of published field data which can serve, and is serving, as grist for the mill of the newer statistical analyses of functional relationships. As we shall see, these functional approaches combine comparative, functional, and psychological techniques in a potentially powerful way and have already generated interesting results. But in addition to a more sophisticated functionalism, there has been significant progress in standards of ethnographic description. Inspired by the success of descriptive (or "structural") linguistics in developing techniques for the precise and unambiguous description of language, American anthropologists have been concentrating on the logical articulation of culture. The structural analysis of culture permits an examination of religion which, because it is concerned to describe rather than explain, is relieved of the need to find the "meaning" of religion in some psychological or sociological function. Although it is necessary to go beyond purely structural accounts if one wishes to "understand" religion, the structural description can often be more objective than a functional one. In the next two chapters we shall attempt to show some of the values of the structural approach.

II

The Anatomy of Religion: The Fundamental Pattern, the Four Major Types, and the Thirteen Regional Traditions

HOW DOES ONE RECOGNIZE a religion? Why does one say that certain behavior is religious? The answer lies in the fundamental pattern, or structure, which the layman and the ethnographer alike recognize when they look at a society and which, whenever it is found, is called "religious," despite the manifold diversity of its forms.

It is the premise of every religion—and this premise is religion's defining characteristic—that souls, supernatural beings, and supernatural forces exist. Furthermore, there are certain minimal categories of behavior which, in the context of the *supernatural premise,* are always found in association with one another and which are the substance of religion itself. Although almost any behavior can be invested with a religious meaning, there seems to be a finite number—about thirteen—behavior categories most of which are, in any religious system, combined into a pattern that is conventionally assigned the title "religion." After reviewing these minimal categories of religious behavior—the things people do when they are behaving "religiously"—we shall consider how behavior of these types is organized into rituals, belief systems, and cult institutions. Within the fundamental pattern of religion, of course, there is great cultural diversity; but this diversity can be conveniently reduced to four major types and thirteen regional variants.

The Minimal Categories of Religious Behavior

The following thirteen specific categories of religious behavior are not intended to represent the only possible classification; indeed, since the choice of level of abstraction must be made intuitively, no one list can ever claim absolute validity. The events to which the categories refer may sometimes be appropriately classified under two or more heads, and the categories are not entirely exclusive even in a logical sense. Nonetheless, they will serve as a rough-and-ready classification of the kinds of actions that most observers recognize as religious.

Prayer. Addressing the Supernatural

In almost every culture in the world there are customary ways of addressing supernatural beings. Such address is generally conducted by speaking aloud while the body is held in a conventional posture and while standardized gestures intended to express fear, love, respect, threat, or other motive are made; the style of speech is also apt to be stereotyped. The purpose and content of the address, of course, vary with culture and, within the culture, with the occasion. Often such address is made in public, at a sacred location and with special apparatus, such as incense or smoke from a fire, to expedite the message.

Perhaps the type of address most readily recognized by the Christian is *prayer*. In prayer the supernatural being is either asked for a favor or is thanked for a past blessing. Prayers may be offered either on behalf of the person praying or on behalf of some other person or persons. The emotional tone may range from abject abasement to demanding arrogance or even threat. Sometimes, of course, prayers are given physical embodiment as written formulas, as in the Buddhist prayer wheel or as inscriptions on monuments and tombstones. Another common type of address occurs in *exorcism*, in which an alien spirit possessing the body of a human being or even an animal or natural object is requested to leave. It is proper also to include in this category *speaking to the soul of a human being*, who may be an ancestral spirit, a ghost, or a temporarily wandering soul, and who may be beseeched to return to the body of its ailing or unconscious host, or to depart and leave the living in peace, or, as in spiritualism, to speak to humans in return.

The variety of possible kinds, occasions, purposes, and techniques of supernatural address is obviously large. Among the Iroquois, for instance, prayer was employed on a number of occasions: members of the Upper Pantheon were regularly asked to favor mankind with the requisite amounts, at the proper times, of rain and sun for the fruitfulness of the crops; wisdom and courage and strength were sought from the divine sponsors of the Great League; the Great Spirit was thanked by Handsome Lake for the blessings of mankind; the False Face, or Great World Rim Dweller, was asked to spare mortals the pain and perils of disease; the Thunders were implored to end drought. The Iroquois maintained a moderately complex civilization, but prayer, exorcism, and speaking to souls occur in the most primitive cultures as well as in the most complex.

MUSIC: DANCING, SINGING, AND PLAYING INSTRUMENTS

Although not all of the performing arts are, even in the simpler societies, exclusively confined to religious situations, there are few, if any, religious systems in which *dancing, singing, chanting, poesy, and the playing of musical instruments* do not play an important part in ceremony. Frequently the formal address to the supernatural is, in effect, sung, chanted, danced, or played; music becomes the vehicle of prayer if not in itself the substance of communication. These musical performances may also be done in honor of, or in the name of, a supernatural being without claiming to be direct address. The native rationalization for the choice of a musical medium of communication may simply be that an address is more effectively transmitted in rhythmic, stylized structure. But we may suspect—and we shall develop the point later—that musical media are preferred because of their effect upon the human performer and his audience and that sometimes, as in "voodoo" dancing and drumming, the participants are consciously aware that musical performance facilitates entry into a desired state of heightened suggestibility or trance in which possession and other ecstatic religious experiences can be expected to occur.

Physiological Exercise: The Physical Manipulation of Psychological State

Efforts to induce an ecstatic spiritual state by crudely and directly manipulating physiological processes are found in every religious system. Such manipulations may be classified under four major headings: (1) *drugs;* (2) *sensory deprivation;* (3) *mortification of the flesh* by pain, sleeplessness, and fatigue; (4) *deprivation* of food, water, or air. The latter two are ways of arousing intense physiological stress (Selye [1950]).

Drugs are often ingested or inhaled for the purpose of inducing ecstatic, and sometimes hallucinatory, experiences of a religious nature. Plains Indians, for instance, eat or drink infusions of *peyote,* a cactus containing a number of alkaloids including mescaline, which is a potent hallucinogen. Ancient Greek celebrants of the great god Pan chewed the intoxicating leaves of ivy to induce ecstatic abandon. The Koryak, Chuckchee, and other Siberian peoples chewed the crimson mushroom fly agaric (*Amanita muscaria*) to bring on episodes of euphoria. Scandinavian *berserkers* ate certain kinds of mushrooms to achieve dissociation. Some modern Americans experiment with such "psychedelic" drugs as lysergic acid dyethylamide (LSD) in the hope of spiritual growth. The religious significance of all such practices lies in the folk interpretation placed upon a basic psycho-physiological reaction to the drug, such that the hallucinatory or other ecstatic experience is phrased for the individual and the group as possession by the divinity or as communication with the divinity (Wallace [1959]).

Comparable quasi-pathological transformations of the normal mode of cognitive function can be achieved by other means, of course. Sensory deprivation has been exploited by mystics, both Eastern and Western, to achieve the higher extremes of beatitude. Sensory deprivation was also exploited by American Indians to secure guardian spirits in visionary experiences. The effectiveness of these procedures in inducing psychological change has been demonstrated, even in a nonreligious setting, by clinical experimentation in the effects of sensory deprivation and in the various "brainwashing" or "thought reform" techniques practiced by agencies of social control in both Western and Communist countries. Physical discomfort produced by torture, prolonged sleeplessness, cold, and fatigue, whether self-applied or imposed by others, can also be effective in inducing cognitive change. Similarly, the deprivation of food, of water, and of normal atmospheric air to breathe can, with varying speeds, produce extreme states of disorientation, dissociation, or euphoria.

In sum, then, one may say that physiological manipulation of the human body, by any means available, to produce euphoria, dissociation, or hallucination is one of the nearly universal characteristics of religion. The ecstatic experience is a goal of religious effort and whatever means, singly or in combination, are found to be effective in reaching it, will be employed by, or on behalf of, at least some communicants.

EXHORTATION: ADDRESSING ANOTHER HUMAN BEING

In every religious system, there are occasions on which one person addresses another as a representative of divinity. The context is one in which one person has closer communion with the supernatural than the other. The one so favored, then, represents the supernatural to his less fortunate fellow man. The shaman, the priest, the minister, the prophet, all occupy their special status by virtue of a unique contract between themselves and the divine to which others are not privy. They are, therefore, addressed by the laity as intermediaries, carrying requests and supplications to the higher being. The clergy (if one may use the term to refer to all sacred specialists) in turn addresses man on behalf of the gods—issuing orders, exhortations, threats, and words of comfort as the occasion demands. Schematically, we might represent the situation thus:

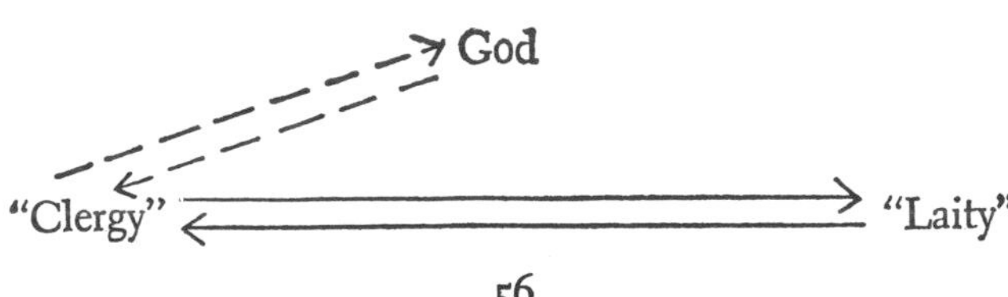

Out of the elementary schema represented in the figure, of course, highly complex organizations often arise. It is a far cry indeed, in regard to complexity, from the simple relation between one shaman and one client to the vast bureaucracy of a great world religion such as Islam or Roman Catholicism. Nonetheless, such organization depends fundamentally upon the principle that one man may have closer relationship with the supernatural than another, and is therefore not merely entitled, but is expected, to exploit this preferred relationship in the spiritual interest of the less fortunate.

Reciting the Code: Mythology, Morality, and Other Aspects of the Belief System

In every society there is a sacred oral or written literature which asserts what is truth in religion. This code contains statements of the *pantheon* and of the *cosmology;* it contains the *myths* which chronicle the activities of divine beings, particularly at the time of the origin of things; and it contains the *moral injunctions* of prophets and of gods. The sacredness of this body of literature depends upon the closeness of its connection with divinity. It is frequently recited in the course of ritual but it may also be told again and again, studied, and discussed in more or less profane settings, provided certain respectful conventions are observed, such as the common North American Indian taboo against the telling of myths in the summertime.

Myths of origin are perhaps the most common of the stories told about the gods. They may describe the origins of the gods themselves, the various adventures which befell them, and their activities in eventually creating the familiar world of man and nature. Some origin myths, which describe the endeavors of a divine or divinely inspired being in bringing to man such cornerstones of his culture as fire, family organization, law and government, and the rules of morality, are sometimes called "culture hero myths." Although such stories are generally serious in tone (however extraordinary and even scatological their content), a class of such origin tales called "trickster myths" is humorous. In trickster myths the successive triumphs and misadventures of an anthropomorphized animal—a raven, a rabbit, or a coyote, for instance —are told in such a way that not only the historical origins of certain features of the world are accounted for, but also a moral is conveyed: the dangers of pride, the risks of gluttony, the perils of boastfulness. Origin myths may be told about the origin, not only of gods, of the world, and of people, but also of particular and recently developed institutions, such as the origin of the Great League of the Iroquois. Origin myths provide answers to questions about how things began; equally important, they also serve to establish an order among values and to justify, by reference to these values, the major customs and institutions of society. Furthermore, the myths, being biographies of the gods, endow the names of the pantheon not only with a list of powers and attributes but also with unique personal identities comparable to those of real human beings. The myths, in other words, describe the supernatural community with which man must interact.

Set compositions purporting to be verbatim or paraphrased accounts of the words of divine beings or of inspired prophets are perhaps not as common as origin myths. Nevertheless, the established great religions all have revealed texts—Bible, Talmud, Koran, the Hindu and Buddhist classics, and so on—and each new revitalization movement usually contains as its intellectual nucleus a formal treatise supposedly communicated by a god to his prophet. Such new codes usually contain elements of origin mythology (new or traditional), together with reflections on the current state of affairs in the society, moral injunctions, and editorial commentary by the prophet and by the subsequent religious leaders, scribes, and scholars who have passed on the Word.

SIMULATION: IMITATING THINGS

Ritual, whether it be explicitly oriented toward the control of supernatural beings or only toward the control of supernatural power, frequently involves some simulation procedure. Simulation is most familiar in those occult performances which Frazer called "imitative magic." The classic illustration is the "voodoo doll" made in the likeness of an enemy and subjected to such maltreatment as being stuck with pins, exposed to foul weather, burned, or stabbed. In this *witchcraft* procedure, it is believed that by the "law of sympathy" between similar objects, what happens to one will happen to the other; thus, in the case of the voodoo doll, as the simulacrum is destroyed the human prototype experiences comparable injury and suffers or dies. Such simulation procedures are familiar in the magic and witchcraft of recent primitives—and, to judge from evidence in Neanderthal and Cro-Magnon caves, where the painted figures and sculptured forms of animals are speared and stabbed, simulation is of great antiquity.

Simulacra are prominent in the practices of *divination*, whereby otherwise unknowable facts are revealed by the examination of an index event which, in some sense, simulates future or distant reality. Thus in scapulimancy, a form of divination common in the circumboreal forests of Asia and North America, an animal scapula is scorched in fire and the resulting cracks in the bone are "read" as if they were a map showing the location and movements of game. The same sort of procedure is followed in *ordeals* applied to men or to animals whereby the physical response of an organism to a physical insult, such as the taking of poison, or being thrown, bound, into a pond, or plunging the hand into boiling water, is interpreted as the equivalent of an otherwise undiscoverable state of guilt or innocence in the accused. Indeed, where the accused himself is not subjected to the ordeal, and an animal is substituted, a double simulation is being practiced: animal for man and physical response to injury for guilt or innocence.

But simulation is not confined merely to the limited arenas of ordeals, witchcraft, and divination. It is also important in ritual and in sacred text directed toward the gods themselves. Thus the man or animal who is sacrificed as a "scapegoat" on behalf of a community simulates the community itself. The painted and sculptured objects to which veneration is shown in many religions are not, in most cases, either divine in themselves or even the residence of divine beings; they simulate divinity and as such are treated "as if" they were divine by the same principle as that by which the voodoo doll is treated "as if" it were the hated enemy. Human beings often impersonate the gods in more or less elaborate theatrical rituals designed, by the principle of simulation, to affect the disposition of the gods in a manner favorable to man. Thus the Iroquois False Face dancers, dressed in rags and wearing grotesque wooden masks, simulate the Great World Rim Dweller, and the treatment accorded them is considered as efficacious as if it were applied to the god himself.

Simulation, then, is an almost universally used religious device. It supposedly produces an effect that would have been impossible to attain by applying energy directly to the object itself, since the object may be distant in space or time, inaccessible in a supernatural realm, or otherwise invulnerable to natural manipulation.

Mana: Touching Things

The passage of valuable qualities from some sacred object—human or non-human, animate or inanimate, part or whole—to a less virtuous subject is often considered to be accomplished by the subject's touching that object. In Christian tradition, for instance, there is the "laying on of hands," by which the virtue of the blessed is conferred upon the novice in virtue. There is also the "relic," which is a part of the body or accouterments of Jesus or of a saint, and which if touched will confer health and good fortune. In vulgar Western folk magic, likewise, the unlucky bettor may touch the gambler who is enjoying a run of luck; the "superstitious" traveler may carry a rabbit's foot on his key chain for good fortune; the seeker of eloquence may kiss the Blarney Stone; the witness in a court of law places his hand on the Bible while he takes an oath to tell the truth. Among the Iroquois, the False Face dancers rub the afflicted part of the patient's body with their hands and the speaker of the Code of Handsome Lake fondles a string of wampum which supposedly once belonged to the prophet. Among the Indians of the Plains, the shaman carries a "medicine bundle" which contains miscellaneous objects that give him "power." The Australian aborigine hides, but periodically handles, the sacred stones called *churinga.*

In all such transactions, power passes from a donor to a receptor. This power may be generalized and omnifacile, as in *mana,* or it may be a specific capacity—for an injured organ to heal; for a healthy body to resist disease or evil magic; for a person, tempted to lie, to tell the truth; for a barren woman to conceive; for an orator to speak eloquently; for a gambler to win; for a traveler to journey safely; for a soul to enjoy innocence. Generally, the transfer of power proceeds automatically, as if mere contact permitted its flow; the source, furthermore, is usually considered to be inexhaustible. The ultimate source of the power may be personalized as a soul or a god, or it may remain an impersonal reservoir of supernormal force like the Melanesian *mana,* the Siouan *wakan,* the Algonkian *manitu,* and the Iroquoian *orenda.* The forms and etiquette governing the act of touching also may be varied. But the fundamental principle is the universal law of power: to acquire a power, touch an object that contains that power.

Taboo: Not Touching Things

Just as, in some instances, sacred things are to be touched in order that one may acquire a power inherent in them, so in other instances sacred things are to be not touched, or are otherwise to be avoided, in order to prevent the power that is in them from injuring the person. (Frazer lumped *mana* and taboo procedures in a common category of "contagious magic.") Such avoided objects are commonly said to be subject to "taboo." Every religious system has some set of taboo phenomena, to come into contact with which under certain conditions is to court disaster. Some religious systems contain so many rules of taboo, and apply them to so many areas of experience, that these faiths are apt to be regarded by Western observers as dominated by taboos. The Polynesians, for instance, maintained an elaborate set of taboos on contacts of one kind or another between status groups, particularly between royalty and commoners. The chief's body could not be touched by the body of a commoner; even if the contact were accidental, death would be the result for the commoner. The commoner could not look down upon his chief from a higher elevation (looking is, in a sense, like touching), and so the chief had to sit upon a raised platform and be carried on a raised litter above the shoulders of his subjects. In India, similarly, elaborate taboos govern the contacts between members of the various castes and even between members of the same caste who are in different states of ritual purity. The consequence of violating these rules, in India, is normally not death but loss of ritual purity, which must be regained at the cost of considerable inconvenience by touching sacred objects (particularly sacred water).

Religious taboos, of course, often govern the choice of foodstuffs, among Jews, Catholics, Eskimos, Australian aborigines, and many other peoples. Religious taboos are also apt to govern the choice of sexual partners by prohibiting intercourse or marriage between certain kinfolk. The classical example of this taboo, celebrated in Greek drama and in the writings of Freud, is the incest taboo. Similar taboos may make women inaccessible during their menstrual periods or when they are nursing children, and men when they are about to engage in or have just returned from warfare. The possible scope of taboos is endless in its variety.

Taboo, like *mana*, is contagious but impersonal. Thus the violation of taboo need not be intentional or even known to the violator for its consequences to be visited upon him. It is as if some impersonal power—the *mana* of which we spoke earlier—resides in the tabooed object in such a degree of concentration that it overwhelms persons who come into contact with the object—as if they had touched a high-voltage wire. Oedipus did not know when he married Jocasta that she was his mother; he was, from a certain moral standpoint, innocent. Yet his act loosed upon him the disastrous fate which automatically befell any violator of the incest taboo. Thus in many primitive societies the person who suffers inexplicable misfortune must search his memory, and the memories of friends and shamans, for evidence that a taboo has been violated—just as in Western society the victim of a neurosis must search, through dreams and free association, for memories and wishes of which no conscious trace remains, in order to explain the symptoms of his neurosis. Indeed, the institutions of *mana* and taboo and some of the symptoms of what the psychiatrist calls the obsessive-compulsive neurosis are so similar that psychiatric literature finds in them a common mode of mental activity.

Feasts: Eating and Drinking

The consumption of food and beverages in a religious context—the *sacred meal*—is a familiar theme in Christian tradition. The Last Supper, and its derivatives in the Catholic and Protestant Holy Communion, are sacred meals in which the communicant partakes, symbolically, of the flesh and blood of the Divinity. This quasi-cannibalistic theme is familiar in some of the more primitive cultures, particularly among the Australian aborigines, in the totem feast, in which the mythical animal ancestor of the totemic group is eaten by his descendants. Among the Iroquois, the congregation during the recitation of the Code of Handsome Lake is expected to drink strawberry juice handed around in pails; the powers of the juice to restore the spiritually and physically ill to health are described in the words of the prophet and hark back to one of the festivals in the annual calendar, the Strawberry Rite, held in June of each year. In general, the sacred meal involves the eating and drinking of materials that contain a supernatural force or power—a "virtue," in the older sense of the word—which can be safely acquired if it is consumed under the proper ritual auspices. This virtue is usually believed to be the property of a particular supernatural being.

The sacred meal can be recognized in more diffuse forms, however. Profane food may be invested with sacred virtue by being blessed, or its natural virtue may be maintained by the observance of appropriate taboos; furthermore, the act of social eating may in itself, even under day-to-day conditions, be considered to have a sacred quality, particularly if it is sanctified by a standard ritual, such as the saying of "grace" before the meal. The taking into one's body of foreign materials is a transaction always fraught with the opportunity for spiritual injury if these objects are under the jurisdiction of, or even material forms of, some supernatural being. The god's attitude toward the use of objects from his domain is of concern to man; the supernatural powers inherent in the objects must be handled with care. There is much clinical evidence to suggest that adult attitudes toward food and eating develop from fundamental psychological attitudes toward the mother's breast, toward the mother herself, and toward the possibilities of identification with both mother and father; this process would evidently provide powerful unconscious motives to most human beings for treating the act of eating as a transaction with spiritual beings.

SACRIFICE: IMMOLATION, OFFERINGS, AND FEES

The powers who populate the supernatural world are usually believed to have an interest in the objects that attract human beings: food, drink, sex, money, household goods, and so on *ad infinitum.* Furthermore, the people and organizations who serve as intermediaries between the natural and supernatural worlds always have need of goods and services, both for their own use and for the purpose of carrying out religious exercises. Thus, the payment of fees and the making of contributions may be rationalized as a sacrificial service to the supernatural beings themselves.

Probably the most widespread instance of sacrifice, certainly the most ancient, is the burying of *grave goods* with a corpse. These articles—food, weapons, clothing, money, and so forth—are intended to provide the soul of the deceased with various things he will need in the life after death. Sometimes offerings to the dead are made out of compassion; sometimes they are intended to forestall the vengeful anger of a frustrated soul. Offerings to the dead may also be made outside the grave at places where the disembodied spirit comes to find food, drink, or other necessities. In our own society the provision of comfortable coffins for well-dressed corpses, perpetual care of the grave, and periodically placed bouquets of flowers are familiar offerings in the same spirit.

Sacrifices and offerings to the gods themselves generally involve concern to secure the favor of the supernatural beings for the major enterprises of the community. A common category of ritual is the *first-fruits* ceremony. Among hunters, this involves the leaving of the first animal of a kind secured during the season; among agricultural peoples, the leaving of a portion of the first corn, the first rice, or whatever the crop may be. The inauguration or completion of any enterprise, in fact, is apt to be celebrated by a humble, prophylactic sacrifice or offering of something of value to any deity who has a measure of control over that area of experience:

thus the launching of a ship, the raising of a house, the return of a war party, the celebration of a marriage, the birth of a child, the opening of a store—all may require the giving up of some valued thing. Occasionally, but rarely, the article sacrificed is a human life.

Now these sacrifices and offerings have in common a quality similar to that of taboo: the giving up of something of value in order to avoid injury from supernatural forces. It is not difficult to infer that such actions are motivated, consciously or unconsciously, by the wish to appease a being toward whom the person making the sacrifice feels guilty. In regard to funeral offerings, for instance, the role of guilt is patent. To the extent that the deceased was the object of hostility during his lifetime, to the extent that his survivors are secretly glad he rather than they died, it is needful to placate the ghost with gifts. In first-fruits sacrifices, to the extent that the new enterprise is motivated by aggressive motives or by challenges to some status quo, a sacrifice is necessary to forestall an anticipated act of retaliation. Sacrifice is based on the hope that it will bring good luck instead of bad luck, that it will elicit a divine blessing rather than a divine curse upon all-too-often selfish and arrogant humans.

Congregation: Processions, Meetings, and Convocations

Religious behavior is always, in at least some of its expressions, social; that is to say, the adherents of a religion on some occasions come together as a group. There they perform (or watch) ceremonies, talk to the gods or to one another, dance and play music, sing, eat and drink, and in other ways engage in acts rationalized by their relevance to the supernatural. Some religious behaviors may be performed by individuals in solitude, but no religion is purely an individual matter; there is always a congregation which meets on some occasions for the joint performance of ritual acts.

Inspiration

Not all religious systems deliberately seek to induce the psychological experiences of revelation, conversion, possession, mystical ecstasy, or other dramatic alterations of mental and emotional states. However, all religious systems recognize some such experiences as being the result of divine intervention in human life. Auditory or visual hallucination, for instance, is generally interpreted to be a communication from a supernatural being. States of dissociation, in which an individual acts out a role foreign to his daily life, are generally regarded as a result of possession by a divinity. Mystical ecstasy is regarded as a temporary union—sometimes of a quasi-sexual kind—with a god.

It is apparently the case that some persons in all human populations are subject to sudden, spontaneous interruptions of mood and thought. Whatever the reasons—psychodynamic or biochemical—for such alterations of mental activity, the belief in supernatural beings offers a ready and universally employed explanation. Religions differ in the extent to which they cultivate such experiences; all interpret them in religious terms.

SYMBOLISM: MANUFACTURE AND USE OF SYMBOLIC OBJECTS

In addition to employing in the course of ritual various tools, furniture, and architecture for such ordinary purposes as lighting fires, sitting down, and keeping off the rain, religious practitioners always employ a variety of representational or symbolic objects. These objects represent either the deities themselves or values, relationships, processes, or events associated with the deity. Sometimes the representation of deity is direct, in the form of idols, ikons, fetishes, paintings, and so forth; sometimes it is less obvious, as in the Christian treatment of the Cross as the symbol of God's love for man. The Iroquois made and wore wooden masks representing the Great False Face Being, the Great World Rim Dweller, and the wearers in ceremonies were believed to possess the power of that divinity. The Australian aborigines made and kept hidden sacred *churinga* stones; the Polynesian inhabitants of Easter Island carved massive stone statues, and African tribesmen of the Ivory Coast carved small wooden ones, as likenesses of their gods.

Thus beyond the tangible, visible representation of deity, there are the more abstruse symbolic representations of supernatural forces, values, and relationships. One thinks of the Christian's Cross, the carved center pole of the Delaware Bear Ceremony, the Star of David, the Yin-and-Yang symbol of the Far East, the quartered circle or *mandala*, and so on. These abstract symbols are sometimes the object of efforts to discover a universal symbolism: the upright pole, wherever it appears in any religious context, may be interpreted as a vestige of an ancient, widespread belief in the *axis mundi* or "world tree," that ladder by which man may ascend to the world of the supernatural and by which the supernatural beings may climb down to visit man. The Cross, the swastika, the more or less quartered circle are seen as variant forms of the *mandala*, the symbol of psychical partition and reintegration. More generally, then, religious art and the objects made for religious veneration are to be interpreted as compressed, symbolic statements of major religious principles and beliefs. Their handling and contemplation, presumably, is efficacious in keeping fresh in mind the structure of the faith.

It should be pointed out, however, that in native thought these symbolic objects usually serve more than the simple role of mnemonic devices or reminders. They are often believed to be charged with force, or virtue, or *mana*, so that the human user is able to derive from them an infusion of power from the supernatural world. The symbol, in other words, somehow comes to possess the power of that which it symbolizes. Indeed, the symbol, being the communication of power, may be thought of as the essence of that power. One is reminded of the opening words of the Gospel according to St. John: "In the beginning was the Word. . . ."

Ritual

In the foregoing review of the minimal units of religious behavior we have selected those phenomena which are manifest and easily observable. We are concerned at this level only to delimit the main categories of the "smallest religious things," in the spirit represented by Marvin Harris in his discussion of the "smallest cultural things" (*vide* Harris [1964]). These are the elements of religion; they are expressed in reality in great variety (thus, for instance, there are thousands of particular dances); and they are combined, usually, in more complex, stereotyped sequences which we shall call *rituals*.

The program of a ritual may be regarded as a succession of discrete events belonging to one or more of the thirteen categories described above; sometimes events of more than one category may be going on at the same time and any event may be classified under more than one category. Thus, for example, a performance of the Condolence Ceremony of the Iroquois, as described by Fenton (1946), involves a clearly specifiable ritual program. This ceremony, which is still held in order to install a new chief whenever a member of the Great League of the Iroquois has died, is explicitly intended to do two things: first, to present condolences to the bereaved moiety in such a way as to preclude not only excessive grief but also any inclination to seek revenge for the chief's death; and second, at the conclusion of ritual mourning, to inaugurate the new chief publicly in an emotional atmosphere of friendship and gaiety.[1] The program of that part of the ritual which was performed at Lower Cayuga Longhouse in 1945, as described by Fenton, was as follows:

Behavior	*Relevant Ritual-Element Category*
1. "Hanging the kettles for the chiefs": collecting and cooking of food for feast by members of the bereaved moiety in the cookhouse near the longhouse.	Feast
2. Sending message to non-bereaved moiety to say that preparations are complete.	Congregation
3. "Clearing the path" for the visitors (kindling small fires of welcome, brushing away leaves and dry weeds).	Congregation

[1] A brief part of this ritual may be seen on film in the Canadian National Film Board's excellent cinematographic essay on Iroquois religion, *The Longhouse People*.

Behavior	*Relevant Ritual-Element Category*
4. "Roll call of the founders of the League" (*Hai Hai*) is sung by visiting moiety's singer as he arrives in procession.	Music; recitation of code; congregation
5. "Welcome at the wood's edge": the visitors and the bereaved meet across fire and bereaved chant welcome.	Music; recitation of code; congregation
6. "Three rare words of requickening": (wipe away tears, open ears, and clear the throat) from mourning hosts to condoling visitors; wampum exchanged.	Exhortation; symbolism; *mana*
7. Reciprocal action by condoling visitors to mourning hosts; wampum exchanged.	Exhortation; symbolism; *mana*
8. Procession of both moieties to longhouse, and sitting down there, while continuing *Hai Hai*.	Music; recitation of code; congregation
9. "The Six Farewell Songs" are sung by clear-minded for dark-minded moiety, beginning with hymn of farewell to the dead chief, and carrying on with songs addressed to various social groupings.	Music; prayer; exhortation
10. Recitation of the Laws of the League.	Recitation of code
11. "Requickening" address by clear-minded to dark-minded; wampum exchanged.	Recitation of code; exhortation; symbolism; *mana*
12. Mourners return condolences by singing the Six Farewell Songs.	Music; prayer; exhortation; address to supernatural
13. Mourners continue to return condolences with abridged version of Requickening address; wampum exchanged.	Recitation of code; exhortation; symbolism; *mana*

Behavior	Relevant Ritual-Element Category
14. "Showing the new chief's face": new chief is introduced by matron and placed by the fire; wampum exchanged; he is quizzed as to his qualifications.	Symbolism; *mana*
15. "Charge to the new chief": he is instructed in his duties in the name of the Founder of the League, Dekanawidah.	Exhortation
16. Feast.	Feast
17. Recitation of dreams.	Inspiration
18. "Rubbing antlers": social dances led by chiefs, including dances in which various familiar animal actions are simulated.	Music; simulation

It is evident that the program of the Condolence Council is a sequence of discrete ritual events, many of them specifically named by the participants, which may be classified under at least eleven of the thirteen minimal categories of the fundamental religious pattern (Items 1, 2, 4, 5, 6, 7, 8, 9, 11, 12, and 13). Item 8, Taboo, which was not mentioned in the tabulation, requires a word of explanation: a "taboo" was placed on the ethnographers, who were permitted to observe but not to record or photograph the ceremony while it was actually under way.[2]

Rituals can be roughly divided into those which are *calendrical* and those which are *non-calendrical.* Calendrical rituals occur on a regular schedule, and the occasion for their performance is always an event in some natural cycle—day and night, the waxing and waning of the moon, the seasons, eclipses, positions of the planets and stars. Indeed, the need to relate ritual performance to natural cycles was the basis for the development of astronomy and led directly to three major triumphs in primitive science: the great solar and lunar astronomical observatory at Stonehenge, the Maya and

[2] This restriction did not apply to rehearsals or to nonsacred performances put on especially for the benefit of scientific observers.

Aztec cosmic calendar and its associated arithmetic, and in the Near East the systematic observations of the movements of planets. Most ethnographers describe an *annual calendar* of ritual events of tribal life. But of equal importance are the non-calendrical ceremonies, which are performed on occasions of crisis. Some non-calendrical rituals (particularly rites of passage) do follow a life-cycle calendar, however. As Titiev (1960) points out, calendrical rituals are almost always communal and attend to regularly recurring needs of the social group; non-calendrical (or, as he calls them, "critical") rituals may or may not be communal. All societies have both kinds of ritual. Thus among the Iroquois, the annual calendar includes a communal Midwinter Ceremony which is concerned to ensure the general renewal of human health and the return of spring; among the non-calendrical, or critical, rituals is the communal Condolence Ceremony which is performed to resolve the crisis produced by the death of a chief. Titiev argues cogently that the division of rituals into two classes, calendrical and non-calendrical, is more useful, and more justifiable, than the old division into magical and religious.

Belief

Much of the work of religion is done by ritual; ritual is not an arbitrary program of meaningless events. On the contrary, the events that comprise ritual are highly meaningful; what makes them meaningful is a system of *beliefs* that rationalize ritual. The belief system may be considered to be composed of *cosmology* and *values*.

A cosmology is a theory of the universe. It includes *pantheon, myth,* and various *substantive beliefs* about such matters as planes of existence (for example, heaven, hell, life, death, sleep, and dreams) and the relations of causes and effects.

The pantheon of a society is simply a list of the supernatural beings whom the members of the community believe to exist. It is generally presented as a hierarchy, the deities being listed in order of importance, from the most powerful gods on down to minor gods, human souls, and the souls of individual animals. The list should, properly, be amoral, in the sense that not only "good" supernaturals are included, but also "bad" ones, if there are any. In most human societies, there is no effort to regard the good and evil deities as constituting two separate systems, although in Christian tradition, or in culture conflict or situations of religious reform where one pantheon is pitted against another for human allegiance, such dualism may be applied. Even the so-called "monotheistic" religions invariably include an elaborate pantheon (remember that we are using the term "religion" in the summative sense and not as the label for a particular cult institution which happens to be monotheistic). Thus, in the small Christian community in which I grew up, "the religion" (in the summative sense) included *at least* the following categories of supernatural beings in its pantheon:

1. God (the high god)
2. Jesus
3. The Virgin Mary
4. The Saints
5. The Devil
6. Ghosts (souls of the dead on earth found in old houses and around cemeteries)
7. Souls in heaven, hell, or purgatory
8. The souls of normal living human beings
9. Witches, who could take on the form of animals and harm people
10. Santa Claus (believed in only by children)
11. The Easter rabbit (also believed in only by children)
12. Souls of animals
13. Fairies (who bring quarters when teeth fall out, and live in closets or in woodsy places)
14. Superstition: beliefs concerning good or bad luck (two impersonal forces immanent in rabbits' feet, wood, cracks in the pavement, Negro women, four-leaf clovers, positions of the planets, the breath while shooting dice, and so forth and so on, and acquirable by touching, saying formulas, carrying on the body, and so forth)

Not everyone "believed in" all of these supernatural beings, at least not at the same time, and the philosophical tradition of reducing all supernaturalism to the expression of one principle led in some cult contexts to a considerable shrinkage of the list: Jesus became an aspect of God the Trinity (along with the "Holy Ghost"), hell was denied, and all other beings and forces except living and after-life souls were expunged, so that the minimal list was:

1. God
2. Souls of living people
3. Souls of the dead in heaven

The situation among the Iroquois was not much different, if (again) one simply adds up the supernaturals into a list of types. There were at least the following categories in the Iroquois pantheon (*vide* Speck [1949]):

1. The Supreme Being (the Creator)
2. The Prophet (Handsome Lake)
3. The Four Angels (or the Winds of the Four Quarters)
4. The Cosmic Deities (sun, moon, thunder, stars)
5. Dekanawidah (the Founder of the League)
6. The Origin Deities (the sky beings, the primal mother, the primal mother's daughter, the good twin, the evil twin)
7. The Patron Deities of the medicine societies
8. The Spirit Forces of the earth (fire, water, food, fruits, forest animals, fish, medicine, plants, grass, and so on)
9. The souls of people
10. Ghosts
11. Dangerous spirits (the Great Stone Giant, snakes, dwarfs, horned monster, and so on)
12. Good and bad luck (*orenda* and *utgon*)

The values that prompt and sanction the performance of ritual are also, generally speaking, the same values that motivate people in their daily lives. But the values that are recognized by religion may also include the sacred goal of spiritual salvation. Furthermore, a strain toward consistency which is missing in the compendia of values collected from miscellaneous contexts is frequently evident in the religious statements of values. Thus, generally speaking, one can usually speak of a religious value system which is, in its own terms at least, not internally contradictory. Among the Iroquois, for instance, it was recognized that individual persons might harbor unconscious wishes (values) which were at variance with their conscious wishes or with the values of the community. It was the contribution of the Iroquois theory of dreams—which was, as a theory of the soul, by definition a religious theory of values—to assert that *all* wishes should be gratified and to specify ritual contexts within which antisocial or personally repugnant motives were either explicitly defined as temporarily tolerable or attributed to supernatural beings.

In most primitive societies, both cosmology and values are expressed in one or more *myths*. Myths are narratives telling of events in the careers of supernatural beings, among themselves and in company with humans. Generally, there will be, at least, a major origin myth, and usually other mythic cycles such as culture hero myths and trickster stories. These myths in effect specify the pantheon, describe the origin of things, explain the nature of reality, and assert the proper organization of values; in other words, they are the formulation of the belief system. In technologically advanced cultures with professional priesthoods, a codified and official mythology (Bible, Koran, and so on) always exists; there are also more or less elaborate auxiliary texts (theology, metaphysics, history, ethics, and so on) which attempt further to integrate the components of the mythology into an intellectually consistent and all-explanatory system. In this task, extremely elaborate processes of symbolic interpretation are usually resorted to in order to justify the particular interpretations of the myth that are deemed to be desirable from the standpoint of internal consistency and external explanation.

With regard to *substantive beliefs*, which are expressed not only in myths but also in the very lexicon of the people, one must recognize that religious belief is inextricably interwoven with secular aspects of the world view and cosmology. One commonly observed ontological belief is that reality is separated into sacred and profane spheres. Usually there are places distinguished as sacred where ritual is performed—for example, the Christian church. But time as well as space may be divided into sacred and profane: for instance, the morning is sacred time, and the afternoon profane, with respect to the recitation of the Code of Handsome Lake, which must cease at noon. Things and people may be sacred or profane. The dichotomy of sacred and profane often is connected with the ideas of *mana* and taboo. In general one may say that the cosmology and values of a people, insofar as they concern supernatural beings, powers, and forces, are an integral part of the whole belief system. While for analytical purposes they can be distinguished, particularly in the context of ritual, in daily life the individual is apt to employ sacred beliefs and values to rationalize all aspects of his behavior.

Cult Institutions

But the "meaning" of such a ritual as the Condolence Council cannot be described simply by enumerating the types of ritual behavior that it contains and citing the elements of the belief system that rationalize it. The Condolence Ceremony itself is explicitly related to at least three other phenomena: the political institution of the League of the Iroquois; the mourning ritual for the dead by their immediate relatives; and the Dekanawidah myth, which describes the origin of the League and is the rationale both for the League as a political structure and for the ritual of condolence. Thus, just as the elementary categories of religious behavior are only to be found organized in specific sequences, called rituals, so these rituals themselves, and their associated beliefs, are parts of larger complexes which may be called (in the most general sense) *cult institutions.*

A cult institution may be defined as a set of rituals all having the same general goal, all explicitly rationalized by a set of similar or related beliefs, and all supported by the same social group. The League of the Iroquois, for instance, may be called a cult institution in its religious aspect, including a myth of origin, a condolence ritual, and the several religious rituals conducted in the context of actual political meetings. The Iroquois, however, maintain a number of other cult institutions, each with its own apparatus of rituals and beliefs. The following would be a minimal list of contemporary Iroquois cult institutions:

1. The League of the Iroquois
2. The Handsome Lake religion
3. The annual calendar of hunting and agricultural ceremonies
4. The medicine societies
5. The dream complex
6. Christianity

Each of these cult institutions is related to others, in one way or another, and many of them join forces in major ritual sequences, dovetailing and overlapping in scheduling, personnel, material apparatus, and beliefs, but each maintaining a distinct and autonomous role. Thus, for instance, some Iroquois attend both Handsome Lake meetings and Christian church services; the medicine societies meet publicly during the calendrical ceremonies; the Code of Handsome Lake is preached both at separate meetings and during the same annual calendar; the dream complex is expressed both in the Condolence Ceremony (a League ritual), in the annual calendar, and on separate occasions. Some cult institutions are, in theory, antithetical to others. Thus, the Handsome Lake religion takes a dim view of the medicine societies; Christianity takes a dim view of Handsome Lake. Yet these more or less autonomous systems of belief and practice, each with its own specific history, rituals, and beliefs, coexist in a more or less coordinated pattern. Furthermore, one must mention a multitude of other supernaturalistic behaviors and beliefs that would be difficult to regard as cult institutions, but which survive as practices carried on occasionally, such as magic and witchcraft, funeral rituals, belief in ghosts, and so forth.

The intermingling of elements from different cult institutions in "the religion" of a society applies to both belief and ritual. Let us consider, for instance, the simple Christian pantheon mentioned earlier (God, living souls, souls in heaven). In the town where I lived, this monotheistic simplification was the theological property of only one kind of cult institution—the liberal religious denominations. The larger pantheon could be conveniently parceled out among at least four major cult institutions:

1. The various denominational congregations: the Catholic parish, the Lutheran Church, the United Brethren Church, the Baptist Church, the Church of the Brethren, a Pentecostal church, perhaps one or two other Protestant denominations, and a few Jews who attended synagogues in larger towns nearby.
2. The religio-political cult: a nondenominational, theistic faith used to rationalize and sanction political, military, and other secular institutions, such as schools, in terms that were then (supposedly, at least) acceptable alike to Protestants, Catholics, Jews, and nondenominational theists. This cult found expression on certain holidays (such as the Fourth of July, Washington's and Lincoln's birthdays, Election Day, Labor Day) and in various observances in schools, banks, post offices, stores, and so on.
3. Superstition: the luck, witchcraft, and powwow cult (growing largely out of Central European magical and religious beliefs), together with miscellaneous beliefs having to do with luck, good and bad, which frequently pretend to a relationship to Christianity.
4. The children's cult: a series of observances arranged, or at least sanctioned, by parents, but believed, in a religious sense, only by children, such as Halloween and Christmas in its Santa Claus aspect.

Just as the inhabitants of my home town would point out that an indiscriminate listing would mingle in one pantheon beings who should be separated into several cult institutions, so the Iroquois do much the same. The benevolent supernatural entities, from the Creator down to the souls of men, are given officially recognized status and priority in the annual calendar and in the Handsome Lake theology; the medicine society beings, the dangerous creatures, ghosts, and luck are relegated, by some religious functionaries, to a secondary position.

Thus we find that both in a "civilized" modern American community, and in a primitive Iroquoian one, a similar principle is at work: "the religion" is, at least with regard to pantheon, in fact a loosely organized federation of beliefs which are more tightly interrelated in the several cult institutions than in any overall system.

The Religion of a Society: A Conglomeration of Cult Institutions

Now the foregoing considerations lead to the final concept: *the religion* of a society. To the extent that the religious beliefs and practices of any community are in fact found largely to exist as appurtenances of more or less autonomous (both conceptually and behaviorally) cult institutions, the term "the religion" of a society must be used with caution. It is essentially a summative notion and cannot be taken uncritically to imply that one single unifying, internally coherent, carefully programed set of rituals and beliefs characterizes the religious behavior of the society or is equally followed by all its members. With the restriction in mind that "the religion" of a society is really likely to be a loosely related group of cult institutions and other, even less well-organized special practices and beliefs, it is sometimes useful to use the term as a collective noun.

RITUAL

Now let us compare my home town and the Iroquois Society to see how the major calendrical rituals of the several cult institutions are distributed over time. In my town, the major events in the calendar were as shown in Table 1 (p. 79). For the Iroquois the calendar was constructed in a slightly different way as shown in Table 2 (p. 80).

It should be noted that the political cult in the American example does not perform all of its rituals calendrically but conducts many in response to specific emergencies, and that the Iroquois dream cult and the curing rituals of the medicine societies for the most part find non-calendrical occasions for their rituals, again because these rituals are invoked ad hoc in response to crises of health. Most of the calendrical rituals are concentrated in the agricultural series, each ceremony in the series containing space for the performance of the rituals of the several other cult institutions. Furthermore, as Fenton points out (1936), there is a basic ritual pro-

TABLE 1

ANNUAL CALENDAR OF RITUAL EVENTS (AMERICAN)

Month	*Denominational Cult* (excluding Jewish)			*"Political" Cult*	*Super-stitious Cult*	*Children's Cult*
1			weekly services	New Year's Day	New Year's Day	
2				Washington's Birthday	Valentine's Day	
3				St. Patrick's Day		
4	Easter (Christ's death)	Lent to Ascension Day				Easter ("Bunny Rabbit")
5				Memorial Day		
6						
7				Fourth of July		
8						
9				Labor Day		
10						Halloween
11				Election Day		
				Thanksgiving Day		
12	Christmas (Christ's birthday)	Advent to Epiphany				Christmas (Santa Claus)

gram which is performed in full at Midwinter, selections from which are repeated in the other ceremonies. Indeed, only the Handsome Lake cult and the Little Water Medicine Society have an annual calendar that is separate and distinct from that of the agricultural cult, and this is only a partial autonomy, since the Code of Handsome Lake is recited not only at the Six Nations Meetings but also at the Midwinter and Green Corn, and the Little

TABLE 2

ANNUAL CALENDAR OF RITUAL EVENTS (IROQUOIS)

Month	*Agricultural Cult*	*Handsome Lake Cult*	*Dream Cult*	*Medicine Societies*
1	Midwinter	Midwinter	Midwinter	Midwinter Little Water Medicine
2				
3	Maple			Maple
4				Traveling False Faces
5	Corn			
6	Strawberry	Strawberry		Little Water Medicine
7				
8	Green Corn	Green Corn Six Nations Meetings		Green Corn Little Water Medicine
9				
10				Traveling False Faces
11	Harvest			
12				

SOURCE: Adapted from William N. Fenton, "An Outline of Seneca Ceremonies at Coldspring Longhouse," *Yale University Publications in Anthropology*, No. 9, 1936, pp. 6–10.

Water Medicine Society chooses to meet, albeit in a separate place, at the time of the Midwinter, Strawberry, and Green Corn. Thus, the annual calendar must be regarded, like the pantheon, as a conglomeration of ritual events, derived from different cult institutions, and only partially given a programed integration in a series. The Iroquois, indeed, have kept their several cults more rationally and programatically integrated than did the people of my home town.

BELIEF SYSTEM: MYTH

The second major component of cosmology, *myth*, generally identifies, describes, and explains the origin, interests, and powers of the supernatural entities of the pantheon, and gives an account of their relation to man which justifies and rationalizes the rituals that are performed in their name. Myth, like pantheon, must be sorted out among cult institutions in order to be understood. Among the Iroquois, for instance, there were at least four classes of myth: the cosmogony, a set of stories that accounted for the creation of the world and its major features, natural and supernatural; the Dekanawidah myth accounting for the origin and ritual of the Great League; the myths of origin of the medicine societies; and the myth (half history, half vision) of the origin of the Handsome Lake religion. These several myths were produced from the dreams and visions, variously remembered and distorted in the telling, of individual Iroquois over a very long period of time. The most recent is the Handsome Lake myth, the most ancient, probably, are the medicine society myths, some of which seem to recall a pre-agricultural era.

Although these myths are all parts of "the mythology" of the Iroquois, they are extraordinarily disconnected. The animal beings to whom most of the medicine society origin myths refer are not even mentioned in the cosmological origin myth, which is devoted largely to deities of agriculture and of war. Handsome Lake invokes a new set of beings, the Four Angels, in his myth; and Dekanawidah stands alone. While the Iroquois have devoted some theological labor to discovering equivalences between the pantheons represented in these cycles, the results are superficial: the Four Angels of Handsome Lake (only three of whom actually appeared to him) are equated by some with the Four Winds of the ancient cosmology; by some Christian Iroquois, the fourth Angel has been interpreted as Jesus; the Evil Twin has been, more substantially, merged into the identity of the False Face or Great World Rim Dweller. But these efforts at developing a unified theological system are continually subverted by the emergence of new deities in dreams and by the autonomy of the cult institutions themselves.

The situation is no different with the people of my home town. The principal mythological document is contained in the Christian Bible, a collection of very old texts, Jewish in origin, divided into two parts. The Old Testament contains cosmological elements that are derived from the earliest written cosmology known to man—the Sumerian and Babylonian—and no doubt reflects a common base of Near Eastern and North African cosmological belief tens of thousands of years old, with later additions specifically Jewish in origin. The New Testament, almost two thousand years old, but recent by comparison, recounts the life and experiences of a Jewish prophet named Jesus. These two myths, which stand in a relation comparable to that of the cosmological origin myth and the Handsome Lake myth, have been the subject of much more intense theological effort than was the case with the Iroquois, but this labor has not succeeded in converting some (the Jews) who still adhere only to the older testament. Moreover, Christians themselves have disputed various theological problems and divided into three more or less antagonistic religious factions—the Roman Catholics, the Orthodox Catholics, and the Protestants (who themselves have further split into denominations).

Although none of these doctrinal divisions originated in my town (which is, after all, only about two hundred years old), the pattern of division is replicated there. The political authorities, to the extent that they are religious, have been intentionally vague and theistic, and, in order to minimize the introduction of religious separation into the secular affairs of the community, have (in conformity with most other communities in the region) proposed the theological doctrine that all religious groups really worship the same Supreme Being, who may simply be called God. Whenever possible, in political ceremonies in which religious ritual is performed, the cosmology and pantheon are kept to a least common denominator of "belief in God"; the coins used by all say simply "In God We Trust"; school children pledge allegiance to "one nation under God." The historical myth here is, simply, that our various ancestors have taken separate paths in the pursuit of goodness. This is not a doctrine that the denominations always accept, since to the Christian in the context of denominational cult—the Jew does *not* worship precisely the same God because he denies the divinity of Jesus. The superstitious and children's cults are even more thoroughly disconnected from the rest; although they, too, contain elements of great antiquity (Babylonian astrology, Egyptian beliefs about cats, medieval European conceptions of witches, and so on), they are for the most part not even recognized as being "religious" at all but rather as being "superstitious." Santa Claus, indeed, is occasionally canonized (by Jews and Protestants as well as Catholics) in order to make it respectable to bring him into the home, but the Easter Bunny and the Halloween beings remain unashamedly pagan, and powwow doctors, four-leaf clovers, witchcraft, and the phases of the moon are dismissed as being irrelevant and of no real consequence to the churches or the political structure. Nonetheless, each of these cults has its own mythology describing the origins of its rituals and the beings or forces that make them work.

The Fundamental Pattern

In sum, the fundamental pattern of religion would seem to be describable in terms of levels of analysis. First is the *supernatural premise*. Second are the thirteen universal categories of religious behavior, which are intuitively recognized by anthropologists, theologians, and laymen alike as *the elementary particles of ritual:* prayer, song, physiological exercise, exhortation, recitation of texts, simulation, *mana* (touching things), taboo, feasts, sacrifice, congregation, inspiration, and symbolism. As a third level we have described the threading of events of these ritual categories into sequences called *ritual* and the rationalization of ritual by *belief*. Fourth, ceremonies are organized into complexes which we have labeled *cult institutions*. Finally, we come to *the religion* of a society, which is describable only as a conglomeration of *ritual* (both calendrical and critical) and *belief system*, including *pantheon*, *myth*, and *values*, whose components are logically well integrated only at the level of cult institutions.

These are the universal formal properties, the skeletal anatomy, the fundamental pattern, of religion. Now we turn to the typology of cult institutions and the regional geography of religious traditions.

The Varieties of Cult Institutions

"The religion" of any community is, as we have pointed out, more a conglomeration than a synthesis of its various cult institutions. The cult institutions of any community have more or less distinct pantheons, calendars, and mythologies; they have distinct histories; they often appeal to different groups of people; and they have different kinds and degrees of social organization. Thus any effort to develop a typology of "religions" must begin with some rough-and-ready classification of the varieties of cult institutions. The major types of religion can only be a group of more or less typical profiles, in each of which one or another kind of cult institutions can be reasonably regarded as predominant.

In studying the varieties of cult institutions in the Judaeo-Christian tradition, sociologists have made use of a familiar dichotomy of ideal types based on differences in social organization: the *church* and the *sect*. Churches—large, stable, mature, socially accepted religious organizations—may be further divided into *ecclesiae* and *denominations* (Nottingham [1954]). Ecclesiae claim to be, and to a reasonably close approximation are, universal established religions within a definable territory—national, international, or even worldwide. A religious bureaucracy unites the religious functionaries and holds the local congregations to a standardized body of ritual and belief. The Roman Catholic Church and Islam are examples of churches that come close to satisfying the requirements of international ecclesiae; the established Anglican Church is an example of a national ecclesia. Denominations, on the other hand, such as the Lutheran, Methodist, and Mormon churches, while they also maintain large bureaucracies, do not demand an exclusive establishment and are willing to coexist with other denominations of more or less similar creeds.

Churches may also be subdivided into three bureaucratic types: the *episcopal*, in which the local priest is responsible to the upper hierarchy rather than to the local congregation or his priestly peers;

the *presbyterian*, in which the local preacher is responsible to the presbytery or body of preachers, his peers; and the *congregational*, in which the congregation selects, and to a large degree controls the conduct of, its own minister.

Sects, in contrast to churches, are relatively small, are alienated from the surrounding world, and may not have the bureaucratic social structure characteristic of churches. Some sects are destined to become churches as they grow larger and attain political power; others remain relatively small, separatist groups, and some are so amorphous in organization as to constitute more a creed than an actual organization. Sects are sometimes further divided into stable, separatist sects proper (such as the Old Order Amish of rural Pennsylvania), religious revitalization movements (like the Black Muslims or the Handsome Lake religion), and cults (like the Negro store-front church), the last being the least-organized groups, with transient memberships and an appeal largely to urban groups.

The sociological emphasis upon organizations that have a more or less bureaucratic structure and are exclusively concerned with religion means, however, that the ecclesiastical typology of cult institutions must exclude such political cults as the Iroquois League and the nondenominational secular creed of my own home town, and must also exclude cult institutions that have ritual and belief but no bureaucracy (such as Iroquois witchcraft, the American children's cult, the Iroquois dream cult, and the home town superstitions). A strictly sociological approach would also tend to eliminate from serious consideration as cult institutions such minimally organized phenomena as shamanism, secret religious societies, family cults, and the magical beliefs and practices of primitive communities, where there is small supporting apparatus of social organization and material. For anthropological, comparative purposes, therefore, we need to begin with a much simpler model of religious organization—a model that will allow us to recognize those culturally institutionalized complexes of religious behavior which, because of the elaborateness of their rituals and beliefs, must be considered cult institutions, even though the associated level of religious social organization is minimally developed.

INDIVIDUALISTIC CULT INSTITUTIONS

In most, if not all, human societies there are cult institutions whose rituals are not performed by specialists. Examples can readily be cited for both primitive and advanced societies: among the Iroquois, the dream cult; among the Americans, the children's cult and the superstitious cult; among the Trobrianders, sailing magic; among the Naskapi, hunting rituals; among Plains Indians, the vision quest and the guardian spirit complex. Invariably, these nonspecialist cults will include mortuary rituals and magic and taboo customs concerning "luck." In such cult institutions, there is no categorical distinction between religious specialist and layman; everyone is his own specialist, entering into a relationship with the deities and powers on occasion of need and requiring no shamanic or priestly intermediary. We may label such cult institutions *individualistic.*

SHAMANIC CULT INSTITUTIONS

Almost as widespread are those cult institutions in which an individual part-time practitioner, endowed by birth, training, or inspirational experience with a special power, intervenes for a fee with supernatural beings or forces on behalf of human clients. We may call these *shamanic* institutions. Shamans are to be found not only in the northern circumboreal and circumpolar regions (whence the term "shaman" derives), but also among most other human communities, including our own. They act as shamans proper (in Siberia), as diviners, as magicians, witch doctors, medicine men, mediums and spiritualists, palm-readers, astrologers, and so forth. It is in the shamanic cult institutions that a religious division of labor is to be found at its simplest level: the shaman in his religious role is a specialist, and his clients in their relation to him are laymen.

COMMUNAL CULT INSTITUTIONS

At a still more complex level of social organization, there are the *communal* cult institutions. In these, groups of laymen are responsible for calendrical or occasional performance of rituals of importance to various social groups ranging in scope from the members of special categories—such as age grades, the sexes, members of secret societies, particular kinship groups, and sufferers from particular diseases—to the whole community. While the ceremonies may employ specialists, such as shamans, professional speakers, or highly skilled dancers, responsibility lies with a lay group whose sacredness is an occasional thing associated with particular role performances. The annual calendar of agricultural rituals among the Iroquois; the political cult among Americans; the ancestor ceremonies of the Chinese and certain African tribes; totemic and puberty rituals among the Australian aborigines—all these are instances of communal cult institutions. Such communally sponsored ceremonies are apt to be associated with a fairly elaborate pantheon of beings and forces whose separate concerns are distributed among a variety of social groups with special interests and problems appropriate to particular deities. The lay organization will have a somewhat bureaucratic social structure, with regular assignment of technical and supervisory responsibilities, but no full-time priesthood or extensive religious hierarchy will exist.

ECCLESIASTICAL CULT INSTITUTIONS

The next, and most complex, type of cult institution is the *ecclesiastical*. At this level we return to the typology developed by the sociologists. Ecclesiastical cult institutions, whether they are churches or sects, have in common the existence of a professional clergy organized into a bureaucracy according to the same principles as the local military, political, and economic institutions. The clergy are neither private entrepreneurs (shamans) nor lay officials (the communal religious functionaries), but rather are formally elected or appointed persons who devote all, or at least a regularly scheduled part, of their careers to the priesthood. They are not primarily responsible for supporting the church with money, labor, contributions, and so forth, these burdens being laid upon the congregation or upon sodalities of laymen. Members of the clergy are exclusively responsible for performing certain rituals on behalf of individuals, groups, or the whole community. Within certain areas of behavior—usually extending beyond ritual itself—they claim authority over laymen. With regard to an ecclesiastical cult institution, therefore, one may speak of a clear-cut division of labor between profane (lay) and sacred (clerical) personnel. The laymen, furthermore, participate in ritual largely as passive respondents, or even as an audience, rather than as active ritual managers.

The pantheon of ecclesiastical cult institutions usually recognizes gods of great power. Where these high gods are several, each of noble and independent character, we may speak of an *Olympian* type of pantheon; where all other supernatural beings and forces are subordinate to, or merely alternative manifestations of, one continuously active and important Supreme Being, the pantheon is called *monotheistic*. The Judaeo-Christian tradition produces, for the most part, a monotheistic ecclesiastical type of cult institution; the ancient Greeks, Egyptians, Babylonians, and Romans, on the other hand, represent the Olympian type.

The Four Main Types of Religion

When one attempts to construct a typology of "religions," one must at the outset recognize that the four major varieties of cult institutions form a scale. In societies containing an ecclesiastical cult institution, there will also be communal, shamanic, and individualistic institutions. Where there is no ecclesiastical institution, but a communal one, there will be also shamanic and individualistic varieties. And where there is neither ecclesiastical nor communal, there will be shamanic and individualistic. Theoretically, there should be—or should once have been—societies containing only individualistic cult institutions, but I know of no surviving examples.

This consideration leads to a fourfold taxonomy of "religions" (in the conglomerative sense of that word): at the most primitive level, *shamanic* religions, containing only shamanic and individualistic cult institutions; *communal* religions, containing communal, shamanic, and individualistic cult institutions; *Olympian* religions, containing an Olympian variety of ecclesiastical institutions, along with the other three; and *monotheistic* religions, with a monotheistic ecclesiastical cult institution, together with communal, shamanic, and individualistic cult institutions.

Examples of these four major types are not difficult to discover. The Eskimos, as described by Lantis (1950), may be taken to represent the shamanic type; the Trobriand Islanders as described by Malinowski (1927), the communal; Dahomey as described by Herskovits (1938), the Olympian; and village India as described by Singer (1959), Marriott (1955), and Harper (1965), the monotheistic. In each case, let us consider the major cult institutions of the society, and then evaluate the classification that we have proposed for it.

THE SHAMANIC RELIGION OF THE ESKIMOS

Among the Eskimos, an uninhibited animism in the old Tylorean sense has populated the world with a numerous pantheon of minor beings—human souls, animal souls, local spirits, trolls, and so on—and with only a few middling-high high gods, principally Sedna the Keeper of the Sea Animals, the Sun, the Moon, and the taboo-sanctioning Spirit of the Air. There would seem to be at least two individualistic cults, which involve no major scheduled ceremonies but which demand constant practice by individuals, and a shamanic cult.

First of all, there is the Spirit Helper Cult, that set of beliefs and practices involving the individual's relationship to his own guardian spirit. Spirit Helpers in many cases are inherited patrilineally; they may also be encountered in personal spiritual experiences. Spirit Helpers are acknowledged in the wearing of amulets, such as little ivory statuettes, bits of animal bodies, and tiny bags containing pebbles, insects, and the remains of shellfish, each item representing a deity with a particular power. One person, especially if he is a child, may have his clothing decorated with dozens of these fetishlike objects. Associated with the promise of help from the spirit come also specific taboos, which have to be carefully observed, against killing or eating the creatures represented.

Second, the Game Animal Cult involves certain universal restrictions on the behavior of all members of the community. General taboos are intended to prevent any action that might offend the major game animals. The flesh of land and sea mammals, for instance, should never be cooked in the same pot or otherwise put together; to do so would bring punishment upon the whole community in the form of illness or starvation. Positive demands are also made. Fresh water, for instance, must be placed in the mouth of recently killed sea mammals; fat must be given to slain land animals. The general motive is so to conduct oneself as to avoid giving offense to the souls, the Keepers, of the game upon which the Eskimos are chiefly dependent for their livelihood. Each person, at all times, privately or publicly, is expected on his own responsibility to observe the various ritual regulations governing contact with game animals, for the sake of the community. Infractions, because they are threatening to the community, must be publicly confessed in order to obviate disaster, and the community itself may join in such a severe discipline as banishment in case of continuing violations.

The third major institution is the Shamanic Cult. The shaman (*angakok*) is a man who by virtue of a spiritual experience and, sometimes, apprenticeship to an older shaman is able to command the attention and aid of a Spirit Helper with great power. The shaman, by calling upon this helper, is able to perform various services for his clients, individually or collectively, and he is paid a fee. The shaman's most important service, in the coastal communities, is his yearly spiritual trip to the bottom of the sea to persuade Sedna the Sea Goddess, Keeper of the Sea Animals, to release the game from her domain so that the Eskimos can live through one more year. The shaman is also called upon frequently to diagnose illness—which means, usually, discovering from his Spirit Helper what supernatural being has been offended by a broken taboo or a slighted ritual. Once diagnosed as a result of taboo violation, the illness may be "spontaneously" aborted or it may have to be directly treated by the shaman. Treatment can consist of the shaman's undertaking a magic flight to recover the soul, or of massage to remove a disease object, or of the victim's confession and ritual expiation in the hope of exorcising a possessing spirit. Sometimes, too, the shamans are reputed to use their power as witches, but ideally the shaman is the community's loyal agent in dealings with the supernatural world.

Beyond these three cult institutions Eskimo religion does not really go. There is no elaborate annual calendar of communal religious rituals; in fact, there are few communal ceremonies of any kind, and the village meetinghouse is as much a secular as a religious center. Such communal rituals as have been occasionally reported are the first to disappear under the impact of acculturation and are only dubiously religious in their ritual rationalization.

THE COMMUNAL RELIGION OF THE TROBRIANDERS

Among inhabitants of the Trobriand Islands, the major cult institution is what may be termed the Technological Magic Cult. All major economic (and, in the old days, military) enterprises associated with a significant degree of uncertainty are carried out with the aid of magical spells. The magical spells are believed to have been handed down from the ancestors of the magicians, beginning with the mythological ancestral culture heroes and passed on by each successive generation. But although the spells have reached modern man through the hands of ancestors, whose spirits still survive and to whom ceremonial deference should be paid, the power of the formulas is inherent and requires no intermediary spirit's aid. The three major traditions of technological magic—garden magic, canoe magic, and fishing magic—involve communal participation in rites presided over by public magicians. The garden magician, in fact, is theoretically also the village chief. Being tied to the cycle of the seasons, these forms of magic arrange themselves more or less regularly into an annual calendar of public rituals in which the leading role, that of the spell-producing magician, is played by a man who, by virtue of his personal possession of the magic, has in a sense the powers of a god and whose spirit, after his death, will become one of the supernatural ancestral beings.

Theologically related to the Technological Magic Cult is a second cult institution: the Cult of the Spirits of the Dead. Although direct interaction between men and supernaturals is minimal in Technological Magic, it is expressed in the beliefs and practices of the Cult of the Spirits of the Dead. Mortuary ceremonies are elaborate, and at the annual harvest feast (a month of food display, dancing, and sexual license) the spirits of the dead are believed to be present as pleased watchers and passive participants. At other times of the year, in dreams, hallucinations, or fits, the spirits of the dead may appear to and communicate with human beings. The spirits of the dead also are responsible for conception. Although the Trobrianders consider that conception usually does not occur in a female until after she has had sexual intercourse, the man's role in conception is believed to be only that of penetrating and enlarging the vagina sufficiently to permit the insertion, by the spirits of the dead, of spiritual matter into the womb. Since this opening can also be accomplished by mechanical means—that is, by the fingers or by other objects—a woman can conceive without intercourse; thus, the onset of pregnancy of a married woman during her husband's absence is no proof of her infidelity.

Professional magic and witchcraft constitute a third cult institution. Professional sorcerers, controlling spells efficacious in causing and curing illness and in handling various other emergencies, are important in the community as agents of individual clients.

Fourth, and finally, a variety of spells is available to individuals working on their own behalf. The individualistic cult institution of private magic is important in matters of love, in protection against the malevolence of certain spirits of the dead, against flying witches, and so on. Trobriand religion thus possesses a remarkably coherent, internally consistent theological and ritual system, which coordinates two communal ritual cults, shamanic services, and individual practice in a well-rationalized system, with individual and regional variability presenting few problems of philosophical integration.

THE OLYMPIAN RELIGION OF DAHOMEY

Our third example, an Olympian type of religious system, will be taken from Dahomey, a West Coast African society, in its days of political independence. In contrast to the Eskimos, who live in very small, isolated, politically self-sufficient villages and are dependent upon the hunt for all subsistence needs, the Dahomeans are a populous agricultural people, supporting large urban centers where trading and manufacturing are carried on and where the political bureaucracy of the kingdom of Dahomey resides. The Dahomeans support a considerable range of cult institutions.

At the simplest level is what may be called the Magical Cult. The common people believe in a miscellany of minor deities, with a few of whom a person may establish a personal relationship and who can be more or less constrained in the form of fetishes. Such powers are useful in magic performed with the help of such fetish objects as monkey skulls, herbs, plant fragments, and lion skins, to bring luck in love, to ensure good fortune in the hunt, and so on.

The Divination Cult, reminiscent of shamanism but attenuated in form, is important in trials and in coping with epidemic diseases. The professional village diviner discovers the proper sacrifice for harvest ceremonies, administers the ordeals that distinguish the guilty from the innocent, prognosticates the fate of proposed economic ventures (such as a new market or a new field for cultivation), and diagnoses the cause of epidemics by identifying the offended god and the sacrifice needed to relieve his ill will. The diviner also sells his services to individual clients needing advice in how to handle the supernatural aspects of various personal affairs.

More elaborately developed are the Ancestral Cults, one of which pertains to each of the thirty or forty sibs. A sib is conceived to include both the living and the dead descendants of an ancient union between a human being and an earthbound deity; often it is localized in a specific village or set of villages. The deities of an ancestral cult are the group of ritually sanctified ancestors. Funeral rituals (within three years after death) are absolutely enjoined, at least in theory, upon the living members of the sib, and annually an elaborate ceremony is required of the sib members to honor their dead. Although it often happens that this calendar is violated by procrastination because of its cost, the ceremonies are always eventually performed when the dangers of ancestral wrath are calculated to outweigh the prospects of financial loss.

The Great Gods Cult has many of the features of an established church, since it is officially supported by, and rationalizes, the feudal monarchy of Dahomey, and since it is endowed with a priesthood and extensive temples. The pantheon of the Great Gods Cult is divided into four major sub-pantheons, the deities in each being related, genealogically, by the creation myth. Each deity is responsible for a major department of nature, and each pantheon is associated with a separate religious order—each with its own priesthood, temples, ritual, and mythology. The Great Gods are humanlike beings with strong (and contrasting) personalities and with an active social life which parallels human life in its concern with sex, with war, and with economic enterprises. The Great Gods have an ongoing and more or less whimsical but essentially moral concern for what happens on earth. They possess human beings temporarily, and act out their roles in public "voodoo" ceremonials.

THE MONOTHEISTIC RELIGION OF INDIA

The exemplification of the fourth, monotheistic, type of religion comes from India. India is notoriously complex and difficult to describe, but in principle is no more intractable to analysis than any other large modern national state. It is, indeed, representative of the contemporary world in many ways, not least in the variety of its religious manifestations. At the sophisticated extreme, there are at least two major (and several minor) monotheistic cult institutions in India: Islam, monotheistic but not monistic; monistic Hinduism; and lesser monotheistic faiths. At the primitive extreme, there are many tribal groups in India which maintain religions of the simpler types. For simplicity of exposition we shall restrict the following discussion to the religion of people who can be classified as Hindu.

Philosophical Hinduism as a cult institution carries monotheism to its theological limit, positing an all-encompassing monistic divinity (the "One") capable of multitudinous manifestations, and hypothesizing a process of spiritual progress in which the individual soul can, theoretically, shuck off the various earthly manifestations of this Oneness in a union with the ultimate sacred reality. Paths of spiritual progress are various—ritual observance, emotional devotion, intellectual control—but all lead, in principle, to Nirvana.

In addition to monotheistic philosophical Hinduism, the so-called Sanskritic or "Great Tradition" of Hinduism maintains a pantheon, a mythology, and a body of rituals, both calendrical and occasional, which can only be classified as Olympian. The Great Gods Siva, Krishna, Ram, Vishnu, and Lakshmi are celebrated in elaborate ceremonials and are the subject of epic myths detailing their characters and the dramatic stories of their lives. Although the Great Gods Cult, like the theosophy, is the product of priestly literati largely resident in temples and urban centers, it extends into small villages and accounts for a substantial proportion of the pantheon, ritual calendar, and mythology at the village level. The Olympian Great Gods Cult in the Hindu Great Tradition, as in the Dahomean, is parceled out, as it were, among a number of ecclesiastical organizations each of which has its own part of the total pantheon, its own priesthood, its own temples, its own rituals.

Rationalized in part by the Great Tradition, but at the village level functioning more as a communal cult institution, is the Caste Taboo system, which involves not only the notorious intercaste rules of avoidance and of labor specialization, but just as importantly, numbers of rules governing states of ritual purity which apply to individual and group behavior within caste boundaries. Some castes also maintain their own communal rituals. The Caste Taboo system, theologically, is rationalized by appeal to the Olympian pantheon, but practically it is preoccupied with a spiritual force that can best be understood as *mana*. Events of defilement and purification are governed by an elaborate, quasi-mathematical theory of transformations.

At the rural village level there is an Ancestral Cult which receives little support from the Hindu Great Tradition but which may be very important to villagers; shrines are erected to departed ancestors of the last few generations. Also quasi-independent of the Great Gods tradition is a Cult of Local Gods, whose pantheon, ritual calendar, and mythology are at the local level interpolated into the Great Tradition; this cult institution, being local, varies from place to place. There is also a cult of various kinds of "holy men" (*gurus*, curers, and so forth). As religious specialists who have more direct and personal contact with the pantheon than do priests, they play a somewhat shamanic role, working directly with individuals in spiritual contract. Finally, there is the residual category that can perhaps most simply be defined as the cult institution of "superstitions" (in relation to the theosophy and the Great Tradition): witchcraft, personal guardian spirits, fertility magic, and so on. The pattern appears to be the same as that in Western national states: an officially recognized national monotheistic tradition, expressed in a variety of separate ecclesiastical domains, overlying a large group of more primitive beliefs and rituals.

An Outline of Religious Culture Areas of the World

Any effort to classify the religious culture areas of the world must be prefaced by apologetic recognition that, if it is to be useful at all, such a classification must vastly oversimplify. In addition to inevitable arbitrariness in choice of defining characteristics, the boundaries of areas are more precise in a book than in nature, enclaves cannot all be separately identified, and difficulties in assigning marginal or mixed types cannot always be adequately met. But with this caveat stated, we shall proceed to suggest a simple culture-area typology of religion. The reader may refer to the accompanying map (p. 98) for location of the types defined below. Briefly, these types are treated as areal varieties of the four major types of religions delineated in the preceding section. The object of classification (and thus the principle of mapping) is not the types of cult institutions themselves but the religions of societies. Thus, for example, if one wished to map the cult institution of shamanism, it would be necessary to show shamanism distributed over the entire world; we delineate, rather, two types of shamanic religions, confined to those areas in which it, together with mortuary cults and individualistic practices, is the only significant aspect of religion. The date of reference will be 1600; since this time, the distribution of religious types has been grossly altered by colonization and by political and economic change. The reader should also remember that the Olympian and monotheistic types of religion both imply the coexistence of communal and shamanistic cults, and the communal implies the shamanic. In these capsule sketches, we shall have little to say about the functions or the processes of historical development and change in religion; these we shall discuss in later chapters. The typology and map here are primarily descriptive rather than dynamically interpretive. Analytical type is represented at the major (Roman numeral) level; regional styles or traditions resulting from diffusion and acculturation are represented at the minor (Arabic numeral) level.

I. SHAMANIC

Individualistic cults (including mortuary and taboo) and shamanistic cults are present; communal, Olympian, and monotheistic cults are absent or trivial. Pantheon does not include many major deities of day-by-day importance; mythology is abbreviated; ritual is mostly critical or non-calendrical rather than calendrical.

1. *Circumpolar shamanism* is found among Eskimos, northern Athapascan and Algonkian hunters, the Paleo Siberians, central Asiatic steppe and forest tribes, and the Lapps. Commonly associated with it is a belief in Keepers of the Game (as in bear and sea-mammal ceremonialism) and a mythological and ritual symbolism involving magical flight and the world-tree motif.

2. *Negrito shamanism* is found among the Andaman Islanders, the Semang of Malaya, African pygmies, and probably wherever surviving Negrito remnant groups are located. It is simpler theologically and lacks, apparently, the circumpolar doctrines of game-keepers, magical flight, and world-tree.

II. COMMUNAL

In addition to individualistic and shamanic cult institutions, there are communal cults which involve a pantheon of major deities controlling departments of nature, either presently or in the past. Rituals are performed in which many lay persons participate actively; a ritual calendar is related to seasonal, life crisis, and other cyclical events. The mythology is rich and variegated, although the gods are not for the most part heroic figures.

3. *American Indian* societies, apart from North American sha-

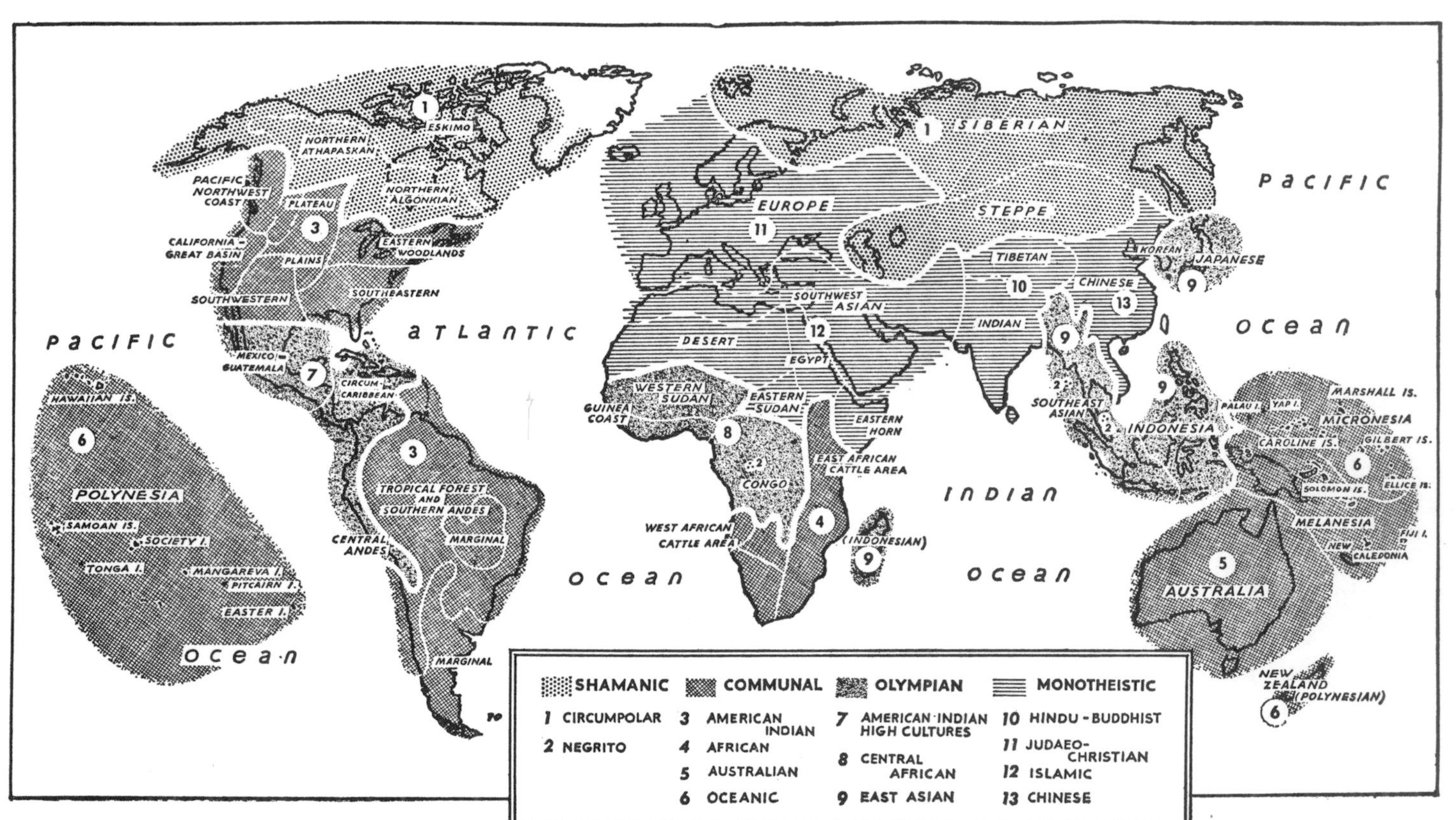

PACIFIC
ATLANTIC
PACIFIC
Ocean
INDIAN
Ocean
Ocean
Ocean
ESKIMO
NORTHERN ATHAPASKAN
NORTHERN ALGONKIAN
PACIFIC NORTHWEST COAST
PLATEAU
CALIFORNIA - GREAT BASIN
PLAINS
EASTERN WOODLANDS
SOUTHEASTERN
SOUTHWESTERN
MEXICO - GUATEMALA
CIRCUM-CARIBBEAN
TROPICAL FOREST AND SOUTHERN ANDES
CENTRAL ANDES
MARGINAL
MARGINAL
HAWAIIAN IS.
POLYNESIA
SAMOAN IS.
SOCIETY I.
TONGA I.
MANGAREVA I.
PITCAIRN I.
EASTER I.
SIBERIAN
EUROPE
STEPPE
TIBETAN
CHINESE
KOREAN
JAPANESE
INDIAN
SOUTHWEST ASIAN
DESERT
EGYPT
WESTERN SUDAN
GUINEA COAST
EASTERN SUDAN
EASTERN HORN
EAST AFRICAN CATTLE AREA
CONGO
WEST AFRICAN CATTLE AREA
(INDONESIAN)
SOUTHEAST ASIAN
INDONESIA
PALAU I.
YAP I.
MARSHALL IS.
MICRONESIA
CAROLINE IS.
GILBERT IS.
SOLOMON IS.
ELLICE IS.
MELANESIA
FIJI I.
NEW CALEDONIA
AUSTRALIA
NEW ZEALAND (POLYNESIAN)
SHAMANIC
COMMUNAL
OLYMPIAN
MONOTHEISTIC
1 CIRCUMPOLAR
2 NEGRITO
3 AMERICAN INDIAN
4 AFRICAN
5 AUSTRALIAN
6 OCEANIC
7 AMERICAN INDIAN HIGH CULTURES
8 CENTRAL AFRICAN
9 EAST ASIAN
10 HINDU - BUDDHIST
11 JUDAEO-CHRISTIAN
12 ISLAMIC
13 CHINESE

manic areas and from the central high-culture region, characteristically maintained communal cult institutions in which seasonal ceremonies were performed in connection with agricultural, hunting, and fishing activities. Frequently, in addition to the calendrical subsistence cults, there were scheduled life-cycle rites of passage, such as puberty rituals, and secret or restricted membership cults.

4. *African* societies, outside of the central African kingdom areas and Muslim North Africa, maintained communal cults emphasizing severe puberty rituals for young men and girls, secret societies, and calendrical subsistence cults, particularly in the eastern and southern cattle areas.

5. *Australian,* presumably Tasmanian, and Melanesian communal cults emphasized subsistence rituals, performed by members of localized totemic groups, and puberty rituals. The major emphasis lay on magical performance by human inheritors (or reincarnations) of great mythological ancestors rather than on intervention by active deities.

6. *Oceanic* (including Micronesian and Polynesian) communal cults stressed fetishes (statuary residences of gods), taboo systems, age-grading, and subsistence.

III. OLYMPIAN

Beyond shamanic and communal cult institutions—these, in some cases, being incorporated into official cults, and in other cases being relegated to the status of popular, or even vulgar, institutions—the society maintained an elaborate cult institution centering in the propitiation of a pantheon of several high gods. These high gods directly sanctioned the political structure and directly controlled the various departments of nature, and the gods themselves were conceived to be busy with both human and their own (humanlike) affairs; they were powerful, arbitrary, and humanly differentiated in character. The worship of these high gods required permanent temples, a full-time priesthood, and political

MAP SOURCE: Adapted from John J. Honigmann, *The World of Man.* New York: Harper & Row, 1959, pp. 136–137 by permission of the publisher.

affiliation of the priestly bureaucracy, sometimes expressed as a divine kingship.

7. *American Indian* high cultures (particularly the Inca, Maya, and Aztec) produced religious cult institutions of an Olympian type, with huge temples, priesthoods, and spectacular public ceremonials on a regular calendar. Calendrical science, indeed, became a specialty among the Maya.

8. *Central African* Negro tribal kingdoms, with their elaborate bureaucracies and incipient urbanism, supported major Olympian cults, as in Ashanti, Dahomey, and Uganda.

9. *East Asian* societies on the edges of China and India (that is, such kingdoms as were found in Burma, Indonesia, Korea, and Japan) traditionally possessed prevailing official cult institutions that would seem to have been of the Olympian rather than the monotheistic type, despite the partial penetration of Islam and Buddhism.

IV. MONOTHEISTIC

Although we have recognized that no religion is absolutely monotheistic, since other spiritual beings are invariably recognized by a large segment of the population as existing apart from "the" one god, nonetheless there are several major, and numberless small, "world religions" of a monotheistic type. Like Olympian religions, they tend to be politically established, or at least politically related, ecclesiastical institutions. For at least some of the elite of the society, however, the theological, mythological, and ritual pluralism of Olympian religion is replaced by a metaphysically simpler belief in one Supreme Being who either controls the other supernaturals or expresses himself through them.

10. *Hindu-Buddhist* monotheism, historically, can be regarded as the legacy of an ancient "Aryan" Olympian cult institution once widespread in Europe and southwest Asia. (We treat Tibetan and other varieties of Buddhism as offshoots, both historically and theologically, of Hinduism.)

11. *Judaeo-Christian* monotheism, similarly, is an outgrowth of Olympian religions of great antiquity which flourished throughout the Mediterranean world from the era of the urban revolution un-

til replacement by Judaism, Christianity, and Islam. In 1600, the Judaeo-Christian monotheism was practically confined to Europe —and, in a sense, defined Europe more adequately than topography.

12. *Islamic* monotheism, which developed slightly later than the Judaeo Christian tradition but is in many respects similar to it, rapidly spread over North Africa and southwest Asia, and made significant penetrations in India, central and southeastern Asia, and Indonesia.

13. *Chinese* monotheism, apart from the devotees of Islam, Buddha, Tao, and other particular monotheistic faiths, is an eclectic mixture of communal (particularly ancestral), Olympian, and monotheistic cults, held together by the teachings and symbolic figure of Confucius, who functions as a kind of humane focus of divine wisdom. Confucian sanctioning of all cults and of the state seems—at least to this Western observer—to serve the same unifying function for religious diversity as does a monotheistic theology, and hence "Chinese religion" is here classified as monotheistic.

III

The Goals of Religion:
Ritual, Myth, and the Transformations of State

THE PRIMARY PHENOMENON of religion is ritual. Ritual is religion in action; it is the cutting edge of the tool. Belief, although its recitation may be a part of the ritual, or a ritual in its own right, serves to explain, to rationalize, to interpret and direct the energy of the ritual performance. It is not a question of priority in time, for, as we shall argue later, even though in some extremely ancient period there may have been rituals without myths, in observed human behavior the two phenomena go together; few if any rituals are any longer instituted before a mythic base is invented to account for them. The primacy of ritual is instrumental: just as the blade of the knife has instrumental priority over the handle, and the barrel of a gun over the stock, so does ritual have instrumental priority over myth. It is ritual which accomplishes what religion sets out to do.

The Primacy and Goals of Ritual

The primacy of ritual has been recognized, in an intuitive way, by most anthropological writers on the subject, although the question of instrumental priority is often confused with the problem of temporal priority. Boas asserted that "The ritual itself is the stimulus for the origin of the myth. . . . The ritual existed, and the tale originated from the desire to account for it" (Boas [1938], p. 617). Lord Raglan asserted the case for instrumental and temporal priority of ritual even more emphatically. After listing thirteen types of rites (a list comparable to in intent, but more specific than, the list given in the preceding chapter), he stated flatly:

> . . . These rites make up religion, as we can see it practised. For the religious, or the vast majority of them, they are not merely a part of religion, but religion itself. Religion, that is to say, consists in the due performance of the rites. Religious belief is belief in the value and efficacy of the rites, and theology, apart from some forms of mystical theology, consists in giving reasons why the rites should be performed. [Raglan, 1949, p. 47.]

And again:

> The purpose of ritual is to confer benefits on, or avert misfortunes from, those by whom or on whose behalf the ritual is performed, by means of actions and words which from a scientific point of view are entirely ineffective, except in so far as they produce a psychological effect upon the participants themselves. This is, of course, not the view of the ritualists, who usually judge the efficacy of the ritual not by its effect upon themselves, but by its supposed effect upon the forces of nature. Many Africans believe that rain will not fall unless there has been a proper rain-making ceremony; if the rain follows the ceremony, then it is clear that the ceremony has been properly performed, and if rain does not follow, it is equally clear that the ceremony has not been properly performed. Where the ritual can be so easily judged by its apparent results, there is no need of a myth.
>
> Usually, however, the supposed effects of the ritual are far less clearly apparent, so that, if belief in its efficacy is to be maintained, a more complex type of faith is required. This is induced by a myth, which not merely links the ritual of the present with the ritual of the past, but actually identifies the present, in its ritual aspect, with a past conceived solely in terms of ritual—a past, that is to say, in which superhuman figures devote themselves to the performance of acts which are the prototypes of the ritual. The stories of their activities, the myths, then perform the dual function of sanctifying and of standardizing the ritual. [Raglan, 1956, pp. 127–128.]

Although Raglan goes on to develop his theories of mythological degeneration over time in so dogmatic a form that myth appears to be almost an appendage to ritual, the essential point is that he recognizes the functional utility of a myth in relation to its ritual.

Kluckhohn's summary of the argument is perhaps closer to the norm of anthropological tradition:

> . . . Hence, although the relative importance of myth and of ritual does vary greatly, the two tend universally to be associated.
>
> For myth and ritual have a common psychological basis. Ritual is an obsessive repetitive activity—often a symbolic dramatization of the fundamental "needs" of the society, whether "economic," "biological," "social," or "sexual." Mythology is the rationalization of these same needs, whether they are all expressed in overt ceremonial or not. Someone has said "every culture has a type conflict and a type solution." Ceremonials tend to portray a symbolic resolvement of the conflicts which external environment, historical experience, and selective distribution of personality types have caused to be characteristic in the society. [Kluckhohn, 1942, pp. 78–79.]

The existing state of opinion, then, is that, by and large, rituals are associated with myths that explain how the ritual came into existence, what it aims to do, and why it should be confidently expected to achieve its goal. The question of temporal priority of origin is, within the range of immediate ethnological inquiry, unanswerable; the two are found together. But, we have argued, ritual has an instrumental priority: the goals of religion are to be achieved by performing rituals; myths are merely extremely valuable, and regularly employed, auxiliary equipment.

This leads us, then, to ask the evident question: What are the goals of ritual—and, therefore, of religion? The answer to this question is not nearly so obscure as one might suppose. Let us dismiss as irrelevant to this stage of the inquiry all speculations about the validity of religious belief, the essence of the religious experience, the meaning of religious symbols, the functions of religion, even the efficacy of ritual itself. We are left with a set of simple and answerable queries: What do the performers of religious ritual say that they are trying to do? What is the intention of the ceremony? What is the purpose of the rite?

An approach to the answers was made in a book by Arnold van Gennep, published more than fifty years ago, and aptly titled *Les Rites de Passage* (1908; in English translation, edited by Solon T. Kimball [1960]). Van Gennep pointed out that all cultures have a class of rituals that celebrate the transition of an individual from one social status to another. Travel, initiation rites (including "puberty rituals"), betrothal and marriage, pregnancy and childbirth, and funerals are the principal occasions of such rites as described by Van Gennep. In any rite of passage, there are three stages: separation, transition, and incorporation. In separation, the individual is taken from a place or group or status; in transition, he is sacred and is subjected to procedures of transformation; and in incorporation, he is formally installed in the new place or group or status. Chapple and Coon, in their textbook *Principles of Anthropology* (1942), have contributed the only major amplification of this classification of rituals. Drawing attention to the fact that rites of passage tend to be related to the life crises of individuals, they suggest adding a new but fundamentally similar category: rites of intensification. These are group- rather than individual-centered and include such ceremonies as New Year, which anticipates the end of winter and the beginning of spring, and hunting and agricultural rites, which aim to renew and to intensify the fertility and availability of game and crops.

Now to such rites of passage and rites of intensification have been attributed various more or less vaguely defined *functions;* however, their goals are, at a certain level, quite explicit. The *goal* of the long Iroquois Condolence Ceremony which we described earlier was to terminate the socially destructive and self-destructive period of mourning by the bereaved survivors of the chief; to preclude the seeking of bloody revenge by kinfolk suspicious of murder by witchcraft; and publicly to install a new chief who had full acceptance by the community. Whether or not the Condolence Ceremony was effective in these aims—whether, in other words, its actual function corresponded to its goal or stated intention—is a question that we shall leave to discussion in the next chapter. But one can recognize without difficulty that what the Iroquois were trying to do, consciously, was to control the behavior of the community in what they considered to be a crisis; the ritual was intended to ensure the passage from a state of mourning to a state of normal social activity of the bereaved, and the passage of a legitimate, qualified, and publicly acceptable candidate for the office from warrior status to that of chief. There is nothing particularly mysterious about the goals of this ritual, nor is there anything mysterious about the garden magic of the Trobriand Islanders. The Trobrianders want the crops to grow and they perform rites of intensification to make as certain as possible a good growing season and a successful harvest. The Eskimos want the seals and whales to visit the coast, the Dahomeans want to secure the good will of their departed ancestors, and so on.

But not all rituals can be conveniently classified as rites of passage or rites of intensification, although these labels do cover a large share of ritual phenomena. Divination, the religio-medical treatment of the sick, the propitiation of the spirits of the dead, the observance of routine food taboos—such ritual events and dozens more cannot be fitted into the schema without a good deal of conceptual pushing and pulling. Is there perhaps a more general characterization of the goals of ritual which will embrace not only rites of passage and rites of intensification, but other ritual aims, and which will serve as a basis for the further classification of ritual goals?

Here again, we find that we are not confronted with a very mysterious problem. All ritual is directed toward the problem of transformations of state in human beings or nature. Sometimes the goal is to ensure the quickest and most thorough transformation into an end state desired by the ritual actor; sometimes the goal is to prevent an undesired transformation from occurring. Sometimes the target is an aspect of nonhuman nature; sometimes it is human. Sometimes the target is an individual; sometimes it is a group. Sometimes the transformation in question is a minor one, a correction which will restore equilibrium and status quo, keep the wobbling of the system within bounds; sometimes it is a question of radical transformation of the system, the attainment of a new level of equilibrium or even of a new quality of organization. The targets of the ritual and the precise nature of the transformations are not esoteric at all: they are the very same things and people, the same variable qualities, that are of day-to-day concern. Ritual control of state differs from secular control only in the recognition by the ritual actor and his audience that a supernatural power—a power apart from that at the disposal of muscles, brain, wind, fire, and other tangible physical sources of energy—is brought to bear. Myth, in the most general sense, is the theory of ritual, which explains the nature of the powers, prescribes the ritual, accounts for its successes and failures. Together, they are religion.

We are now in a position to make a new and more analytical definition of religion. From this vantage point, we can say that *religion is a set of rituals, rationalized by myth, which mobilizes supernatural powers for the purpose of achieving or preventing transformations of state in man and nature.* We find no advantage, in this formulation, in distinguishing radically between those rituals that invoke supernatural beings (to which some writers restrict the term "religion") and those that invoke an impersonal supernatural force, such as *mana* (which some writers like to denote separately by the term "magic"). As Hsu (1952), Titiev (1960), and others have said, the aims, the social context, and often even the rituals themselves are indistinguishable. Furthermore, while we recognize the usefulness of Van Gennep's category of rites of passage, and Chapple and Coon's rites of intensification, we shall work with a less abstract classification of the transformations intended by religious rituals, closer to the consciously stated purposes of the actors. Five categories of transformations of state would seem to suffice to partition the aims of ritual: ritual as *technology*; ritual as *therapy and anti-therapy*; ritual as *social control*; ritual as *salvation*; and ritual as *revitalization.*

Let us now proceed to discuss in more detail the kinds of rituals these five categories include.

Ritual as Technology

Technological rituals are rituals intended to control various aspects of nature, other than man himself, for the purpose of human exploitation. There are two obvious and ubiquitous kinds of technological ritual: *divination* and hunting and agricultural *rites of intensification.* Ritual that aims to extract useful information from nature is called divination. Ritual that purports directly or indirectly to control the availability and fertility of game (fish, fowl, insects, mammals, or whatever), of flocks and herds, or of wild and cultivated vegetable crops is called rites of intensification. We may also add a third category: *protective rituals,* intended to prevent or avoid a diversity of ills or disasters—broken tools, floods, fires, flawed carpentry, cracked pottery, earthquakes, mechanical breakdown, volcanic eruptions, lightning bolts, plagues of insects, and the like.

DIVINATION

Probably no human society, even in modern, thoroughly secularized urban areas, is without many people who practice divination. Divination is performed when a decision must be made that the actor feels should be based on more information than is available or on more valid principles of judgment than he commands. In such a situation, divination is intended to provide the missing information or principle of judgment by direct, if apparently arbitrary, advice from supernatural authority. Even the most militant atheist is apt to turn to simple divinatory practices when neurotic uncertainty or real information gaps make choice difficult. Such a procedure as flipping a coin to decide between two alternatives—which movie to attend, who shall pay the check, whether to take one route or another—is the very prototype of divination. Of course, the secular coin flipper regards the rite as merely a means for random selection between equally attractive alternatives in order to hasten decision or obviate dispute. But to the religious diviner, such a ritual is believed to reveal something about nature, including its future, which is hidden from the senses and which requires supernatural complicity to unravel.

Religious divination is always practiced in the context of a mythological belief in a doctrine of signs. The logical structure of this belief is that one aspect of nature will, when the appropriate power is invoked by the rite, act as an index variable to the phenomenon of interest. In the United States, for instance, dowsing or water-witching is a common practice for finding well water, particularly where geological advice is wanting, ambiguous, or discouraging. In one common procedure, the dowser holds in his hands the two forks of a willow branch (willow, being a tree that prefers river banks, is "sympathetic" to the presence of water). The dowser walks across the property of his client, holding the wand, and expects that when he stands above water, the wand will bend downward, thereby indicating the place to dig or drill the well. The action of the wood, in other words, is an index of the conformation of another aspect of nature—water; the two are connected by some bond of sympathy; and a supernatural power (in this case, an impersonal force like *mana*) acts physically to ensure that the indicator communicates the information desired.

Finding water for wells is evidently an important problem for agricultural people living in a scattered settlement pattern of individual homesteads without access to a communal well, lake, or stream. Among hunters, finding game, particularly migratory game, is a comparable issue. The Naskapi—the caribou hunters of the Labrador peninsula—commonly use another form of divination called scapulimancy, involving the scorched shoulderblade of a caribou or other game animal. Among these people, there is a cult of dreams as well as a divination cult. The dream cult is similar to that reported for the Iroquois: the dreamer's soul expresses its wishes and wisdom in dreams, which are carefully interpreted and obeyed by the dreamer. When the hunter wishes to find game, he performs a ceremonial sequence which has three stages: a dream-induction rite, involving a sweat bath and drumming or shaking a rattle; in the evening, before sleep, a vision, hypnagogic image, or dream of seeing or securing game; and finally, scapulimantic divination. The divination ritual is necessary to discover where to go to find the game prognosticated by the dream and what hazards and other pertinent circumstances may be found along the way. In the divination rite, the shoulderblade of the animal is conceived to be a blank chart of the hunting terrain; the charred spots and cracks which appear as the bone is scorched over the fire represent the filling in of the map with various landmarks, such as rivers, lakes, and mountains, with signs for game, and with data about such relevant considerations as the depth of snow and the presence of other humans. In difficult territory, the hunter may have recourse to divination as often as every three or four days. Furthermore, analogous procedures may be used not just for locating game, but also for predicting good or bad luck and for obtaining answers to all kinds of important questions: When will the missing hunters return to camp? Is so-and-so practicing some chicanery? How deep is the snow to the south? How soon will the broken leg heal?

The example of Naskapi scapulimancy will be discussed again in Chapter IV on the functions of religion. Here it may suffice to point out two things: first, that scapulimancy is a widespread custom found not only among the Indians of Labrador and among most of the northern Algonkian and Athapascan hunters of the boreal forest and tundra in North America, but also in a wide belt across Asia and Europe, including Japan, China, India, the sheep-raising regions of the Old World, and among the hunters and herdsmen of central and northern Asia; and second, that although on superficial inspection it might appear that this form of divination is a mechanical magical procedure, there is in fact a theology and a mythology which explain and support it, so that it would be impossible to differentiate this "magical" rite from other rituals involving supernaturals. In fact, this is true all over the world: divination and oracular rituals tend to occur in widely distributed forms and are rarely if ever devoid of a supernatural connection.

HUNTING AND AGRICULTURAL RITES OF INTENSIFICATION

Although divination will usually be employed to secure information relevant to hunting and agriculture, there is always a group of rituals intended to control those physical processes of nature that are relevant to success in the hunt, in herding, or in the fields. The rituals may be almost purely magical, as among the Trobriand gardeners who invoke only otiose deities in mechanically efficacious spells and formulas; or they may be almost purely spiritual, as among the Iroquois gardeners who invoke the sympathetic interest of gods who are living presences. The communal hunting and agricultural rituals of a society are, very often, concerned with fertility: birth of spring after death of winter, and more specifically, the birth of a new generation of animals and the sprouting and growth of plants. Without the annual renewal of the natural world in all its variety, man's own life would soon come to an end.

Rites of intensification mobilize, focus, and intensify those natural processes which must periodically achieve such a renewal.

In general, because of their relationship to the cycle of the seasons, these rituals are calendrical and are performed on occasions marked by solar or planetary events, or by related events in nature such as the appearance of vegetation of one kind or another or the arrival of migratory birds, fishes, or mammals. The Iroquois annual calendar exemplifies such a pattern well. The New Year, celebrated on the fifth day of the new moon which follows the zenith of the Pleiades, inaugurates the cycle. It is followed, as we saw earlier, by rituals scheduled to take place shortly after various index events in the vegetable world have occurred: the rising of the sap in the maples, the ripening of strawberries, the maturing of the corn, and so on. Such a calendrical cycle of rituals occurs in all agricultural societies and in many hunting and gathering societies as a series of communally sponsored celebrations in which the whole community participates. But not all hunting and agricultural rituals are calendrical. Crisis rites of intensification are also needed on occasion—to bring rain to end a drought, for instance—and these crisis rites may be as elaborate in ceremonial as the calendrical celebrations.

Some hunting rituals, however, are not so much concerned with the ensurance of fertility as with the good will of the animals being hunted. Not only must there be an ever-renewed supply; the animals, being intelligent and willful, and perhaps under the guidance and protection of an even more intelligent and willful Keeper of the Game, must be willing to be caught. Thus a large class of hunting rituals is concerned with measures for avoiding the giving of offense to the spirits of game animals, for flattering them, for supplicating them, in order that they should not refuse to be caught. The hunt is, in some respects, apt to become a mystic encounter. Even the urban worker reading Hemingway's *The Old Man and the Sea* can respond to the fisherman's intense concern that he give due respect to his prey, lest somehow it escape him or even destroy him; even more do hunters, whose lives depend on the animals, feel a need to ensure that the animals are treated in a way that will actually motivate them to become victims of the hunt. Earlier we made note of the Eskimo shaman's annual voyage to the bottom of the sea, to comb the hair of Sedna, the Goddess of the Sea Game, and so flatter and pacify her that she will forget the broken taboos and release the game once more. A similar and even more ancient and widespread tradition is the cult of bear ceremonialism (*vide* Hallowell [1926]), which like scapulimancy was distributed over much of the Northern Hemisphere. According to this widespread cult institution, individual bears have souls, and there may also be a Great Bear Being who is the guardian of the bear as game. In order not to offend bears, or the Keeper of the Game, and so make them shy, difficult to find, and hard to kill, it is necessary to speak to them with respect, to dispose of their bones with care; in some groups, bear cubs should be raised and killed with ceremony. Even where the game animals are not the object of a shamanic or communal cult, it is common for individual hunters to call upon guardian spirits or to carry "medicine-bundles" containing talismans having the power to dispel the animals' doubts or conquer their shyness or confuse their minds and make them willing victims of the hunter's art.

PROTECTIVE RITUALS

Divination and hunting and agricultural magic would seem to be the major categories of what we have been calling *technological rituals*. It should be recognized, however, that ritual may be employed to improve technological control of any fractious part of physical nature. One could develop an encyclopedia of mariners' rituals, for instance, devoted to ensuring the efficiency and safety of vessels, to calming the stormy sea, to securing favorable winds, and so on; a catalogue of husbandmen's rituals to cope with sick or strayed animals; a handbook of gardeners' rituals to prevent or cure plagues of locusts, blights, borers, and so forth. Where the people depend upon an annual flood to irrigate their fields, not only the flood waters themselves, but the hydraulic works by which the water is stored and channeled, must be blessed. Where artifacts are used as tools, ritual may be employed to protect them from breaking, to ensure that they function truly and smoothly; just as the gambler breathes luck onto his dice, so the driver of a combat vehicle gives it a name and pampers it with cozening rituals so that it will not fail him in a critical hour.

In sum, then, all of these ritual attentions, divinatory and manipulative, are aimed at one goal: the transformation of man's external environment into states favorable to man. In divination, the goal is to make some department of nature transparent, self-revealing, so that man may make an informed decision. In manipulative ritual, the aim is to transform the state of nature from a stale, cold, dry, lagging condition to a vigorous, fertile condition; to transform the will of an animal from resistance to compliance; to transform the tool from unreliability to reliability. These aims are intensely pragmatic; they are rarely, if ever, pursued without corresponding activities that are practical and "rational" (by which we mean efficacious in terms of the cause-and-effect relationships recognized by scientific knowledge). And they may involve either or both mantic and spiritual religious rituals.

Ritual as Therapy and Anti-therapy

In this section we consider those rituals that aim to control human health, principally for therapeutic purposes but also for anti-therapeutic purposes. Because much of ritual therapy is concerned with the treatment of ritual anti-therapy, let us discuss ritual anti-therapy—or witchcraft—first.

Witchcraft

The ills that the human flesh and mind are heir to sometimes have readily recognizable immediate causes: gunshot wounds, falls, disappointments in love, bereavement, and so on. But the immediate causes of many human disorders are difficult to discover, even in an age of science, and without the conceptual and technological apparatus of modern medicine, most disorders are impossible to understand in any naturalistic way. Infectious diseases, psychosomatic complaints, allergies, nutritional and metabolic disorders, senile conditions, and chronic neuroses and psychoses are particularly likely to find their explanation in supernatural intervention; even broken bones, cuts and bruises, and drowning may invite speculation about possible supernatural responsibility for the concatenation of circumstances that led to the injurious event and for undue reluctance of the body or mind to heal.

Witchcraft is an almost, if not completely, culturally universal explanation for illness, injury, and slow recovery. Indeed, witchcraft is probably far more commonly used as an explanation for human misfortune than as an actual practice. Theoretically there could be societies in which illness and death are regularly ascribed to witchcraft, in which the techniques of witchcraft and the identities of witches are commonly known, and yet in which there are no persons who regard themselves as witches or who practice the black art. But in most societies there are persons who, as professionals working on behalf of clients (or even to vent their own spleen), or as individual laymen carrying out do-it-yourself rituals, do attempt to practice witchcraft.

Witchcraft may be defined as an individual's use of religious ritual to control, exploit, or injure unsuspecting, or at least uncooperating, other persons. Witches do not bewitch themselves. Furthermore, despite the connotation of evil, witchcraft is not necessarily directed toward socially disfavored aims. Although acts of witchcraft often do aim secretly to injure or kill a member of the witch's own group and are therefore regarded as bad, criminal, or evil, witches often perform socially valued services such as punishing a wrongdoer or incapacitating the enemy in war or an opposing team in competitive sports. A wide range of witchcraft is, in a sense, ethically neutral in the value system of its society: the use of love magic, for instance, to compel the favors of the hostile or indifferent loved one or of spells to injure thieves in the orchard. Thus, although to Western eyes witchcraft has an invariable connotation of evil and is associated with notions of more or less organized professionalism, nevertheless in cross-cultural perspective it is to be seen as a spectrum of acts, performed by both professionals and laymen, ranging in local ethical status from the extremely reprehensible to the highly valued.

The ethically dual nature of witchcraft (as we have just defined it) can be seen in the religious beliefs of the Lugbara, a central African Negro tribe of village-dwelling agriculturists. The Lugbara, as described by Middleton (1955), use the same term, *ole rozu,* to refer to the practice of two kinds of witchcraft, one socially sanctioned and the other not. *Ole* is a term used to refer to the unpleasant emotional feeling associated with being left out, slighted, neglected; *rozu* means "to bring sickness by mystical means." The socially approved kind of witchcraft involves the curse of an individual—usually an older, more responsible person than the one cursed, and in most cases a man—upon a kinsman who has offended him personally, particularly if the offense itself was a publicly recognized breach of proper behavior (such as a son's refusing to obey his father). The curse invokes the common ancestor of the witch and his victim; the ghost brings sickness (in extreme cases, death) upon the offending person, and the sickness can be removed only by making reparation to the offended elder and by sacrificing beer and perhaps animals to the ghost.

The socially disapproved kind of witchcraft is perpetrated by irresponsible persons, usually excessively friendly or excessively withdrawn people, whose maleficent activity is also generated by spite, but a spite that has no proper justification. The souls of these spiteful people, who sometimes are from neighboring villages and sometimes from within, steal into the victim's hut at night in the form of animals and bring disease by spitting or vomiting on the victim or on a place where he will step. Sometimes they go about by day and spit on children's heads just to see them waste away and die; sometimes they make persons sick with the evil eye or perform rituals using the corral ropes of a neighbor in order to bewitch his cattle. These witches do not invoke ghosts; their mantic power is their own. And, finally, there are specialists in medicines and poisons who can bring sickness to a victim, but their activities are placed by the Lugbara in a different category from *ole rozu.*

Witchcraft, then, must be regarded as a complex of activities which can, in any society, include both acceptable and unacceptable goals of personal coercion and punishment. The techniques, furthermore, may vary from the more or less spiritual invocation of higher powers to the application of the mantic resources of the practitioner, who may be a professional or a layman. The ritual techniques are similarly various: curses (the invocation of supernatural wrath), magic poisons (introjected substances whose efficacy depends in part on supernatural properties), simulation (as with the "voodoo doll"), touching (as with rites involving the bodily exuviae or artifacts associated with the victim), and so on down the catalogue of ritual types. Rarely is witchcraft exclusively practiced, or believed to be practiced, by a special cult group organized in a witches' sabbath, as the medieval European fantasy had it, although on occasion communities do organize—in Africa, among North American Indians, and in Europe, for example, to combat the subversive influence of supposed witch cults (*vide* Bohannon [1958]; Kluckhohn [1944]; and Murray [1921]).

THERAPY

As Clements (1932) has pointed out, there are six main primitive theories of disease and for each of them there is a corresponding therapeutic theory. The six disease theories are: natural causes; imitative and contagious magic; disease-object intrusion; soul loss; spirit intrusion; and breach of taboo. The corresponding types of treatment are: herbs, ointments, bone-setting, and the like; reverse magic; massage and sucking; bringing or enticing the wandering soul back to its body; exorcism; and confession. The "natural causes" category of disease, treated by natural means, is a major or minor part of every primitive medical system; all the other theories of disease and of treatment, however, involve religious ritual. The second, third, and fourth combine, in a general way, into a category of witchcraft theories; the fifth and sixth categories involve other supernatural agencies; Clements regards the former complex as more ancient than the latter.

Although it is not necessary to agree with this historical interpretation, it is fair to say that witchcraft, in one setting or another, does use techniques of imitative and contagious magic (such as the "voodoo doll" and the abuse of the victim's exuviae), disease-object intrusion (in which a ball of hair, or a bone, or other foreign "poison" is magically introduced into his body), and the theft of the victim's soul, leaving his body to sicken and die. In both groups the aims of the therapeutic rituals are simple and direct:

the cure of the illness. Although Clements' treatment is perhaps too simplified to represent adequately the complexity of the interaction in any one society of ideas of witchcraft and of direct supernatural intervention, both in the cause and cure of disease, he provides a useful way of sorting out the main ingredients of the concepts.

Once again, it must be pointed out that therapeutic rituals may be performed both by laymen and professional curers. A simple example of a lay ritual for minor burns in use among the Oklahoma Cherokee is given by the Kilpatricks (1964). After a burn is experienced, the sufferer takes a small quantity of water, preferably newly drawn fresh-flowing water, into the mouth and blows it onto the burn in four parts. After each spraying, he recites the following spell (p. 18):

> Water is cold
> Ice is cold
> Snow is cold
> Rime is cold
> "Relief!" I will be saying.

It should be noted that the magical quality both of the four-part treatment and of the spell, which invokes four cold things, is (presumably) enhanced by the fact that four is a sacred number. Whatever supernatural power is being invoked by this procedure, it evidently involves both naturalistic treatment (cold water feels good on minor burns and may actually benefit them) and ritual involving both supernatural address and simulation.

For more serious conditions, whether or not the victim is grossly incapacitated at the moment, the ritual treatment will generally involve the ministrations of a shaman of one kind or another (as diviner, oracle, medicine man or leech, or shaman proper) and of interested spectators from among the sufferer's kinsmen and friends. Ritual treatment will generally involve two major phases: diagnosis, during which the immediate nature and final cause of the condition are determined by observation of symptoms, etiological inference, and divinatory procedures; and treatment, during which the appropriate actions indicated by the diagnosis (and, in general, following Clements' prescription) are performed. These ceremonies may require hours or days for completion, and involve a wide selection of ritual types from the basic repertoire. Gillin (1948) provides a careful account of the treatment of a sixty-three-year-old Guatemalan Indian woman suffering from *espanto* ("magical fright" or "soul loss"). The woman's symptoms were a mixture of the physical and the emotional. She complained of diarrhea, aches and pains in her stomach, back, and legs, loss of appetite, and occasional fever. She was depressed, neglectful of household duties and of her pottery making, and avoided her friends; her moods alternated between agitated anxiety—with whining talk and jerky, tremulous movements—and extreme lethargy. The physical symptoms did not respond to standard quinine treatment for malaria. She believed that she was suffering from *espanto* and that she would eventually die, but she did not have enough money to pay a competent native curer for treatment until the anthropological field worker contributed some funds and encouragement.

The first phase of therapy was the diagnostic session. The native curer, the *parchero,* talked to the patient in her one-room thatched hut, in the presence of her husband, a male friend of the family, and two field workers. The curer first took her pulse in each wrist, for about thirty seconds each time, while gazing directly into her eyes; when she tried to drop her eyes, he told her to continue to return his stare. After taking the pulse, he informed her that she definitely was suffering from *espanto.* Next the curer interviewed her to discover what had so frightened and startled her that her soul had fled. He first announced what he knew to be a fact: that she had once become *espanto* near the river, when she saw her husband deceiving her with a prostitute. He demanded that she tell the whole story. She proceeded to recount the history of her life, beginning with her childhood and proceeding through the chronicle of an unhappy marriage to an improvident, drunken, sexually unsatisfying ne'er-do-well. She had been *espantado* seven times before. The curer now wanted to know what it was that had precipitated the present attack of *espanto.* She then described a recent quarrel with her husband when they walked by the spot at the river where he had been unfaithful to her; she had berated him and he had struck her with a rock. This had set off the current attack.

After this recital, she seemed more calm. The *parchero* now declared that her condition was curable, and gave instructions for the curing session proper to be held four days later. This would be a feast and in preparation for it she was to secure a variety of herbs, drugs, and foods; these preparations would require so much work that she must persuade a friend or kinswoman to be her "servant" for the next several days. Together the woman and her helper cleaned the house, decorated the house altar with a picture of the household saint, and covered the floors and walls with pine boughs and pine needles. About four in the afternoon on the day of the feast the house began to fill with guests, including two principal religious persons—the curer himself and one of the six Principals of the town. The Principals of villages of this kind are, in the absence of resident priests, the local Catholic religious authorities and, although their power is not recognized by the national government, constitute also a kind of informal political leadership among the Indians.

The curing ceremony itself is best described in Gillin's detailed and vivid account:

After dusk a delegation left for the church in the center of town to pray to the saints, explaining to them the necessity for this cure, and to plead for their aid and benign interest. The delegation consisted of the curer carrying a large bundle of candles, the Principal carrying a native-made clay censer in which copal incense burned, and the patient's son carrying a large armful of pine boughs with which to decorate the altars of the various saints in the church. The curer and the Principal prayed together at the main altar and set up large candles before it and at the church door. Then the curer began a long series of prayers in Pokomam before each of the 14 images of saints in the church. All prayers were much the same. The curer knelt with two lighted candles in his right hand and swung the copal censer with the left hand while he explained in somewhat stylized fashion the loss of the soul of Alicia and invoked aid in its recovery. At the end of each prayer he placed two lighted candles before the saint and swung the censer in the sign of the cross, while the patient's son decorated that particular altar with pine boughs. When each of the saints had been properly appealed to, both the curer and the Principal knelt before the main altar and prayed long and loud to the Virgin and to Jesus Christ. Then two extra candles and another prayer were offered to San Marcos "because he is said to be the saint of the *brujos* (evil witches)." After this the group returned to the patient's house where the curer explained what had been done. The prayers had lasted about two hours.

The function of this part of the cure seems to be primarily to relieve the patient's anxiety concerning the Christian saints. From the phrasing of the prayers it is also evident that all participants in the "cure," including the medicine man himself receive reassurance against the fear that the Christian deities may intervene unfavorably in what is essentially a pagan proceeding. For soul loss itself lies outside the realm of Christian affairs and the recovery of a soul involves dealing with renegade saints and familiar spirits certainly not approved of by God Almighty.

After we returned to the house a large meal of native dishes was served. The scene was lighted with pine splinters. The patient did not eat but looked on, complaining about the efforts she had put forth, but clearly enjoying her misery. The guests and the curer complimented her on the food. Then the curer asked that the herbs and essences and other medicines which had been procured be brought out so that he could inspect them and give instruction to the women as to how they should be prepared.

During this phase also the curer was engaged in making a pair of small images, representing "Don Avelín Caballero Sombrerón" (the chief of the evil spirits) and "his wife." These images, made from a ball of beeswax which he carried in his pocket, were about three inches tall. The male figure had a wide-brimmed hat, and the female figure displayed a typical married woman's hairdress, arranged in a sort of crown or filet around the head. The female figure had a needle placed in her hands. The curer explained that if the appeal to Avelín for the return of the patient's soul was unsuccessful, he would implore the wife who would prod her husband with her "lance."

The patient was instructed to stand in her clothes before the house altar. The curer took two eggs in the shell from a gourd plate included in the collection of necessities for the cure. Holding one egg in his right hand he passed it over her forehead, then down her neck to the inside of her right forearm, stroking the inside of the right forearm 12 times from below elbow to wrist. With a second egg he repeated the process on the left side. Then he took more eggs, one in each hand. After making the sign of a cross before her face, he moved both eggs, one on each side, up her arms to her head, down her back and legs all the way to her feet, up the inside of her legs to the crotch, and over her abdomen and breasts to her mouth. He placed the four eggs which he had used in a gourd plate and lighted a small candle on the house altar. This, explained Manuel, removes some of the sickness from the body into the eggs. The eggs are taken to "The Place" where the fright occurred and constitute evidence to be offered to the spirits of the harm which has befallen the patient as the result of soul loss.

The native theory here is that the organism is seriously weakened at the time the soul is frightened out of the body and that in this condition *aires* (evil winds) may enter the body. The physical symptoms of a person suffering soul loss are believed to be caused by the "*aires de espanto*." The eggs used in this fashion have the effect of drawing the *aires* into themselves and out of the patient's body. This in itself, however, is not a sufficient "cure," according to the local theory of etiology, for the soul has not yet been restored to its owner and consequently the patient is still in a "weakened" condition, peculiarly susceptible to invasion by other *aires*.

The curer and the Principal, together with two male helpers, now went to "The Place" where the precipitating fright of the present *espanto* occurred. They carried with them in a gourd the four eggs just used to draw the *aires* out of the patient, digging sticks, pine splinters for light, two candles, and a collection of gifts to be offered the evil spirits. These gifts included a cigar, a bunch of handmade cigarettes, an earthen pitcher of *chilate* (a maize gruel used as ceremonial drink among the Pokomam), four cacao seeds, some sweet biscuits, and a small bottle of drinking alcohol. We walked in single file through the darkness, following a dim path among the bushes upstream along the river. Finally we came to a spot about ten feet above the river which the curer announced was "The Place" where Alicia had lost her soul. A pine splinter was lighted. While the two men helpers started digging a hole in the ground, the curer and the Principal turned their backs and faced across the river to the west. All previous prayers had been in Pokomam, but now the curer spoke in Spanish and in familiar, man-to-man terms. He addressed five spirits, calling them by name and addressing them as *compadres* (a form of ceremonial kinship). The names of the five were "Avelín Caballero Sombrerón, Señor Don Justo Juez, Doña Maria Diego, Don Manuel Urrutia, and San Graviel (Gabriel)." After saluting the others he directed his remarks to Don Avelín. He explained in detail that he had brought them a feast to eat and alcohol to drink. He explained that here Alicia had lost her soul through a *susto* [magical fright]. He dwelt upon her symptoms and said that the eggs would bear him out. He said that he knew that his *compadres* knew where her soul was hidden and that they had it in their power to return it to her. As a favor to him, the curer, would they not help him to secure the lost soul? And so on. This discourse delivered into the darkness lasted about twenty minutes. During it the old Principal stood by the curer's side, saying nothing but swinging the smoking censer in a regular rhythm. The two wax images of Avelín and his wife were set on a stone, the food and other offerings were laid out, drinks were poured for the spirits. Then everything was buried in a shallow hole, and we departed for the patient's house. Some earth and pebbles dug up by the helpers were placed in a gourd dish and carried back with us. "That the soul might follow," the earth and pebbles were rattled in their gourd container as we walked through the night.

This step in the cure was the crucial one from the native point of view. The theory is that the evil spirits, which the Indians call *tiéwu* in their own language and *diablos* (devils) when speaking Spanish, hide a disembodied soul somewhere in the mountains. Only a medicine man who has established friendly relations with these occult powers is able to persuade them to release the soul.

As we left the spot a roll of thunder rumbled through the mountains as the rainstorm which had been going on all evening moved off toward the west, and a flash of lightning illuminated the slope across the river. The curer remarked that this was a "good sign."

We were met at the door of the house by the patient. She showed an intense desire to know if the mission had been successful. The curer spoke noncommittal but comforting words.

The curer and the Principal set up two large candles on the house altar and prayed in Pokomam, explaining to the picture of the household patron saint why it had been necessary to talk with the spirits and to make offerings to them.

A ground altar was laid out on the tamped earth outside the door of the house in the form of a square about a yard on each side. Each corner was marked by a stake to which a pine bough was tied upright. Each side faced one of the cardinal directions. Now the curer with the Principal beside him knelt on a goatskin and began a long series of prayers in Pokomam. First they knelt on the south side facing north, then on the north side facing west, then on the west side, and finally on the east side. The whole sequence of prayers was repeated in each position. Although the cardinal directions were not named or personified, this procedure seems to be a survival of earlier Mayan beliefs in the sacredness of the directions. The prayers were actually directed to Jesus Christ and a list of 44 saints, "if you happen to be now in the north (south, east, west)." The ground-altar phase lasted about ninety minutes and ended about 1:30 A.M.

The house was purified and sanctified. The Principal set up two candles at each inside corner of the house, while the curer, holding the copal censer swinging from his hand, prayed over each pair of candles in Pokomam. Then he knelt before the house altar once more explaining briefly to the patron saint what he had done. He perfumed the altar with copal smoke and went into the yard and did the same to the ground altar. He came back into the house and sat down to smoke a cigarette while he wiped the weariness from his eyes.

The son and daughter-in-law of the patient now began to grind the medicinal herbs and to mix the magic potions under directions of the curer. When the mixture was completed a gourd bowlful of greenish liquid was handed to the curer who muttered an invocation over it and placed it on the altar.

Under instructions from the curer all the guests sat down on the floor, leaving a small open space in front of the altar. The curer took off his jacket and shirt, tying the arms of the shirt around his neck so that it hung down his back. The patient, her mumbling complaints silenced for once, took off her clothes and tied a scanty piece of cloth around her loins, just sufficient to cover her genitals. The curer took a long drink of *aguardiente* (beverage alcohol). The patient cried and whimpered, standing naked before the company. She and the curer stood for a moment facing the altar while he prayed. It was now about 2:00 A.M.

The curer went out of the house and the patient followed. He walked about a hundred yards into the cornfield. The rest of the party was instructed to stand about in such a way as to form a crude square. The only light was a single burning pine splinter. The sky had cleared, and the night air was uncomfortably chilly. The patient stood naked in the center of the square, facing north. The curer offered her the bowl of magic potion. She took a quick gulp, making a face as she did so and whining with complaint.

The curer put his lips to the bowl and took a large mouthful, stepping back from the patient about three feet. For approximately sixty seconds everyone present stood rigid. Suddenly and without warning a blast of fine spray burst from the curer's mouth straight into the face of the patient. The shock of the alcoholic liquid in the cold air rocked her. He continued, systematically spraying her whole body—front and rear—with the medicine, ignoring her protests and her shivering. A stool was brought and the patient sat down trembling while the curer rinsed his mouth with a bowl of water. After she had sat for about ten minutes the curer gave her a bowl of the mixture and she drank it all, about a pint. Then everyone returned to the house.

A mat was laid on the damp earth floor in front of the altar, and the patient, still naked and shivering, stretched out on it. The curer took off his shirt entirely and with a gourd plate of six eggs in the shell in his hands he offered a short prayer before the altar. First he took two eggs in his right hand and massaged her right arm, front of her body, trunk, head, and ears. A third pair of eggs were used to massage both legs. Then four eggs, two in each hand, were pressed against each side of her chest. She turned over, and the whole back side of her body was similarly massaged. This whole procedure was not superficial but a systematic and thorough rubbing of skin and muscle. Although the curer did not touch the genitals, he did not hesitate to massage the nipples. Gradually her shivering and complaints ceased. She was obviously enjoying the treatment and was relaxed. The curer removed one of his sandals and with it massaged all parts of her body.

The patient rose and put on her clothes and was led to the rustic platform bed where she lay down and was covered with blankets. She emitted a long humming sigh of relaxation. One of the assistants placed a broken pot full of coals under the bed, and the curer crawled through the smoke and placed under the bed the gourd of earth and pebbles brought from "The Place" of fright. As he did so the copal suddenly burst into flame. "Ha," said the medicine man, "the soul is here."

As the smoke cleared away a large gourd bowl half full of water was brought to the curer. He broke the six eggs he had used in the massage one by one into the water, forming swirling shapes. For a long time the curer gazed into the bowl by the vague light of the candles on the altar behind him. Then he nodded affirmatively, saying that he saw that all was confirmed in the eggs. He went through the entire history of the patient's eight *espantos* pointing out proofs in the eggs. Then as the whites sank slowly to the bottom of the bowl he said that this showed that all previous *sustos* had been cured and that the present symptoms would shortly disappear. He pronounced the cure finished. The patient roused herself briefly on the bed and shouted hoarsely, "That is right." Then she sank back into a deep snoring sleep.

The curer, the Principal, and guests left the patient's house about 5:00 A.M., leaving her in the care of her son, her daughter-in-law, and her husband. [Gillin, 1948, pp. 391–394.] *

Next day the patient was in bed with a fever of 105° F., and happy. The curer refused to visit her, despite the worried bulletins of the anthropologist, saying that the return of the soul often disturbed the body; if she died, as such patients sometimes did, at least she would die with her soul immanent and need not fear the awful prospect of the spirit's eternal wandering on the earth. As it turned out, in a week the patient was on her feet, well, and busy with her household tasks. Furthermore, she seemed to have developed a new personality: her depression, withdrawal, and anxiety all had disappeared; her hypochondriacal complaints of aches and pains were gone; the fever vanished. Although, in view of her past history of similar episodes of *espanto,* the anthropologist doubted that the cure would be permanent, it was adequate to resolve the immediate emergency.

In this instance, it may be noted that the disorder to which the shaman directed his therapy presented a mixture of physical and mental or emotional difficulties. It is worth observing that, whether or not a culture recognizes any sort of categorical distinction between physical and mental disorders (and many cultures, even primitive ones, do make such a distinction), the rituals of religion are generally applied both to organic and psychological difficulties and to that vast potpourri of conditions which in Western medicine are loosely termed "psychosomatic."

The Shaman

The shaman, as we have noted earlier in a discussion of types of cult institutions, is a ubiquitous figure in the religious life of the

* From John Gillin, "Magical Fright," *Psychiatry,* 11 (1948), 387–400. Reprinted by special permission of The William Alanson White Psychiatric Foundation, Inc. Copyright, 1949, by The William Alanson White Psychiatric Foundation.

world. He is an individual practitioner who performs ritual for a fee on behalf of individuals or groups. Although the services of the shaman are, in principle, capable of being directed at any religious goal, he tends to concentrate on the diagnosis and treatment of illness. Because of his association with therapy, he is also often linked with witchcraft and may be suspected of selling his skills to control, coerce, or injure human beings.

The central ritual experience of the shaman himself, however, is very different from that which he sells to his clients. The shaman is usually not just a skilled ritualist who, after observing and participating in many rituals, with or without a tutor, assumes a professional role. Quite the contrary: for him the standard rituals are of minimal benefit; he usually undergoes (for reasons of personality dynamics which we shall discuss in the later section on salvation) a more dramatic and radical religious experience, one to which he does not subject his clients. Although he becomes witch or curer, he has not undertaken his role as a result of being bewitched or of being—in the ordinary ritual manner—cured. Let us defer, then, the discussion of the shaman's "own" religion until later.

Religion as Ideology

Just as therapeutic and anti-therapeutic rituals are efforts to control the behavior and welfare of the individual, for his own sake as an individual or for the sake of the individual manipulator, so "ideological" rituals are rituals intended to control, in a conservative way, the behavior, the mood, the sentiments and values of groups for the sake of the community as a whole. The term "ideological" in this sense is drawn from the work of Karl Mannheim, who in *Ideology and Utopia* (1929) pointed out the tendency in any society toward one set of beliefs and rituals, the ideological, which are conservative, aimed at the repair and perfection of the existing system, and toward another, the utopian, which are directed toward the attainment of a revolutionary change for the achievement of a new and better world.

Ideological rituals may be said to have as their aim social control in a cybernetic sense; they intend to instruct, to direct, and to program individuals as they enter upon new tasks, and to correct the "wobbling" of the system of society which would result if individuals strayed too far from the roles they have assumed. Much of the concern of ideology is with morality, ethics, and values; but this term does not adequately cover the ritual phenomena, for, as we shall see, there are also ideological rituals in which immoral or rebellious behavior is sanctioned or even required as a catharsis or purgation of anti-ideological motives. And we should note that much of what is written about "religion" deals almost entirely with its ideological rituals and their functions; this is perhaps because the anthropological observers of religion tend to come from conservative institutions in conservative societies. Indeed, to many Western persons, religion *is* ideology—and that which is ritualistic and supernaturally rationalized, but is not ideological, is either ignored or dismissed as pathological or merely superstitious.

Rites of Passage

In all societies there are two types of mobility, or passage, to the successful accomplishment of which ritual is directed: role change and geographical movement. In both cases, the persons undertaking the passage from one state to another must abandon certain attachments and habits and form new ones; they must, in other words, learn. Role changes occur more or less regularly and predictably in the life cycle of individuals; and, although these role changes, and their timing, vary from one culture to another, they often maintain a general connection with physiological maturation. Birth, puberty, and death are universal objects of ritual, for at these times the individual enters into a new relationship to the world and to the community, subject to new opportunities, new dangers, and new responsibilities. In many societies, however, other stages in the life cycle are ritualized. Marriage, schooling, joining of age grades and other social groups, taking on occupational tasks and relinquishing them are subjects of rites of passage. And, of course, not all role changes can be easily fitted into a neat life-cycle framework. Especially in adulthood, the assumption and renunciation of specialized roles and new relationships of marriage, friendship, business association, military association, and group memberships of various kinds may present a kaleidoscope of shifting roles, each role change requiring its proper rite.

As Van Gennep (1908) has pointed out, rites of passage always involve three stages: separation from the old group or relationship, transition, and incorporation into a new group or relationship. It is important to recognize that the target of the ritual is not just the individual who is making the move; equally important are the persons being left behind and the group the initiate is joining. All must be reminded of or instructed in their proper behavior, whether it be renunciation or acceptance or both. Furthermore, the change being celebrated is culturally standardized; that is to say, many persons make it, sometimes in whole cohorts, but in any case the class of event occurs again and again.

The classic examples of rites of passage at times of role change are puberty and mourning rituals. All societies ritually recognize in some way a social transformation from childhood to adulthood in both males and females which occurs about the time of physiological puberty. Sometimes puberty rituals, particularly the ceremonies for boys, involve extensive communal ceremonies; of these, the bloody and orgiastic initiations of the Australian tribes are perhaps the most notorious, with their combination of circumcision and subincision. But elaborate initiation ceremonies may also be provided for girls, particularly in Negro Africa, where in some tribes the sexual mutilation of clitoridectomy is performed. Although the rigors of these initiation ceremonies not only frighten many of the aspirants but also offend the sensibilities of Western observers (who tend to circumcise only infant males), it is necessary to point out, first, that some overt attention to sex is not surprising in puberty rituals, and second, that the purpose of the ceremony is not merely to issue a sexual license to properly chastened adolescents, but also to instill a more general set of values regarding the rights and duties of adulthood. Thus, in preparation for the dramatic culmination of puberty rituals, there is generally a more or less protracted period of separation from the familiar household, of hazing, and of didactics, with a variety of temporary and irksome taboos on food, bathing, and other creature comforts. The triple-staged program of the rite of passage—separation, transition, and reaggregation—is thus carried through.

Less elaborate in a ceremonial way, but equally intense, are the puberty rituals of the Plains Indians. Here the youth does not undergo a communal initiation; however, although his experience is solitary, it involves a similar program. The boy is gradually weaned from his family by being scolded and neglected around the dwelling and encouraged to go out and seek "power" by a vision. Instructed by his elders, he retires to some lonely spot, supplied with little food or water or hunting equipment; there he remains, day and night, until he receives a vision. In this hallucinatory experience, a supernatural being in the form of some animal, bird, or insect speaks to the lad and promises to be his guardian and protector. Fortified by the vision and its promise of companionship, the young man returns from the wilderness able to accomplish the transition from childhood dependence and irresponsibility to adult independence and responsibility.

The situation of bereavement offers similar ground for ritual action. An individual, not long ago committed to the living and to whom the living were emotionally attached—in either a positive or a negative way, or both—has died. An emotional separation must be achieved. The departed soul and the survivors must be released from each other; otherwise, the living will remain miserable in their frustrated devotion and the departed soul will be unhappy. Once again, the goal of ritual is to separate effectively the living from the dead, to accomplish the transition, to bring about the incorporation of the dead into its proper place in the hereafter, and to reconstitute the mourners with each other and with the community. That this passage be satisfactorily completed is always a matter of community interest, for the actions of the mourners and of the ghost are relevant not only to themselves but to the rest of the group.

It is hardly necessary to point out that this ritual theme of passage—of separation, transition, and incorporation—is applicable to any situation in which an individual, or individuals, are expected to take up new roles in the community. Accordingly, the number and nature of such rituals in any culture are directly related to the role transitions that the particular society recognizes and enjoins. Birth, for the mother and child and for the father; getting a name; joining organizations; completing courses of training ("commencement"); marriage and divorce; taking on a job or office—all these are likely to be celebrated by some ritual of passage. And we may notice, in addition to the separation-transition-incorporation form of these rituals, another formal property: a combination of instruction and executive command. The rite of passage includes both some statement, or reminder, of how to play the expected role, and then a directive to commence its performance; first, "This is what to do," and second, "Now do it."

A second type of ritual of passage, which differs in an important sense from those just described, must now be mentioned. This is the ceremonial handling of geographical passage; that is to say, the crossing of boundaries on the ground. The preceding rituals were intramural, as it were—devoted to the accomplishment of role transformations within the community itself. But there are occasions in which persons move physically across the geographical boundaries of communities, as visitors, invaders, immigrants, traders, and so on. Ritual is apt to occur when community boundaries are crossed, to ensure that the new arrival is properly prepared to interact satisfactorily with his willing or unwilling hosts. These rituals have a particular importance for the conduct of intergroup relations; they serve to give strangers a defined place in a foreign community and thus pave the way for clear and explicit understanding.

Social Rites of Intensification

Earlier we discussed the hunting and agricultural rites of intensification; now we shall take up certain kinds of ritual which have comparable intent with respect to society itself. Just as nature requires ritual attention in order to ensure that its fertility and benevolence shall not flag or fail, so the community of people from time to time needs to be restored in its attachment to the values and customs of its culture. The most familiar example to Western readers is the regularly occurring worship service of the Judaeo-Christian and Mohammedan traditions: the Sabbath, the

Mass, the Sunday morning service, the daily muezzin-call, and the like. These are, as it were, broadcast ritual, compulsory but impersonal, which aim not at affecting any particular life-crisis but at maintaining the general value-tonus of the community by symbolic reminders of the mythology and by exhortation to apply the religiously sanctioned values to the routine problems of daily living. It is as if the cult institution recognized an entropic tendency for faith to slide away and the necessity to correct this constant randomization of motives by repetitive reminders. Where faith has slipped too far, of course, and religious demoralization has occurred, there is need for a more enthusiastic and revolutionary revival, of a type which we shall discuss later under the rubric of revitalization movements. Here we are concerned with a continuous, essentially conservative, effort to keep faith alive by symbol presentation, by exhortation, by sentimental reminders, by threats, cajolery, and the reiteration of brief, highly meaningful fragments of larger rituals.

Although most rituals no doubt have this function, not all have religious intensification as their explicit goal. The examples that come most readily to mind are taken from cults of an ecclesiastical type which have a conscious eye on the problem of social control. In simpler cult institutions, however, the same intent is sometimes expressed in more casual exercises: in the recitation of myths and legends by storytellers before informal spontaneous groups in the wintertime (never in the summer) among American Indians; in the moral injunctions, threats of supernatural punishment, and occasional lectures directed at children by their parents or guardians; in the casual ritual devotions addressed to shrines and household "idols" and icons. But it would seem that until a professional clergy has evolved, responsible *to* an ecclesiastical institution and *for* the community as a whole, a deliberate program of regular, calendrical rituals explicitly designed for the maintenance of the faith, rather than for any other ritual aim, does not occur. Society does not consciously become an object to itself until there exists a class, or professional specialty, responsible for the care of selected aspects of that society's welfare and maintaining a bureaucracy sufficiently large and sufficiently free of routine subsistence demands to perform the necessary rituals regularly and frequently.

Thus, for example, it is not until the middle of the nineteenth century, when they were beginning to work for industrial enterprises, that the Iroquois Indians began to hold regular meetings at which the Code of Handsome Lake was recited as a means of maintaining the faith; before this, although Handsome Lake was able to launch a revitalization movement, the Iroquois had not calendrically performed large rituals of social intensification in a purely religious sphere. They had, however, for generations performed the Condolence Ritual, which—in addition to being a rite of passage on occasions of bereavement—was also, and quite consciously, a ritual of political intensification, intended to keep alive faith in the Great League, a political institution. Indeed, we may hazard the guess that the first major calendrical programs of religious ritual of the social intensification variety may have been developed in connection with political institutions and have been taken up by religious specialists only when an ecclesiastical organization budded off, as it were, from political organization in the early stages of urbanization.

TABOOS AND OTHER ARBITRARY CEREMONIAL OBLIGATIONS IN SOCIAL INTERACTION

In complex societies there are frequently customary restrictions on the nature of social interaction permissible between members of differently ranked social classes, races, or ethnic groups, and between differently ranked members of particular organizations, such as the military, the clergy, economic enterprises, and even the family. Generally speaking, this kind of rank-based restriction on behavior is not found among the simpler hunting peoples except on occasions of individual dominance by an outstanding warrior, a feared shaman, or (perhaps) a sharp-tongued matron. But in simpler societies equally stringent restrictions, based on concepts of sex, of age, and of kinship, may be applied to sexual and household relationships.

Wherever such formally differentiated roles occur, whether on the basis of rank or class, sex, kinship, or age, there are likely to be certain formalities which are intrinsically necessary to the performance of mutual work roles and therefore are strictly enjoined. These arbitrary formalities are, in effect, rituals, and are explained and rationalized by reference to mythology; thus they come into the purview of religion. They would seem to be readily divisible into two general classes: *taboos*, or ritual avoidances, and what (for want of a better term) we shall call *courtesies*, positive actions rather than avoidances. Needless to say, there are also taboos and courtesies that do not receive a religious rationale; collectively they may all be termed "etiquette."

The taboo variety of religious etiquette is most conspicuously exemplified by the Hindus and the Polynesians. Although details differ, in both groups there is strict observance of ceremonial avoidance behavior between members of differently ranked social groups and between differently ranked members of the same group. The philosophical rationale involves a notion of *mana*: the higher the inherent virtue, or *mana*, of the person, the more careful must he be to avoid loss of this virtue by discharging it upon a person with less virtue with whom he comes into contact directly or indirectly. The Hindu Brahman, for instance, can at any one time be in only one of three states of ritual purity; he may lose a degree of purity by contact even with a Brahman in a lower state and of course can lose it by contact with a member of a lower caste. A Polynesian commoner, by indiscreet physical or even visual contact with a royal personage, can be overwhelmed by the discharge of *mana* from his superior. In less gross fashion, similar ritual taboos may be found in many cultures. The purpose of the avoidance is explicit enough: to prevent the depletion of the higher or the oversaturation of the lower person in the interaction through the flow of power from one to the other.

Not all interpersonal taboo systems are as formally elaborated in the social structure as these, of course. Three familiar, and widespread, examples of interpersonal taboo systems that can be found in both the most primitive and the most civilized cultures are the taboos on sexual intercourse between kinfolk, on sexual and other sorts of contact between menstruating women and their menfolk, and on intimacy of any kind between a man and his mother-in-law. In the case of the incest taboo, the avoidance behavior is motivated by a desire to avoid dangerous amounts of *mana* or direct supernatural punishment. While the boundaries of kinship are of course variable, and while even the banning of incest in the nuclear family is not quite universal, the incest taboo is so nearly ubiquitous in some form that the exceptions are chiefly of interest in the search for an understanding of the rule. With regard to menstruating women, violation of the taboo is expected to bring an automatic *mana* disorder or the anger of supernaturals. In the case of the mother-in-law taboo, the sanctions are less stringent and the avoidances less dramatic, but the flavor is much the same: the son must turn his face when he addresses his mother-in-law, he must not make sexual references in her presence, and so on, lest some evil befall him. This last example is instructive because it introduces another motive: respect. Not only is the social avoidance motivated by fear of supernatural retribution; it is, more positively, motivated by a desire to secure, or to show, respect between the persons in interaction. The respect, indeed, may seem to go one way, and to find contempt on the other side; but the failure of the lower-ranked party, in the case of ranking systems, to practice appropriate avoidance behavior, is apt to be understood as a signal of disrespect.

The importance of respect in the motivational complex of these arbitrary social rituals is even more evident in the positive ceremonial obligations. Many such ritual obligations are, of course, secular. Familiar Western examples are military courtesies between ranks, such as saluting, standing at attention, and the use of "sir" to indicate mutual respect for "the uniform" (not necessarily, it is carefully pointed out, for the man inside the uniform), and the courtesies between the sexes, such as the male's doffing of his hat, holding doors open, and walking on the curb side of the pavement. But many other such courtesies between members of role groups do have religious sanction and, particularly in ecclesiastical societies, their omission may entail supernatural retribution. One thinks of the multitudinous obeisances and respectful salutations required of those approaching the person of a "divine king" in African societies; of the respectful attentions of wives to husbands in Japan; of the use of respectful terms of address such as "father," "brother," "sister," toward the clergy in many Christian denominations. In all such instances, the behaviors are reciprocal: the respect must be mutual, whether or not it recognizes a difference in rank.

Such formalities have been treated by Goffman (1956, 1959) as a dialogue of identity in which both parties normally express deference to the other's demeanor. Each experiences extreme dismay if the other refuses to play his part in the exchange. The aspects of identity that we are considering here tend to be those based on group or class membership and the relevant courtesies are evidently and consciously intended to reinforce precisely those sentiments that will promote the continuous and effective execution of the complementary roles which members of these groups or classes play in various publicly recognized tasks. The purpose of religious cults in sanctioning these courtesies is not to multiply "empty rituals," but to animate the participants in real and important transactions with precisely those feelings of respect and, in some cases, subordination or dominance, which are believed to be necessary to efficiency. How effective these courtesies are in maintaining readiness to act appropriately may be questioned, and in the next chapter on the functions of religion we shall consider this question. But the belief that they are effective is manifest.

Rituals of Rebellion

So far in this discussion of the ideological goals of religious ritual, we have dealt with rituals that are intended to ensure that people do the "right" thing. In the category of behavior that has been conveniently labeled "rituals of rebellion" we are confronted by rituals in which people are permitted, or even required, to do precisely the "wrong" thing (*vide* Norbeck [1961, 1963]). The paradox, however, is only a seeming one, for the ultimate goal is still the same: the maintenance of order and stability in society. Rituals of rebellion are intended to contribute to this order by venting the impulses that are chronically frustrated in the day-to-day course of doing what is required. They are, in effect, a ritualized catharsis for precisely those motives that are suppressed by conformity to the ideology.

In my home town, at least two ceremonies on the annual calendar are the occasion for rituals of rebellion. For children, Halloween is a time when children are encouraged to gratify a number of wishes that are formally proscribed during the rest of the year: vandalism; impersonating persons of the opposite sex; harassment of neighbors; indulgence in sweets; staying out late; concealment of identity; demanding of gifts; identification with animals, devils, malevolent ghosts, monsters, and other unlikely creatures. Stuffy, crabby, and unduly respectable members of the community are particular targets of this annual revolt (Mead [1960]). New Year's Eve is a comparable occasion for adults, permitting them to wear unusual clothes, to carouse, and to mingle more exuberantly than on most other occasions.

These two rituals, Halloween and New Year's Eve, are relatively restrained examples of a large subclass of rituals of rebellion which can be referred to as saturnalia. In saturnalia, the object is the venting—and dispelling—of wanton impulses accumulated during a preceding period of routine propriety. The rebellion is an intramural one, directed against the rules and regulations imposed by the community on itself. Mardi Gras, Carnival, the Roman Saturnalia proper are familiar ceremonials of this kind in a Latin tradition. Many American Indian tribes incorporated into their ceremonial sequences a series of burlesques by clowns who parodied serious rituals, introduced obscenity into sacred places (by drinking urine, eating feces, and simulating sexual intercourse), and showed open disrespect to the gods themselves. Among the Swazi of southeast Africa, ritual rebellion includes the singing of traditional songs ridiculing the king; yet the Swazi themselves assert that the rituals "strengthen kingship" and confirm the royal family's title to the throne (Gluckman [1954]). Such occasions of license thus temporarily elicit "contrary" behavior of precisely the kinds that are normally subject to the most stringent and irksome taboos. If the avoidance of incest is a preoccupation, then the *corroboree* permits the father to have intercourse with his daughter; if the soundness of marriage is emphasized throughout the year, then the holiday permits promiscuity; if the authority of the political structure is sternly enforced, then the ceremony encourages its ridicule. Ribaldry, buffoonery, and the burlesque of well-established institutions become the rule; instead of sobriety, high humor is the mood.

A similar cathartic release of pent-up wishes whose routine expression would be considered destructive also can be directed at oppressive outsiders. Among American Indians, the buffoons have at times performed comic dances expressing hatred and contempt for the white people. On one occasion, for instance, Zuñi clowns made ribald fun of the United States Army and of Mexican Catholicism, some dressing in cast-off army clothing, others wearing imitation priestly garments (including white-painted goggles), one parading as a girl, and some strutting about naked. They put on a parody of missionary Catholic ritual, concluding with an obscene imitation of the Mass in which urine took the place of wine.

> The dancers suddenly wheeled into line, threw themselves on their knees before my table, and with extravagant beatings of breast began an outlandish and fanciful mockery of a Mexican Catholic congregation at vespers. One bawled out a parody upon the pater-noster, another mumbled along in the manner of an old man reciting the rosary, while the fellow with the India-rubber coat jumped up and began a passionate exhortation or sermon, which for mimetic fidelity was incomparable. This kept the audience laughing with sore sides for some moments. . . .
>
> The dancers swallowed great draughts (of urine), smacked their lips, and amid the roaring merriment of the spectators, remarked that it was very, very, good. The clowns were now upon their mettle, each trying to surpass his neighbors in feats of nastiness. One swallowed a fragment of corn-husk, saying he thought it very good and better than bread; his *vis-à-vis* attempted to chew and gulp down a piece of filthy rag. Another expressed regret that the dance had not been held out of doors, in one of the plazas; there they could show what they could do. There they always made it a point of honor to eat the excrement of men and dogs. [Norbeck, 1961, p. 208.]

Among the Cherokee, the ancient Bugger Dance similarly pokes fun at European invaders. But it may be doubted that such intergroup ritual rebellion is often couched in terms of religion; more commonly, perhaps, it is a secular ritual, performed in small private groups or by individuals, as seems to have been the case with the American Negro. Ritual rebellion against external political authority is, perhaps, too dangerous: it may too easily slide off into futile revolt or precipitate savage punishment, unless the rebellious have consciously accepted the rightness of their subordinate relationship. And if they have accepted that inferior role, they are likely to consider themselves to be a caste or class, and the rituals become intramural, as before.

In all of the ideological rituals, the aim is manifest: to ensure that the members of the society enter into, and remain constantly in, a state of readiness to respond with culturally appropriate behavior in circumstances of importance to society. The transformation is conservative; it aims to standardize, to replicate in the new generation the growth process of the last, to correct the minor wobbles and strayings, the rents and tears, to which the social structure is subjected by the vicissitudes of time. Its goal is to make people want to do what they have to do.

Ritual as Salvation

In the past section we drew attention to the importance of ritual courtesies in the continuous validation of the social identities of holders of complementary roles. By social identity we mean those rights and duties that are culturally recognized as pertaining to all persons who hold a certain classificatory position in society; and, of course, such social identities are always complementary, so that the rights of one correspond to reciprocal duties of the other (Goodenough [1965]). Religious ritual is often aimed at validating and confirming these identities and has the connotation of mutual respect for the participants.

As Goffman (1959), Wallace and Fogelson (1965), and others have pointed out, however, denial of ritual reciprocity in an identity relationship is interpreted by the snubbed person as an assault upon his identity; he feels insulted, his self-esteem is threatened, and he experiences fear, rage, despair, or other intense negative emotions. Systematic refusal to show deference to the demeanor of another, in both ritual and substantive interactions, can indeed lead to profound emotional disorganization. This technique is used as a means of deliberately destroying the existing self-image of a victim by the keepers of such "total institutions" as prisons, concentration camps, mental hospitals, the military services, boarding schools, and monastic orders (Goffman [1956]). In less coercive circumstances, an interruption of the deference-and-demeanor reciprocity can lead to an escalating identity struggle between and among increasingly antagonistic individuals and groups (Wallace and Fogelson [1965]).

But there are other aspects of identity than those that can be neatly packaged as a bundle of reciprocal rights and duties or of deferences and demeanors. In a more general psychological sense, a person's identity is the whole set of images of self which over a given span of time that person maintains. It is possible to distinguish, therefore, a number of areas of identity, including those implied in the concept of social identity, but including also various aspects of the self in which the individual wishes to feel adequate but which may not easily be translated into terms of reciprocal social rights and duties. Estimates of physical prowess, moral virtue, beauty, intelligence, sexual fulfillment, supernatural power or influence, and so on, may in one instance or another be personal rather than social, absolute rather than relative, amoral rather than moral or immoral. If these categorical areas of identity, as well as—or rather than—the reciprocal ones, are put in question, the person's response is often an even more desperate emotional crisis than if his social identity has been questioned. And, of course, the two kinds of identity may be so thoroughly fused—indeed, in some cultures, such as the Chinese, it has been said that they cannot be distinguished—that any question of social identity is also a threat to the personal identity. In Western tradition, by contrast, the two kinds of identity are theoretically and ideally sharply distinguished. A familiar literary plot involves the person whose social identity (usually a high one) is unquestioned, but whose personal identity is weak, and who is confronted by a person whose social identity is obscure but whose personal identity is strong. But, granting the cultural variability in concepts of identity, and the intricacy of the structure of identity components, we can declare with confidence that serious damage to the self-esteem of a person is, universally, a life crisis of the first magnitude, whether by social abuse, as occurs in identity struggles and brainwashing, or by an internal disillusionment, as seems to occur in neurosis and psychosis, in brain damage, and in consequence of various physical and emotional accidents.

When identity is seriously impaired, therefore, we can expect that the experience will call for strenuous efforts to understand and repair the damage to self-esteem; the deeper the impairment, the more desperate the efforts to find a solution. Sometimes, of course, the efforts at resynthesis of identity are inadequate to maintain or restore a tolerable level of self-esteem; but frequently, if the effort is supported and guided by others and if some sort of model of the transformation process is provided by the culture, the effort is successful. And, although there are many avenues to identity renewal, they all involve some kind of identification with an admired model of the human personality, and differentiation from a despised model. Perhaps the most ancient, most widespread, and most successful of these procedures is provided by religious ritual. In religious identity renewal—salvation, to use the familiar term—the identification is with, or the differentiation is from, a supernatural being. Let us now discuss the three common types of rituals of salvation: possession, becoming a shaman, and mysticism.

Possession: The Socially Sanctioned Alternation of Identities

We have already encountered the concept of possession in our review of religious ritual as therapy. One of the widespread explanations of illness, either physical or mental, is that an alien spirit has entered the body of the victim and is using it for its own purposes at the expense of the host. Hence exorcism of the possessing spirit is the indicated treatment. Little in the way of identity conflict is revealed in many such experiences, particularly where the symptoms are physical, as in real organic disorders and many conversion hysterias. But if the symptoms are chronic behavioral and emotional troubles of certain other kinds, then the victim's own experience, as well as native theory, will inevitably involve split identity. The possession theory, however, while it may be intellectually satisfying to the victim as an explanation for his condition, will not bring relief, and the search for exorcism becomes a search for the path to salvation itself.

The type of disorder in question is the classic obsessive-compulsive neurosis, in which the victim is compelled against his conscious will to perform certain acts, to say certain things, to think certain thoughts, to experience certain bodily sensations which are felt to be foreign to his true nature. The experience, even for sufferers not inclined to use a possession theory as explanation, is of an intrusive alien mental system, partly or occasionally capturing the body's physical and mental apparatus. Thus the victim may, against his will, bark like a dog and walk on all fours, shout curses on the most sacred occasions, be plagued by inexplicable fears and doubts, be preoccupied with sexual thoughts which are, to him, obscene and disgusting, or be irresistibly forced into nymphomaniacal or satyriacal excesses which yield no lasting emotional satisfaction.

How grim this experience may be depends on the extent to which it weakens or invalidates the individual's self-esteem. Among the Iroquois, for instance, persons who suffered from impulses to walk on all fours, grunting like a bear, were regarded as being possessed by the spirit of the bear, and were treated by the cathartic rituals of the Bear Society, a medicine society which provided ritual occasions for the performance of these acts; kleptomaniacs were, by analogous reasoning, subjected to the rituals of the Chipmunk Society (Speck [1949]). These possessions do not seem to have represented any danger of a catastrophic identity collapse. Nor, for native practitioners, do the highly stereotyped rituals of possession in African and Haitian voodoo represent any denial of identity. Here, the experience of possession is more like that of true multiple personality: the victim who is "mounted" by a deity, and for several hours acts out dramatically that god's or goddess's role (however dissonant it may be with the victim's daily character), does not experience other than a sense of enhanced value and worth at being chosen to serve as the vehicle for an Olympian divinity (*vide* Métraux [1959]; and Deren [1953]).

But if the intrusive mental system is, by reason of idiosyncratic personal significance or cultural definition, experienced only as a contradiction of the person's true and valued identity or as a failure to live up to the ideal—if it is, in other words, *not* recognized as an invasion by an evil spirit or the Devil himself—then the matter is more serious. Maya Deren, a dancer from New York, described in graphic terms her fright at the awareness that, under the monotonous iteration of drum beats and the suggestion of the crowd, she was becoming possessed at a voodoo ritual in Haiti:

> At first the drummer is considerate and "breaks" often enough to permit the limbs to relax and rest. But as the dance goes on, these "breaks" become more rare and the sense of fun gives way to a sense of great effort. The air seems heavy and wet, and, gasping, I feel that it brings no refreshment into my laboring lungs. My heart pounds in the pulse at my temple. My legs are heavy beyond belief, the muscles contracted into an enormous ache which digs deeper with every movement. My entire being focuses on one single thought: that I must endure.
>
> I cannot say, now, why I did not stop; except that, beneath all this is always a sense of contract: whether, in the end, one be victor or victim, it is to be in the terms one has accepted. One cannot default. So focused was I, at that time, upon the effort to endure, that I did not even mark the moment when this ceased to be difficult and I cannot say whether it was sudden or gradual but only that my awareness of it was a sudden thing, as if the pace which had seemed unbearably demanding had slipped down a notch into a slow-motion, so that my mind had time, now, to wander, to observe at leisure, what a splendid thing it was, indeed, to hear the drums, to move like this, to be able to do all this so easily, to do even more, if it pleased one, to elaborate, to extend this movement of the arms toward greater elegance, or to counterpoint that rhythm of the heel or even to make this movement to the side, this time. As sometimes in dreams, so here I can observe myself, can note with pleasure how the full hem of my white skirt plays with the rhythms, can watch, as if in a mirror, how the smile begins with a softening of the lips, spreads imperceptibly into a radiance which, surely, is lovelier than any I have ever seen. It is when I turn, as if to a neighbor, to say, "Look! See how lovely that is!" and see that the others are removed to a distance, withdrawn to a circle which is already watching, that I realize, like a shaft of terror struck through me, that it *is* myself, for as that terror strikes, we two are made one again, joined by and upon the point of the left leg which is as if rooted to the earth. Now there

is only terror. "This is it!" Resting upon that leg I feel a strange numbness enter it from the earth itself and mount, within the very marrow of the bone, as slowly and richly as sap might mount the trunk of a tree. I say numbness, but that is inaccurate. To be precise, I must say what, even to me, is pure recollection, but not otherwise conceivable: I must call it a white darkness, its whiteness a glory and its darkness, terror. It is the terror which has the greater force, and with a supreme effort I wrench the leg loose—I must keep moving! must keep moving!—and pick up the dancing rhythm of the drums as something to grasp at, something to keep my feet from resting upon the dangerous earth. No sooner do I settle into the succor of this support than my sense of self doubles again, as in a mirror, separates to both sides of an invisible threshold, except that now the vision of the one who watches flickers, the lids flutter, the gaps between moments of sight growing greater, wider. I see the dancing one here, and next in a different place, facing another direction, and whatever lay between these moments is lost, utterly lost. I feel that the gaps will spread and widen and that I will, myself, be altogether lost in that dead space and that dead time. With a great blow the drum unites us once more upon the point of the left leg. The white darkness starts to shoot up; I wrench my foot free but the effort catapults me across what seems a vast, vast distance, and I come to rest upon a firmness of arms and bodies which would hold me up. But these have voices—great, insistent, singing voices—whose sound would smother me. With every muscle I pull loose and again plunge across a vast space and once more am no sooner poised in balance than my leg roots. So it goes; the leg fixed, then wrenched loose, the long fall across space, the rooting of the leg again—for how long, how many times I cannot know. My skull is a drum; each great beat drives that leg, like the point of a stake, into the ground. The singing is at my very ear, inside my head. This sound will drown me! "Why don't they stop! Why don't they stop!" I cannot wrench the leg free. I am caught in this cylinder, this well of sound. There is nothing anywhere except this. There is no way out. The white darkness moves up the veins of my leg like a swift tide rising; is a great force which I cannot sustain or contain, which, surely, will burst my skin. It is too much, too bright, too white for me; this is its darkness. "Mercy!" I scream within me. I hear it echoed by the voices, shrill and unearthly: "Erzulie!" The bright darkness floods up through my body, reaches my head, engulfs me. I am sucked down and exploded upward at once. That is all. [Deren, 1953, pp. 258–260.]

The hysterical medieval prioress Soeur Jeanne, preoccupied with orgiastic dreams, sexual fantasies, and ecstatic devotion to her confessor, saw her obsession at first only as a personal failure of fidelity to Christ:

"I did not then believe that one could be possessed without having given consent to, or made a pact with, the devil; in which I was mistaken, for the most innocent and even the most holy can be possessed. I myself was not of the number of the innocent; for thousands upon thousands of times I had given myself over to the devil by committing sin and making continual resistance to grace. . . . The demons insinuated themselves into my mind and inclinations, in such sort that, through the evil dispositions they found in me, they made of me one and the same substance with themselves. . . . Ordinarily the demons acted in conformity with the feelings I had in my soul; this they did so subtly that I myself did not believe that I had any demons within me. I felt insulted when people showed that they suspected me of being possessed, and if anyone talked to me of my possession by the demons, I felt a violent emotion of anger and could not control the expression of my resentment." [In Huxley, 1952, p. 116.]

Soeur Jeanne did not achieve any relief until she had been convinced of her possession, bound, and exorcised in a kind of public debauchery, replete with obscene yells, convulsive seizures, and forcible enemas. The consequence, however, of this forcible effort at exorcism was tragedy: she accused the priest she loved of being a witch; he was in due course burned alive. She then attempted suicide herself, and spent the next thirty years of her life in heroic efforts to resolve, by way of mystic union with God Himself, the catastrophic contradictions of her soul. One suspects that had she been allowed to act out some of her sexual fantasies, in a state of socially sanctioned possession, or in more or less routine exorcistic "treatments," she would never have become so ill or have had the need to destroy her platonic lover.

Salvation by possession, then, involves the *acceptance* of two (or even more) mutually contradictory identities, each being permitted, or even encouraged, to take executive control of the body at certain times, with more or less mutual ignorance or indifference. Exorcism, in such a case, must be in effect not the casting out of devils but the ritual acceptance and recognition of these intrusive identities in a place and on an occasion allotted to them; the identities are encapsulated, insulated from one another, each permitted its share of fulfillment.

Becoming a Shaman: The Substitution of One Identity for Another

In the manipulation of possession for the sake of salvation, the victim of identity conflict is not merely permitted, but is ritually encouraged, to accept a lapse into an alternate identity. But the lapse is occasional, circumscribed by time and place, and leaves the victim free during profane periods to go about his daily life unimpeded by the inconvenience of intrusive thoughts and compulsive acts. Where, however, neither exorcism nor ritually segregated episodes of possession bring relief, a more extensive transformation of identity is required. Such an extensive process of identity transformation occurs generally in the process of becoming a shaman; indeed, it is often the procedure by which potential shamans are recruited and trained.

The potential shaman is very often a sick human being, suffering from serious mental and physical disorders which spring from or involve profound identity conflict. The ritual procedures of developing a shaman are intended both to cure the potential shaman and to produce a specialist of value to the community. Sometimes the ritual is self-imposed; sometimes it is conducted by another shaman or by other knowledgeable members of the community. A classic description of the process among the Zulus of South Africa is retold by an early missionary, Canon Henry Callaway:

> The condition of a man who is about to be an inyanga [1] is this: At first he is apparently robust; but in process of time he begins to be delicate, not having any real disease, but being very delicate. He begins to be particular about food, and abstains from some kinds, and requests his friends not to give him that food, because it makes him ill. He habitually avoids certain kinds of food, choosing what he likes, and he does not eat much of that; and he is continually complaining of pains

[1] Diviner, physician, or shaman.

in different parts of his body. And he tells them that he has dreamt that he was being carried away by a river. He dreams of many things, and his body is muddled and he becomes a house of dreams. And he dreams constantly of many things, and on awaking says to his friends, "My body is muddled today; I dreamt many men were killing me; I escaped I know not how. And on waking one part of my body felt different from other parts; it was no longer alike all over." At last the man is very ill, and they go to the diviners to enquire.

The diviners do not at once see that he is about to have a soft head.[2] It is difficult for them to see the truth; they continually talk nonsense, and make false statements, until all the man's cattle are devoured at their command, they saying that the spirit of his people demands cattle, that it may eat food.

So the people readily assent to the diviners' word, thinking that they know. At length all the man's property is expended, he being still ill; and they no longer know what to do, for he has no more cattle, and his friends help him in such things as he needs.

At length an inyanga comes and says that all the others are wrong. He says, "I know that you come here to me because you have been unable to do anything for the man, and have no longer the heart to believe that any inyanga can help you. But, my friends, I see that my friends, the other izinyanga,[3] have gone astray. They have not eaten impepo. They were not initiated in a proper way. Why have they been mistaken, when the disease is evident? For my part, I tell you the izinyanga have troubled you. The disease does not require to be treated with blood. As for the man, I see nothing else but that he is possessed by the Itongo. There is nothing else. He is possessed by an Itongo. Your people move in him.[4] They are divided into two parties; some say, 'No, we do not wish that our child should be injured. We do not wish it.' It is for that reason and no other that he does not get well. If you bar the way against the Itongo, you will be killing him. For he will not be an inyanga; neither will he ever be a man again; he will be what he is now. If he is not ill, he will be delicate, and become a fool, and be unable to understand anything. I tell you you will kill him by using medicines. Just leave him alone, and look to the end to which the disease points. Do you not see that on the day he has not taken medicine, he just takes a mouthful of food? Do not give him any more

[2] A *soft head,* that is, impressible. Diviners are said to have soft heads.

[3] Plural of inyanga.

[4] *Your people move in him,* that is, the Amatongo, a class of spirits.

medicines. He will not die of the sickness, for he will have what is good given to him."

So the man may be ill two years without getting better; perhaps even longer than that. He may leave the house for a few days, and the people begin to think he will get well. But no, he is confined to the house again. This continues until his hair falls off. And his body is dry and scurfy; and he does not like to anoint himself. People wonder at the progress of the disease. But his head begins to give signs of what is about to happen. He shows that he is about to be a diviner by yawning again and again, and by sneezing again and again. And men say, "No! Truly it seems as though this man was about to be possessed by a spirit." This is also apparent from his being very fond of snuff; not allowing any long time to pass without taking some. And people begin to see that he has had what is good given to him.

After that he is ill; he has slight convulsions, and has water poured on him, and they cease for a time. He habitually sheds tears, at first slight, and at last he weeps aloud, and in the middle of the night, when the people are asleep, he is heard making a noise, and wakes the people by singing; he has composed a song, and men and women awake and go to sing in concert with him.

In this state of things they daily expect his death; he is now but skin and bones, and they think that to-morrow's sun will not leave him alive. The people wonder when they hear him singing, and they strike their hands in concert. They then begin to take courage, saying, "Yes; now we can see that it is the head." [5]

Therefore whilst he is undergoing this initiation the people of the village are troubled by want of sleep; for a man who is beginning to be an inyanga causes great trouble, for he does not sleep, but works constantly with his brain; his sleep is merely by snatches, and he wakes up singing many songs; and people who are near quit their villages by night when they hear him singing aloud, and go to sing in concert. Perhaps he sings till the morning, no one having slept. The people of the village smite their hands in concert till they are sore. And then he leaps about the house like a frog; and the house becomes too small for him, and he goes out, leaping and singing, and shaking like a reed in the water, and dripping with perspiration.

At that time many cattle are eaten. The people encourage his becoming an inyanga; they employ means for making the Itongo white, that it

[5] Literally, we see the head, *viz.* that it is affected in that way which is followed by the power to divine.

may make his divination very clear. At length another ancient inyanga of celebrity is pointed out to him.[6] At night whilst asleep he is commanded by the Itongo, who says to him, "Go to So-and-so; go to him, and he will churn for you emetic-ubulawo, that you may be an inyanga altogether." Then he is quiet for a few days, having gone to the inyanga to have ubulawo churned for him; and he comes back quite another man, being now cleansed and an inyanga indeed.

And if he is to have familiar spirits, there is continually a voice saying to him, "You will not speak with the people; they will be told by us everything they come to enquire about." And he continually tells the people his dreams, saying, "There are people [7] who tell me at night that they will speak for themselves to those who come to enquire." At last all this turns out to be true; when he has begun to divine, at length his power entirely ceases, and he hears the spirits who speak by whistlings speaking to him, and he answers them as he would answer a man; and he causes them to speak by asking them questions; if he does not understand what they say, they make him understand everything they see. The familiar spirits do not begin by explaining omens which occur among the people; they begin by speaking with him whose familiars they are, and making him acquainted with what is about to happen, and then he divines for the people.

This then is what I know of familiar spirits and diviners.

If the relatives of the man who has been made ill by the Itongo do not wish him to become a diviner, they call a great doctor to treat him, to lay the spirit, that he may not divine. But although the man no longer divines, he is not well; he continues to be always out of health. This is what I know. But although he no longer divines, as regards wisdom he is like a diviner. For instance, there was Undayeni. His friends did not wish him to become a diviner; they said, "No; we do not wish so fine and powerful a man to become a mere thing which stays at home, and does no work, but only divines." So they laid the spirit. But there still remained in him signs which caused the people to say, "If that man had been a diviner, he would have been a very great man, a first-class diviner."

As to the familiar spirits, it is not one only that speaks; they are very many; and their voices are not alike; one has his voice, and another his; and the voice of the man into whom they enter is different from theirs. He too enquires of them as other people do; and he too seeks

---

[6] That is, by the Itongo in a dream.
[7] People, *viz.* the dead, the Amatongo.

divination of them. If they do not speak, he does not know what they will say; he cannot tell those who come for divination what they will be told. No. It is his place to take what those who come to enquire bring, and nothing more. And the man and the familiar spirits ask questions of each other and converse.

When those who come to seek divination salute him, he replies, "O, you have come when I am alone. The spirits departed yesterday. I do not know where they are gone." So the people wait. When they come they are heard saluting them, saying, "Good day." They reply, "Good day to you, masters." And the man who lives with them also asks them saying, "Are you coming?" They say, they are. It is therefore difficult to understand that it is a deception, when we hear many voices speaking with the man who has familiar spirits, and him too speaking with them. [Callaway, 1870, pp. 259–267.]

Although not all potential shamans invariably go through such a profound episode of emotional disorder or such heroic measures of transformation, the statistical association of shamanism with emotional disorder is marked and has been commented on by many observers. In the case of the treatment of the Guatemalan woman who suffered from magical fright, which we cited in detail earlier, the curer himself was diagnosed as probably psychotic by the anthropologist and by his colleague, a psychiatrist. Gillin remarks:

The curer, Manuel, from all points of view would probably be labeled as a schizophrenic in North American society. This diagnosis is unequivocally brought out, according to Dr. Billig, in his Rorschach protocol. Also, behavioristic material tends to support such a diagnosis. Manuel exhibits the typical masklike countenance, flat emotional reactions, high development of fantasy life which is unshared with others, and typical disregard of opinions and reactions of the members of his social group. However, in the society of San Luis, Manuel does not occupy a position corresponding to that of a schizophrenic patient in our own society. On the contrary, he fills a highly respected status as an important and much respected curer who has had considerable success. He carries on his farming with skill, and he manages his business affairs, such as renting and trading new plots of lands, with a certain shrewdness. His income is considerably more than that of an ordinary Indian because of the fees which he collects for curing sessions. Many people come to him for advice which he gives in a calm and rather dissociated manner. In short, whatever the final diagnosis of Manuel may be, there is a recognized and, from the local point of view, a useful place for him in the social structure of San Luis. As Dr. Billig says in his Rorschach report, "His society does not exert any pressure to bring his drive-dominated fantasy life under a more rigid control, and it does not regard thorough testing of reality as necessary. It enables Manuel not only to live in a dream world of his own but also enables him to find an accepted escape for others, as in the case of Alicia's difficulties, by the powerful convictions evolving from the symbolic strength of his own traumatic experiences."

It may be interesting to note that the five other Indian curers on whom we have life-history material and Rorschach protocols exhibit fairly uniform personality structure. All share, according to Billig's Rorschach results, basic "introversive tendencies," and in our society would be considered "schizoid." Nevertheless, although all the shaman curers in the Indian sector of San Luis society exhibit similar status personalities, and occupy similar positions in the social structure of the community, they are, as regards other personality traits, rather distinct personalities whose types vary throughout a certain range.

In a tentative way, we may say that the Indian curers are all people whose basic personality is in some way "peculiar," but that they have found an application of their talents and a toleration of their peculiarities in the status of shaman curer as recognized among the Indians of San Luis. [Gillin, 1948, p. 396.] *

Similar comments are made about Eskimo shamans (Lantis [1950a]), Nuba shamans in the Sudan (Nadel [1946]), and northern Asiatic shamans (Czaplicka [1914]). The general process of becoming a shaman is, indeed, remarkably similar throughout the world: a phase of schizoid identity dissolution is followed by a phase of paranoidal identity restitution, the new identity being that of the shaman, and with community support and encouragement for the development of a controlled hysterical dissociability during which the shaman is able to visit, speak to, see, or be entered by his supernatural alter ego.

It is important to emphasize that the support and encourage-

* From John Gillin, "Magical Fright," *Psychiatry*, 11 (1948), 387–400. Reprinted by special permission of The William Alanson White Psychiatric Foundation, Inc. Copyright, 1949, by The William Alanson White Psychiatric Foundation.

ment of the community and the availability of technical instruction or apprenticeship in the arts of the shaman are indispensable not merely for satisfactory role performance but for the sustenance of the shaman's new identity. The shaman is, in a psychological sense (and often, as Eliade [1950] points out, in a mythological sense, too) being reborn at the time of his transformation and also on the occasion of his magical flight or possession, and like all neonates he needs succor. Without a community to help him through the crisis, the shaman may languish in a withdrawn, apathetic, or wildly disturbed schizophrenic state. In the case of the Zulu described earlier by Callaway, the prognosis for the potential shaman's illness is poor unless his identification with the possessing spirits is permitted and ritually encouraged by the community. Potential shamans, lingering in a deteriorated schizophrenic condition, may be seen on the back wards of any American state hospital. I recall a case in a state hospital in the eastern United States which illustrates the point elegantly. An urban Negro, addicted to heroin and jailed following a conviction for car theft (presumably motivated by the need to gain money to support his habit), experienced a hallucinatory episode while he was in jail. He heard God's voice adjuring him to renounce drugs and to found a new organization of an "addicts anonymous" character which would help others to shake the habit (or, in the language of possession, to get the monkey off their backs). His fellow prisoners objected to his loud preaching and singing, however, and the warden called in a panel of physicians, who declared him insane. Instead of being recognized and supported in his shamanic resynthesis, the prisoner was thereupon carted off to a state hospital. His condition there rapidly deteriorated: he was soon incoherent, incontinent and smearing feces—and there he has remained for years.

A process very similar, but less regularized, occurs in the lives of many religious prophets who go beyond the limited role of the shaman to become leaders of revitalization movements, but this is a topic we shall discuss in the next section. Suffice it here to remark that in the interest of curing a hysterical or schizophrenic person, societies all over the world have discovered that ritual support for a transformation of state which involves the abandonment of a collapsed secular identity and a new identification with a supernatural being is an effective means for producing the shaman. He receives support for the maintenance of the new identity not merely from the shaman's initiation rituals but also from the rituals that he performs for others, wherein periodically he may identify with powerful supernaturals, claim arcane knowledge, and act out restitution fantasies of saving lives, finding lost objects, and forestalling community disaster.

The Mystic Experience

Very similar to the process of becoming a shaman, but less closely tied to a specific helping role in the community and less dependent upon a schizophrenic identity crisis for its inauguration, is the mystic experience. This experience is, to many religious persons, the heart of religion. It may range in intensity from the relatively brief "conversion experience" of our forefathers to the intense ecstasies of Christian, Islamic, Hindu, and Buddhist mystics who ritualized certain systematic procedures for achieving the sense of union with God. Although the nature of this experience no doubt is shared under many names (including that of "becoming a shaman") by people in cultures of every religious type, the particular kind of ritual regime denoted by the term "mysticism" seems to be associated with monotheistic cults, where the only deity with whom it is permissible, or perhaps even possible, to identify is the Supreme Being.

The prolegomena to the mystic experience must be, as with the shaman, a profound sense of dissatisfaction with one's secular identity, a feeling of anxiety or fear, a desperate sense of the need to be saved before being damned by some final disaster. The path to salvation therefore requires an abandonment of the old self. The achievement of salvation is experienced as an intense ecstasy, which may be metaphorically described in sexual terms, or as a more diffuse sense of floating away on an infinite ocean, or simply as a deep sense of confidence and release from fear in the certainty of divine benevolence and concern.

The ritual procedures for accomplishing the mystic transformation are no less specific than those required for managing possession or for producing a shaman; but they differ in several respects because they are aimed at a different identity problem. Whereas the rituals of possession are directed toward hysteria, and the shamanic toward schizophrenia, the rituals of mysticism are focused on depression. Depressed persons may reach just as profound a depth of misery as hysterics and schizophrenics but depression may also be found as a far less climactic condition than either the identity conflict that produces the personality dissociations of hysteria or the identity collapse that produces schizophrenia. Depression may be merely a nagging, chronic sense of unworthiness, inadequacy, and dissatisfaction with life, for which the remedial action—the mystic search for salvation—may be either postponed or avoided altogether.

The ritual techniques for achieving the mystical experience of salvation are various, depending on individual temperament and cultural repertoire. In our society today, Zen Buddhism may provide a path that satisfies some; for others, the revivalist enthusiasm of the Protestant camp meeting or the quiet discipline of the Catholic nunnery or monastery is the way. In all these mystic ways, however, there is a common theme: renunciation of "the world," with its temptations for the flesh and the intellect, and withdrawal into an intense and preoccupying interest in the state of the soul and its relationship to the Absolute.

Underhill (1955) has attempted to codify the mystic way into a series of five universal stages: awakening, purgation, illumination, the dark night of the soul, and union. She describes these stages as follows:

(1) The awakening of the Self to consciousness of Divine Reality. This experience, usually abrupt and well-marked, is accompanied by intense feelings of joy and exaltation.

(2) The Self, aware for the first time of Divine Beauty, realizes by contrast its own finiteness and imperfection, the manifold illusions in which it is immersed, the immense distance which separates it from the One. Its attempts to eliminate by discipline and mortification all that stands in the way of its progress towards union with God constitute *Purgation:* a state of pain and effort.

(3) When by Purgation the Self has become detached from the "things of sense," and acquired those virtues which are the "ornaments of the spiritual marriage," its joyful consciousness of the Transcendent Order returns in an enhanced form. Like the prisoners in Plato's "Cave of Illusion," it has awakened to knowledge of Reality, has struggled up the harsh and difficult path to the mouth of the cave. Now it looks upon the sun. This is *Illumination:* a state which includes in itself many of the stages of contemplation, "degrees of orison," visions and adventures of the soul described by St. Teresa and other mystical writers. These form, as it were, a way within the Way: a *moyen de parvenir,* a training devised by experts which will strengthen and assist the mounting soul. They stand, so to speak, for education; whilst the Way proper represents organic growth. Illumination is the "contemplative state" *par excellence.* It forms, with the two preceding states, the "first mystic life." Many mystics never go beyond it; and, on the other hand, many seers and artists not usually classed amongst them, have shared, to some extent, the experiences of the illuminated state. Illumination brings a certain apprehension of the Absolute, a sense of the Divine Presence: but not true union with it. It is a state of Happiness.

(4) In the development of the great and strenuous seekers after God, this is followed—or sometimes intermittently accompanied—by the most terrible of all the experiences of the Mystic Way: the final and complete purification of the Self, which is called by some contemplatives the "mystic pain" or "mystic death," by others the Purification of the Spirit or *Dark Night of the Soul.* The consciousness which had, in Illumination, sunned itself in the sense of the Divine Presence, now suffers under an equally intense sense of the Divine Absence: learning to dissociate the personal satisfaction of mystical vision from the reality of mystical life. As in Purgation the senses were cleansed and humbled, and the energies and interests of the Self were concentrated upon transcendental things: so now the purifying process is extended to the very centre of I-hood, the will. The human instinct for personal happiness must be killed. This is the "spiritual crucifixion" so often described by the mystics: the great desolation in which the soul seems abandoned by the Divine. The Self now surrenders itself, its individuality, and its will, completely. It desires nothing, asks nothing, is utterly passive, and is thus prepared for

(5) *Union:* the true goal of the mystic quest. In this state the Absolute Life is not merely perceived and enjoyed by the Self, as in Illumi-

nation: but is *one* with it. This is the end towards which all the previous oscillations of consciousness have tended. It is a state of equilibrium, of purely spiritual life; characterized by peaceful joy, by enhanced powers, by intense certitude. To call this state, as some authorities do, by the name of Ecstasy is inaccurate and confusing: since the term Ecstasy has long been used both by psychologists and ascetic writers to define that short and rapturous trance—a state with well-marked physical and psychical accompaniments—in which the contemplative, losing all consciousness of the phenomenal world, is caught up to a brief and immediate enjoyment of the Divine Vision. Ecstasies of this kind are often experienced by the mystic in Illumination, or even on his first conversion. They cannot therefore be regarded as exclusively characteristic of the Unitive Way. In some of the greatest mystics—St. Teresa is an example—the ecstatic trance seems to diminish rather than increase in frequency after the state of union has been attained: whilst others achieve the heights by a path which leaves on one side all abnormal phenomena.

Union must be looked upon as the goal of mystical growth; that permanent establishment of life upon transcendent levels of reality of which ecstasies give a foretaste to the soul. Intense forms of it, described by individual mystics, under symbols such as those of Mystical Marriage, Deification, or Divine Fecundity, all prove on examination to be aspects of this same experience "seen through a temperament."

It is right, however, to state here that Oriental Mysticism insists upon a further stage beyond that of union, which stage it regards as the real goal of the spiritual life. This is the total annihilation or reabsorption of the individual soul in the Infinite. [Underhill, 1955, pp. 169–170.]

After the achievement of union, the mystic may remain withdrawn from the world; or, secure in his salvation, he may return to the world and do good works. But it would be a mistake to suppose that the heroic spiritual exploits of the "great" mystics, both Eastern and Western, to whom Underhill devotes her principal attention, are the models for all mystical experience. Far more common, indeed, is a more modest and mundane experience, which goes deeply enough to relieve depression and generate a sense of salvation without requiring the violent, almost cyclothymic, oscillations of mood which the "great" mystics describe.

In addition to the psychological disciplines which lead to a more or less spontaneous mystical experience, there are also some commonly used techniques for inducing ecstatic religious states in persons who may or may not be suffering from emotional disorder. The so-called "psychedelic" drugs, such as mescaline and lysergic acid dyethylamide (LSD) and mixtures of these or similar substances found in the peyote cactus, various mushrooms, and products of various plants, can lead to intensely gratifying and insightful experiences, sometimes hallucinatory. Prolonged physical pain, fatigue, sleeplessness, sensory deprivation, and other physiological insults to the organism may induce cognitive and emotional changes of a mystical kind. Folk knowledge of such chemical and physiological techniques for inducing mystical experience is found in many cultures and is exploited to provide means for accomplishing major role transformations or salvation. Thus the vision quest of the Plains Indians depended upon knowledge of the probable effectiveness of fatigue, sleeplessness, fear, and sensory deprivation, combined with prior suggestion, in inducing appropriate visions of a guardian spirit helper in pubescent youths. (Benedict [1922]). Other American Indians employed peyote, a cactus containing mescaline, to stimulate hallucinatory experience in members of the Native American church (Slotkin [1952]). And some of the contemporary popularity of the psychedelic drugs such as LSD among American intellectuals is based upon the quasi-religious conviction that the mystical experience often achieved during their use is of profound therapeutic value, in a virtually salvational sense.

EXPIATION: PENANCE AND GOOD WORKS

In contrast to the salvation rituals that exploit possession, shamanic transformation, and mysticism, the way of penance and good works appeals to those whose identities are reasonably intact but who in some specific aspect of identity may experience severe shame or guilt, and suffer in consequence chronic anxiety and the accompanying physiological stress. A person may, for instance, have violated a taboo, committed a sin, or persistently avoided a specific kind of social obligation. This single flaw, gross though it may be, does not invalidate the entire identity structure but does call for action to rebuild identity in this one respect. Ritual that punishes the transgressor can remove guilt, wipe the slate clean, and assert that the flaw in identity is no longer there; good works maintain the repair thus accomplished. On the other hand, persistent failure to expiate the fault may ultimately prejudice the entire identity structure and lead to emotional or physiological collapse. Thus, while expiation is repair work, it is relevant to salvation in a prophylactic sense at least because it precludes a later dissolution of identity.

Rituals of expiation take many forms: public confession (as in the Handsome Lake religion), private confession with penance (as in Catholicism), baptism (as in Christianity generally), pilgrimages (as in Mohammedanism), flagellation and other forms of self-punishment and self-deprivation, the giving of alms, and so on. Less dramatic than the other rituals of salvation, and more closely related to ideological concerns, expiatory rituals may nonetheless be performed with grim devotion by those who feel that such rituals alone maintain the integrity of personality.

Ritual as Revitalization

As we have seen, when the person's identity (or image of self) is unsatisfactory, religion is a source of ritual to which he may turn in order to achieve salvation. Most, if not all, cultures recognize at least some such identity problems in individual instances and provide culturally standardized ways for the unfortunate victim of identity conflict to achieve relief, by way of possession, becoming a shaman, mystical withdrawal, or good works.

A crisis comparable to the identity crisis of the individual may occur to an entire community. When most, or even many, of a community's members are unable to maintain a satisfying image of self because their culture or their fellow citizens, or both, are making it impossible for them to realize the values they have learned to take as goals and models, then the customary individualized procedures for achieving personal salvation may no longer be effective. For one thing, more people may require the rituals of salvation than existing institutional resources can accommodate: there will be too few exorcists to deal with possession, too many potential shamans for the community to employ, too many mystics withdrawn from kinship, economic, and political obligations. For another thing, the effectiveness of these same traditional rituals of salvation will probably be reduced, even for those who are fortunate enough to secure them, because a pervasive disillusionment with the community and its culture will continuously vitiate the self-respect of those who consider themselves, willy-nilly, to be members of, and identified with, that community. Under circumstances of anomie (Merton [1938]) and pervasive factionalism (Beals and Siegel [1960]), a new religious movement is very likely to develop, led by a prophet who has undergone an ecstatic revelation (comparable to becoming a shaman), and aimed at the dual goal of providing new and more effective rituals of salvation and of creating a new and more satisfying culture.

STAGES IN A REVITALIZATION MOVEMENT

Although the ritual and mythological content of revitalization movements are as diverse as the cultures in which they rise, the general course of such movements follows a remarkably uniform program. A type case, that of the Iroquois religious revival led by the prophet Handsome Lake, was described earlier in the course of a discussion of a "revitalization theory" approach to religion. A successful revitalization movement includes the following stages (*vide* Wallace [1956, 1961b]).

THE STEADY STATE

This is a period of moving equilibrium. Culture change occurs during the steady state but is of a relatively slow and chainlike kind. Stress levels vary among interest groups and there is some oscillation in organization level, but disorganization and stress remain within limits tolerable to most individuals. Occasional events of intolerable stress for groups may stimulate a limited "correction" of the system, but some incidence of individual ill health and deviance is accepted in principle as a price society must pay for stability.

THE PERIOD OF INCREASED INDIVIDUAL STRESS

The sociocultural system is being "pushed" progressively out of equilibrium by various forces, such as climatic and biotic change, epidemic disease, war and conquest, social subordination, or acculturation. Under these circumstances, increasingly large numbers of individuals are placed under what is to them intolerable stress by the failure of the system to accommodate their needs. Anomie and disillusionment become widespread as the culture is perceived to be disorganized and inadequate; crime, illness, and individualistic asocial responses increase sharply in frequency. But the situation is still generally defined as one of fluctuation within the steady state.

THE PERIOD OF CULTURAL DISTORTION

Some members of the society attempt, piecemeal and ineffectively, to restore personal equilibrium by adopting socially dysfunctional expedients. Alcoholism, venality in public officials, the "black market," breaches of sexual and kinship mores, hoarding, gambling for gain, "scapegoating" by attacking other groups or a central bureaucracy, and similar alienated behaviors which, in the preceding period, were still defined as individual deviances, in effect become institutionalized efforts to circumvent the evil effects of "the system" or "the Establishment." Interest groups, losing confidence in the advantages of maintaining mutually acceptable interrelationships, may resort to violence in order to coerce others into unilaterally advantageous behavior. Because of the mal-coordination of cultural changes during this period, such changes are rarely able to reduce the impact of the forces that have pushed the society out of equilibrium and, in fact, are likely to lead to a continuous decline in organization.

THE PERIOD OF REVITALIZATION

Once severe cultural distortion has occurred, it is difficult for the society to return to a steady state without the institution of a revitalization process. Indeed, without revitalization the society is apt to disintegrate as a system: the population will either die off, splinter into autonomous groups, or be absorbed into another, more stable, society. Revitalization depends on the successful completion of the following functions:

Formulation of a code. An individual or group of individuals constructs a new, utopian image of sociocultural organization. This model is a blueprint of an ideal society or *goal culture.* Contrasted with the goal culture is the *existing culture,* which is presented as inadequate or evil in certain respects. Connecting the existing culture and the goal culture is a *transfer culture*—a system of operations which, if faithfully carried out, will transform the existing culture into the goal culture. Failure to institute the transfer operations will, according to the code, result in either the perpetuation of the existing misery or the ultimate destruction of the society (if not of the whole world).

Not infrequently the code, or the core of it, is formulated by one individual in the course of an hallucinatory revelation. Such prophetic experiences tend to launch religiously oriented movements, since the source of the revelation is apt to be regarded as a supernatural being. In such religious movements, ritual is a principal element of the transfer culture. Nonhallucinatory formulations usually are found in politically oriented movements. In either case, the formulation of the code constitutes a reformulation of the author's own identity and brings to him a renewed confidence in the future and a remission of the complaints he experienced before.

Communication. The formulators of the code preach the code to other people in an evangelistic spirit. The aim of the communication is to make converts. The code is offered as the means of spiritual salvation for the individual and of cultural salvation for the society. Benefits promised to the target population need not be immediate or materialistic, for the basis of the code's appeal is the attractiveness of identification with a more highly organized system, with all that this implies in the way of self-respect. Indeed, in view of the extensiveness of the changes in values, promises of material and social benefits meaningful in the old system would often be pointless. Religious codes offer spiritual salvation, identification with God, elect status; political codes offer honor, fame, the respect of society for sacrifices made in its interest. Refusal to accept the code, on the other hand, is usually defined as placing the listener in immediate spiritual, as well as material, peril with respect to his existing values as well as new ones. In small societies, the target population may be the entire community; but in more complex societies, the message may be aimed only at certain groups deemed eligible for participation in the transfer and goal cultures.

Organization. The code attracts converts. The motivations that are satisfied by conversion, and the psychodynamics of the conversion experience itself, are likely to be highly diverse, ranging from the mazeway resynthesis characteristic of the prophet and the hysterical conviction of the "true believer" to the calculated expediency of the opportunist. As the group of converts expands, it differentiates into two parts: a set of disciples and a set of mass followers. The disciples increasingly become the executive organization, responsible for administering the evangelistic program, protecting the formulator, combating heresy, and so on. As the executive part of the movement, the disciples also increasingly become full-time specialists in the work of the movement. In this they are economically supported by the mass followers, who continue to play their roles in the existing culture, devoting part of their time and money to the movement. The tricornered relationship between the formulators, the disciples, and the mass followers is given an authoritarian structure—even without the formalities of older or bureaucratic organizations—by the charismatic quality of the formulator's image. The formulator is regarded as a man who has been vouchsafed, from a supernatural being or from some other source of wisdom unavailable to the masses, superior knowledge and authority which justify his claim to unquestioned belief and obedience from his followers.

Adaptation. Because the movement is a revolutionary organization (however benevolent and humane the ultimate values to which it subscribes), it threatens the interests of any group that obtains advantage, or believes it obtains advantage, from maintaining or only moderately reforming the status quo. Furthermore, the code is never complete; new inadequacies are constantly being found in the existing culture, and new inconsistencies, predictive failures, and ambiguities are discovered in the code itself (some of the latter being pointed out by the opposition). The response of the code formulators and disciples is to rework the code, and, if necessary, to defend the movement by political and diplomatic maneuver, and, ultimately, by force. The general tendency is for codes to harden gradually, and for the tone of the movement to become increasingly militant, nativistic, and hostile both toward nonparticipating fellow members of the group, who will ultimately be defined as "traitors," and toward outsiders, who are "enemies."

Cultural transformation. If the movement is able to capture both the adherence of a substantial proportion of a local population and, in complex societies, of the functionally crucial technological apparatus (such as power and communications networks, water supply, transport systems, and military establishment), the transfer culture and, in some cases, the goal culture itself, can be put into operation. The revitalization, if successful, will be attended by a drastic decline in quasi-pathological individual symptoms of anomie and by the disappearance of cultural distortions. For such a revitalization to be accomplished, however, the movement must be able to obtain internal social conformity without destructive coercion and must have a successful economic system.

Routinization. If the preceding functions are satisfactorily completed, the reasons for the movement's existence as an innovative force disappear. The transfer culture, if not the goal culture, operates of necessity with the participation of a large proportion of the community. Thus the movement's function shifts from the role of innovation to the role of maintenance. If the movement was heavily religious in orientation, its legacy is a cult or church which preserves and reworks the code, and maintains, through ritual and myth, the public awareness of the history and values that brought forth the new culture. If the movement was primarily political, its organization is routinized into various stable bodies—administrative, police, military, and so on—whose functions are to make decisions and to maintain morale and order. Charisma can, to a degree, be routinized, but its intensity diminishes as its functional necessity becomes, with increasing obviousness, outmoded.

THE NEW STEADY STATE

With the routinization of the movement, a new steady state may be said to exist. Steady-state processes of culture change continue, many of them in areas where the movement has made further change likely. In particular, changes in the value structure of the culture may lay the basis for long-continuing changes in other areas. An example of this would be the train of economic and technological consequences that followed the dissemination of the Protestant ethic after the Protestant Reformation.

Thus, in addition to changes the revitalization movement accomplishes during its active phase, it may control the direction of the subsequent equilibrium processes by shifting the values that define the cultural focus. The record of the movement itself, over time, is subject to cumulative distortion and eventually is enshrined in myths and rituals which elevate the events that occurred and persons who were involved in them into quasi- or literally divine status.

TYPOLOGY OF REVITALIZATION MOVEMENTS

Although the above characterization of the *stages* of a revitalization movement appears to be generally valid, a broadly useful typology or subclassification of the *kinds* of revitalization movements has proved difficult to construct. This has in turn hampered efforts to derive more specific and testable hypotheses relating variation in movements to variation in other factors (*vide* Kopytoff [1964]).

The most readily available subclassifications of revitalization movements are based on culture area. Major and recognized subtypes particularly associated with culture areas or regions can be listed as follows:

Type	*Area*
1. Cargo cults	1. Melanesia
2. *Terre sans mal* movements	2. South American tropical forest
3. Mahdist movements	3. Islamic areas

4. Millenarian movements	4. Christian areas
5. Messianic movements	5. Judaic areas
6. Nativistic movements	6. North American Indian
7. Separatist churches	7. African Negro

While it emphasizes the tendency for processes of cultural conservatism and diffusion to maintain a certain common flavor in the doctrinal content of movements in broad cultural regions, such an area-based classification does not lead to the formulation of analytical categories. A number of dimensions of variation have been proposed as a basis for systematic classification, starting with Ralph Linton's (1943) fourfold classification along the polar dimensions of magical versus rational and revivalistic versus perpetuative. Other writers have suggested a number of additional characteristics or variables for consideration: syncretism; utopian (future) orientation; militancy versus withdrawal or passivity; reformativeness; assimilationism; nationalism; and so on.

All of these descriptive concepts are useful in characterizing at least some movements, but in sum they generate an impossibly complex typology and, furthermore, still leave the boundaries of the whole revitalization concept fuzzy. The problem of boundaries is further complicated by the facts that both religious and political movements are included and that, although in principle only movements that aim to revitalize the whole society are intended, revitalization processes (if not movements proper) can have as a target only a segment, smaller or larger, of a whole society—for example, a particular cult institution, a school system, a family group, a political organization, or an artistic tradition.

From the standpoint of this book, a typology of a different kind may be in order. As we have pointed out, a religious revitalization movement has two aims: to provide immediate personal salvation to the presently afflicted and to reorganize the culture in such a manner that a better way of life is brought into being to take the place of the old.

In the preceding section, we showed that there were four main kinds of rituals of salvation—possession, becoming a shaman, mysticism, and penance and good works. The salvation rituals proposed in the doctrines of revitalization movements can be characterized as emphasizing one or another of these four. The Ghost Dance (*vide* Mooney [1896]), for instance, offered salvation by possession, which was induced in the dancers by marathon dancing; the peyote cult, on the other hand, turned its devotees to mysticism; and Handsome Lake (*vide* Parker [1913]) emphasized confession, penance, abstinence, and good works. Few, if any, movements depend on the process of becoming a shaman as a path for the multitude to follow, although the prophet and many of his disciples very often experience essentially this process. Thus, with respect to the goal of salvation rituals, we are left with three attributes: *possession, mysticism,* and *good works.*

With regard to the goal of cultural reorganization, it would seem useful, as well as reasonably conventional, to emphasize the attitude of the movement both toward the community's own culture and toward the cultures of other communities (including, particularly, dominating societies in acculturation situations). Four attitudes would seem to be common: *revivalistic,* which aims to restore a golden age believed to have existed in the society's past and which ignores or expels the alien group; *utopian,* which aims to achieve a golden age believed to lie in the future, but to be implicit in the evolving patterns of the present, and which also ignores or expels the alien group; *assimilative,* which aims to import many of the customs of the alien (usually dominant) group, to combine them syncretistically with native customs, and to dissolve social boundaries between the two societies; and *expropriative,* which aims to import many of the customs of the alien group and to combine them with native customs, but to expel alien persons. The *terre sans mal* movements were utopian; the Ghost Dance, revivalistic; current American Negro civil rights movements are assimilative (except for the Black Muslims, which are revivalistic); cargo cults, expropriative.

In the next chapter we shall consider the causes and functions of revitalization movements. Here we may point out that even though a movement may be relatively ineffectual in bringing about the changes in culture toward which it aims, it can still bring the sense of salvation to people afflicted with feelings of conflict, inadequacy, and confusion springing from the identity problem generated by situations of anomie.

IV

The Functions of Religion:
Relations among Cause, Intention, and Effect

IN OUR REVIEW of the goals of religion we found that the intentions of the performers of particular religious rituals are explicit. They aim to control nature, make people sick or well, organize human behavior, save souls, or revitalize society. But now we must ask: How successful is religious ritual in achieving these goals? And, in the course of answering this question, we must confront several others: What are the actual effects, intended or not, of religious belief and practice? How are these effects accomplished? Under what conditions will there occur the institutionalization of one or another kind of religious behavior? These are questions about the *functions* of religion.

Before proceeding to review some of the answers that have been offered to these queries, we must take a position on several conceptual issues. First of all, we must remind ourselves what it is, in this book, that we have been making generalizations about. This "object" is not any particular "religion," such as Christianity, Judaism, Islam, or the New Religion of Handsome Lake. Each such "religion" is, in our terminology, a particular ecclesiastical cult institution, local variants of which will be accepted in a number of communities. The object of our attention is, rather, the sum total of religious cult institutions—individual, shamanic, communal, or ecclesiastical—which are, in fact, institutionalized in a given society. We use the term "society" to denote any organized, perennial, self-reproducing social group, from small community, band, or village, to tribe, to national state. Thus, when we inquire into the functions of religion in a particular society, we do not restrict our attention to the official or respectable or predominant cult institution but include all those cult institutions that are culturally established there. This does, to be sure, open up a Pandora's box of mutually inconsistent beliefs and rituals; but this inconsistency is an aspect of religious organization, and there are good reasons for the religion of a society to be a potpourri of rituals and beliefs assembled in ritual sequences and cult institutions without much regard to logical elegance. Furthermore, in both developed, industrialized nations and developing, mixed peasant-and-industrial societies intergroup conflict is far more intense and flux in cultural and social arrangements far more rapid than in the relatively stable "primitive societies" which are largely represented in most statistical compilations. In complex and conflict-ridden modern societies, functional hypotheses are indeed difficult to prove.

The Meaning of Function

The term "function" itself requires some discussion, not only because it means different things to different people in the social sciences, but also because certain of its uses are poorly suited to the needs of scientific study. All scholars, I think, agree in one essential: that the statement of the function of a piece of culturally standardized behavior—a trait, custom, complex, pattern, or institution—must *at least* include either some statement regarding the consequences of performing the behavior in a particular community, or some statement regarding the consequences of not performing it, or both. In other words, the function of a cultural element is the effect of its performance or nonperformance in a given cultural setting.

Beyond this point of agreement, however, usages diverge. Some scholars are interested both in the *biological* needs that the behavior satisfies, directly or indirectly, and in the *instrumental* utility of the behavior in the technical sequence of behaviors that lead to the satisfaction of the need. Thus a biological function of a certain hunting technique is to satisfy hunger; this is an effect of using it. That technique, however, may be only a part, albeit a necessary part, of the whole procedure of hunting. It may be necessary to use tracking techniques, for instance, in order to find the animal, and only after finding it can killing techniques be employed; thus tracking has as its instrumental function the putting of the hunter in a position where he can make the kill. Other investigators are more interested in the *psychological* effects of behavior, its psychodynamic function in relieving or intensifying emotional tensions by presenting the actor with an array of symbolically meaningful information whose pattern affects his emotional state. Thus, from the psychodynamic viewpoint, a hunter in tracking an animal may experience an increase of tension because the game unconsciously represents the feared and hated authoritarian father; the killing of the animal may bring relief, because the hunter has, symbolically, dispatched the dangerous adversary in his internal psychic drama, a psychodynamic function arising from an unconscious legacy of unresolved interpersonal conflicts. To sociologists and social anthropologists, the function of an element of culture is the contribution that it makes to the *survival of the society* by inculcating the motives (values, sentiments, attitudes) necessary to the accomplishment of vital tasks and to the tolerance of inevitable burdens. The units of discourse, in sociological usage, tend to be relationships between people and between groups rather than attributes of individuals or of the culture. Thus a function of hunting, in the sociological sense, is the reaffirmation of the uniqueness of the male's role in relationship to the female; hunting serves to inculcate and maintain certain masculine values, to confirm male solidarity vis-à-vis females, to provide reinforcement to certain areas of male self-esteem which domestic relationships leave unsupported or even challenge.

Now it is important to recognize that these kinds of functional interpretation are not mutually exclusive. Thus it is always hazardous to conclude that because *a* function has been shown to be plausible, or even been demonstrated to exist, therefore it is *the* function and there is no other. Furthermore, it is necessary to point out that none of these functions—biological, instrumental, psychodynamic, and sociological—is *necessarily* the same as the conscious intention of the actor; the motive of a deed, and its effect, may be very different. Still further, it is absolutely essential to keep in mind that neither intention nor function is a sufficient *cause*. The cause of the establishment of an institution is a sequence of antecedent circumstances. It is a common methodological error to read back into the past the intention and/or the effect of an act and to imply that the instititution of that act exists today "because" people wished then to achieve a goal that is identical with the effects of the institution now and/or that is the goal of the institution now. In the discussion of function, therefore, we shall attempt to avoid presenting the function of religion as the explanation of religion.

Function may be thought of, in relation to a particular custom, in two senses. If the sequence of events is

$$A \longrightarrow B \longrightarrow C$$

then *B* is a function of A and *C* is a function of B.

Thus although answers to functional questions of the form "What is the function of religious behavior?" do not lead to causal understanding of how religious behavior came to be, there is another form for functional questions about religion: "What is religious behavior a function of?" Here religious behavior is treated as the effect of some other kind of behavior, and the explanation *is* causal with respect to religion. Thus, for example, the assertion that a certain looseness in authority structure leads to the proliferation of witchcraft fears and accusations is an assertion that the form of authority determines an aspect of religion, and one would expect to find that change in the authority structure will be followed, historically, by a change in the prevalence of witch fear in a given society. But, again, assumptions of intention as being equivalent to effect must be eschewed.

Although these two forms of the functional question ("Is *B* an effect of *A*?" and "Is C an effect of *B*?") thus imply different causal sequences, they are not always easy to separate in cross-cultural statistical studies of function. Statistical investigations of the sort that we shall review in this chapter can demonstrate covariation but not temporal sequence. Ideally, historical evidence is required for the latter demonstration, and causal interpretation of statistical correlations must be based on deduction from other premises. Accordingly, we must be cautious in making our conclusions about religious behavior as an effect of social structure, and about socialization, anxiety-reduction, and cultural revitalization as an effect of religion.

In our presentation of function of religion, we shall follow the scheme of organization used in the preceding chapter, and consider the goal of the ritual as the point of departure.

Functions of Technological Rituals

Technological rituals, including divination, hunting and agricultural increase ceremonies, and protective rites, are intended to control nature so as to yield information, food, and other benefits. It is generally agreed among most educated men that technological rituals are useless; that is to say, whatever effect they may have, it is not what was intended. These rituals are only intermittently reinforced; they are the most likely of all rituals to be disconfirmed by experience or scientific test; laymen and "respectable" religious establishments are likely to condemn them as "superstition." Yet technological rituals have survived, even in the most advanced countries, in defiance of the most determined intellectual, political, and religious onslaughts and in the face of an uninterrupted sequence of actual failures that is probably hundreds of thousands of years old. The efficacy of intermittent reinforcement, as described by learning theory for pigeons and rats, can hardly be stretched to account for this phenomenon in man. Evidently technological rituals have a function, a positive and regular reinforcement function, which is different from their avowed intention but which in some circumstances permits deluded practitioners to survive where wise men perish or move away. Let us first consider divination for some interesting and plausible hypotheses about the critical function.

The Function of Divination in Decision-making

There are two problems in decision-making which affect both primitive and civilized men: the problem of indecisiveness in the face of ignorance or neurosis and the problem of disagreement in group decision. Divination, when scrupulously practiced, will provide a solution to both problems. A mechanical device for picking one of a set of alternative solutions, no one of which appears on the basis of available evidence to be preferable, makes it possible to do "something" which may work. One is reminded of the ancient parable of the ass who starved to death between two bales of hay; divination would have saved him by telling him that one bale was juicier than the other. Furthermore, where a group must make and jointly execute a decision and no convincing argument for one alternative is possible, there is apt to be disagreement; in such cases, divination can point the way and no one need feel that he has been disregarded by his colleagues, for the choice was made by an outside power.

Moore (1957) in an interesting analysis of northeastern Algonkian scapulimancy points out that, in some rather special types of situations, divination may have still another beneficial effect on the decision-making process. Moore bases his considerations on game theory. Game theory is a mathematical approach to decision-making which generates estimations of best moves against an opponent based on calculations of probable countermoves and possible losses or gains. Moore points out that in the situation of the northern Indian hunter, who at a certain season year after year must find a herd of migrating caribou, some distance away, whose direction he never knows from one year to the next, the strategy with the least likelihood of repeated failures (ending in the catastrophe of starvation) is to randomize his choices each year. It is only too easy, even for supposedly sophisticated persons, to bias their attempts to make random choices in all sorts of unconscious ways; the only reliable method for truly randomizing decision is to use a mechanical device. For such purposes, reading the irregular pattern of cracks and charred spots on the burned scapula of a caribou is as good a technique as any.

Vogt (1952), in his study of water-witching in the contemporary United States, points out that a similar function may be performed by "dowsers." Where deep wells must be dug by farmers and ranchers in an arid environment with a complicated geological structure, so that the underground water table has variable depth, rational or even "scientific" techniques for locating water are not always successful. Here dowsers ply their ancient trade, carrying a forked stick in both hands over the ground, and claiming to locate water wherever the stick is pulled downward so that its point aims at the earth. Although the movement of the stick is undoubtedly controlled, consciously or unconsciously, by the dowser himself, and although the dowser's success is, as a matter of fact, slightly less than that of the user of other methods, *no* method is thoroughly reliable, and the water diviner is usually able to attract a steady following. The effect of his ritual is to make a decision for the homesteader, a decision couched in terms of certainties rather than probabilities. As Vogt points out, "The *certain* answers provided by the dowser relieve the farmer's anxiety about groundwater resources and inspire confidence to go ahead with the hard work of developing farms" (p. 185).

Thus, the hypothesis would seem to be highly plausible that the practice of divinatory rituals has the effects of: reducing the duration of individual indecision; accomplishing a more rapid consensus within a group, with minimal offense to the members; and inspiring the persons who must execute the decision with sufficient confidence to permit them to mobilize their full skills and energies, unimpeded by anxiety, fear, or doubts about having made the best choice among the alternatives available. We may, if we wish, speculate with Malinowski (1925) that divination will be practiced most, because it has most value, in precisely those areas or on those occasions of human endeavor where empirical or scientific knowledge is least adequate and where uncertainty most prevails.

The Function of Rites of Intensification in Mobilizing Human Effort

In some human enterprises, there is no problem about knowing what must be done and there is no useful purpose in asking fatalistically whether or not the program will be successful; hence divination is not the ritual need. The perceived need is to maximize the likelihood of success in the human task by enlisting the cooperation of nature and the supernaturals. This is the object of those technological rituals which we have called "rites of intensification": hunting magic, agricultural fertility rituals, rain-making ceremonies, and the like. Their practitioners, as Malinowski points out (1925), know very well the necessity for hard, efficient human work; they know that the arrow kills the deer, that plants need rain, that animals must have food, that mating is followed by pregnancy in animals as well as man. But human knowledge, whether it be folk empiricism or modern science, always leaves a measure of uncertainty. The arrow sometimes goes astray, the rains are late, the creatures starve, the cattle are inexplicably barren. In this zone of uncertainty, technological ritual is seen as the only way of affecting the outcome.

Now such rituals are actually worthless in any technological sense; they do not affect the flight of the arrow, the condensation of moisture, the growth of vegetation, or the breeding of animals. But the suggestion of many writers is that technological rituals nevertheless do have a positive function which far outweighs their direct economic cost and, in primitive societies, the cost they have in inhibiting the inquiry that could lead to better technology. This positive function is their effect on the practitioners of the rituals. They serve, it is argued, to reduce the anxiety of the native hunter or agriculturist in the face of uncertainty about the efficacy of his efforts to supply himself and his kinfolk with food. Food anxiety is not a principal emotional experience to most Western populations now; but to many primitive and peasant societies, and to the urban poor, food is not a thing to be taken for granted. People do hunger, and waste, and starve.

But food anxiety can also spring from, or be reinforced by, anxieties that derive from other sources than a realistic concern over success in subsistence enterprises. There is good reason for agreeing with the claim of psychoanalysts that some food anxieties in individuals are the relics of infantile frustrations or overindulgences which have been only partially outgrown and which persist into adulthood as distorted replicas of early anxieties about the breast and the relation to the mother. To the extent that such neurotic anxieties—and the related unconscious motives, which may be ill-suited to efficiency in the food quest—do affect the attitudes of adults to their subsistence activities, ritual may serve at least to reduce the poignancy of the experience of anxiety.

The importance of reducing food anxiety, whether realistic or neurotic—and, for that matter, other anxieties about the effectiveness of subsistence practices—does not lie merely in the elimination of an unpleasant feeling, so that life looks brighter and people can enjoy themselves more. Its importance lies in the improvement of the total efficiency of the food quest. While mild amounts of tension do improve the effectiveness of human effort, serious chronic anxiety and uncertainty reduce the effectiveness of behavior; the hand is less steady, movements are slower, the readiness to respond flexibly to emergency is dulled, behavior becomes rigid and regressive and cooperation among members of a team is more difficult. Thus the improvement of confidence in the likelihood of success may very well be an important ingredient in achieving that very success. Ritual, by reducing anxiety and increasing confidence in hunting, agriculture, and other important activities, may very well be of material aid in mobilizing maximum human efficiency in direct proportion to the magnitude of the real risks involved.

The interaction of realistic and neurotic anxiety in relation to the food quest, and the role of ritual in attempting to reduce it to a level where technical efficiency remains adequately high, can be illustrated both in cultures that are, realistically, relatively secure with regard to food and in those that are marginal. Among the Alorese, an East Indian population of relatively prosperous, neolithic agriculturists described by Cora Du Bois (1944), food anxiety is extremely high. Despite the fact that they produce more food than they can eat, the Alorese, like many other primitive agriculturists, periodically organize extensive communal ceremonies, a principal feature of which is the lavish public display of piles of yams and other agricultural products, which are deliberately allowed to rot. The manifest intent of this display is to gratify the hunger of supernatural beings who, in return, will ensure a bountiful harvest the next year. The actual function, of course, is not to guarantee a good harvest, but to reassure the Alorese of the effectiveness of their food-getting methods by providing visible evidence of success both in the gardens and in paying off the gods.

In addition, however, according to Kardiner, the analyst who interpreted the Alorese data, this display of economic braggadocio serves to relieve a neurotic anxiety characteristic of most Alorese. This anxiety stems, not from realistic uncertainty about technology, but from an infantile fixation on food, which was established by an experience of extremely casual and indifferent mothering. In this view, their unhappy, frustrating relationships with their mothers have left the Alorese plagued by emotional difficulties. Since they unconsciously regard food as a symbol of motherhood, they comfort themselves for their maternal deprivation by boasting about the adequacy of their food supply. Perhaps no small benefit is derived from this self-mothering, for, because of their mutual jealousies and tendency to sudden tantrums which threaten to disrupt collective effort, the Alorese find cooperative living difficult. Anything, like a food ceremony, that soothes the irritated feeling of being let down and imposed upon by others will help them to survive.

The coastal Eskimos present a different economic situation. They are heavily dependent upon sea mammals for food and other economic necessaries; and sea-mammal hunting is both dangerous and uncertain. A seasonal decline in the number of animals available, or an unfortunate combination of wind and ice and ocean currents, may bring a village to the edge of starvation. The hunt is therefore preceded by the shaman's ritual trip to the bottom of the sea, to release the sea mammals from Sedna's care once more and permit the people to survive another year. Furthermore, the conduct of the hunt and the processing of the foods, skins, bones, and other parts of the animals taken are surrounded by an aura of constant danger of giving offense to Sedna and the animals taken. Taboos must be scrupulously observed lest, in retaliation for a breach of courtesy, the goddess withdraw her favor.

It is not implausible to suppose that the observance of these rituals reduces, to some degree, a very realistic anxiety about the food quest, which must be suppressed or dispelled in order to free the hunters for full engrossment with their task. But it is also difficult not to sense a neurotic component even here. The animals themselves are emotionally very important—as are the game animals of other primitive peoples—and they are regarded with intensely ambivalent feelings. Both undue sympathy, which might reduce the "courage" of the hunter, and undue hostility, which might arouse an equally inconvenient sense of guilt (akin to "buck fever"), must be kept in check. Furthermore, it is not easy to disregard the implications of the Sedna myth itself. It says, in effect, that the sea mammals upon whom all Eskimos' lives depend are in the care of a dirty, bitter, unkempt old woman at the bottom of the sea. Sedna got that way a long time ago because her father threw her out of the boat and, when she clung desperately to the gunwales, pleading to be let back in, chopped off her fingers one by one until she sank. Food, and life itself, in other words, are in the hands of an angry old woman who hates fathers who go out in boats. The unconscious meanings of this tale do not need to be explored in detail in order for one to reach a conclusion that the Eskimo hunter's anxiety about food, however realistic, is supplemented by an anxiety that is built on some features of his relationship with other human beings.

This observation leads us, then, to a second observation: not only should technological ritual function to increase the efficiency of individuals in the performance of their mechanical tasks; it should also serve temporarily to resolve, in a symbolic way, such conflicts in human relationships as may interfere with the effectiveness of the cooperative team effort to get and distribute food. Thus we find that the dual functional pattern that seemed to apply to divination—the promotion of efficiency in both task performance and group cooperation—probably is true for rites of intensification as well.

Functions of Therapeutic and Anti-therapeutic Rituals

The Clinical Efficacy of Witchcraft and Ritual Medicine

In evaluating the functions of witchcraft and medicine, we cannot, as we did in discussing technological rituals, be so confident that the function is different from the goal. Both witchcraft and therapeutic rituals do, under some circumstances, have as an important part of their effect the bringing of injury or help to their human targets. With regard to witchcraft, as Cannon (1942) has pointed out in his classic paper on "voodoo death," the victim of a witch's arts may indeed sicken and even die. He suffers, however, not because of any direct efficacy in the ritual itself but because he knows, or thinks he knows, that he is the target of a malicious practice which he believes to be efficacious. His response, in proportion to the certainty of his belief, may be a real physiological disorder, particularly of those endocrine systems involved in the stress reaction. Believing himself to be under deadly attack, from which deliverance may be unlikely, he may actually sicken and die from the consequences of prolonged stress, despair, starvation, and inanition. Cannon cites the case of an Australian aborigine who believed that he was bewitched by bone pointing, and who after the initial shock of realization, stoically crawled away to his hut to die. In more recent parlance, such victims of witchcraft are suffering from the deteriorating effects of a prolonged continuation of the General Adaptation Syndrome, or stress reaction, which if not relieved may indeed result in serious illness or death. To be sure, the effectiveness of the ritual depends entirely upon the intended victim's awareness that it is being performed; he must be, in other words, the object of a communication from the witch, a communication of implacable and irresistible hate.

If witchcraft rituals can, by arousing stress, bring about illness, then it is reasonable to suppose that therapeutic rituals, intended to turn the spell back upon the witch, can cure the same illness; and so Cannon, on the authority of other observers, does claim. But this principle can obviously be more widely applied. Not only in instances of illness produced by the belief that one is bewitched, but also in other psychosomatic conditions, the ministrations of the medicine man are at least to some degree efficacious. The general principle is that if therapeutic ritual can reduce the anxiety associated with some complex of thoughts and feelings, then emotional and physical symptoms will to some extent be alleviated. The origin of the anxiety in cases of "witchcraft illness" can be, in part, circumstantial; but even here a large component of neurotic guilt toward the suspected witch or his employer may very likely play some role. Similarly, in organically established diseases, such as cancer, or in infectious diseases, the illness may well be complicated not only by the fear of pain and death, but also by guilty interpretations in terms of witchcraft, of punishment for violation, or of possession, all of which may contribute to the sum total of disorder. And, of course, the functional mental disorders, springing at least in part from neurotic emotional conflicts of long duration, but aggravated by local and temporary circumstances, may very well be relieved to a degree by the soothing reassurances of support offered by the shaman and the victim's relatives and by the cathartic experiences of confession, of being indulged, of dream interpretation, of bodily massage, and so on.

Even theoretically unsympathetic observers have recognized the effectiveness of primitive therapeutic rituals. The Jesuit priests, for instance, who watched the Iroquois use of dream interpretation and indulgence of dream wishes, were reluctantly forced to admit that these devilish practices were at least partially effective. Father Le Jeune described the case of a woman who, judging from her symptoms—dizziness, disturbed dreams, and involuntary muscular contractions—suffered from conversion hysteria. Her dreams were of being given public honors, feasts, and rich gifts; and when these desires were gratified, she was "much better." Although the cure was not complete, it was impressive enough to force the good father to admit that the devil had done a good piece of work (Father Le Jeune, in Kenton [1927], 1:393–401). Thus if, by one means or another, ritual is able to increase or decrease stress, it can exacerbate or diminish the symptoms of emotional and/or physical disorder. And where, as is sometimes the case, actual physical adjuncts are employed—such as poisonous or helpful drugs, physical medicine, bone-setting, or blood-letting—the effect may be more markedly therapeutic or anti-therapeutic (*vide* Ackerknecht [1942a]).

But the functions of these ritual devices for manipulating the symptoms of health and disease are not limited to clinical efficacy. Both witchcraft and ritual medicine serve two other major functions: as measures for social control and as a general palliative for social conflict prompted by the emotional lesions left by traumatic child-rearing experiences.

Witchcraft as a Function of Social Structure

The fear of witchcraft and the fear of taboo violation both serve, as a number of anthropologists have pointed out, as an extremely effective system for maintaining social control in societies where secular means of ensuring a necessary level of conformity and for resolving interpersonal disputes are inadequately developed or have been disallowed by unwise administrative fiat. In such societies, where there is threat of retaliation by witchcraft or supernatural wrath, behavior must be discreet, circumspect, and careful lest one give offense. If one does a wrong thing, disease or ill luck may strike him down; indeed, this revenge may be inflicted not only upon the offender, but upon his kinsmen, or even the whole community. The fear of disease thus becomes a major weapon of the social conscience; it extorts compliance from anyone who believes that failure to act properly and cooperatively may bring upon himself, his kinfolk, or his friends the revenge of the wrathful neighbor or insulted god. To be sure, the emotional flavor of this pervasive sanction is a bitter one and it may yield a situation of superficial politeness that conceals a generalized fearfulness in human relationships.

The prevalence of fear of and accusations of witchcraft seems to be determined both by the natural cleavage lines in the social structure and by the success of the society in handling conflict by such secular means as court proceedings and arbitration. In colonial African societies, for instance, where European administrators have interfered with the jurisdictions of native courts, a flourishing of witchcraft anxiety is apt to occur. Participants to disputes, unable to find resolution for their disagreements in court, fear that their antagonists will seek recourse by witchcraft. Further, since accusations of witchcraft are not even recognized by European courts, this fear of witchcraft leads in turn to the formation of antiwitchcraft secret societies, whose extralegal efforts to annihilate witches compound the difficulty. It would appear to be a general rule that wherever there is a breakdown of secular procedures for resolving conflict, or where there is an increase in the number of conflicts requiring settlement beyond the capacity of these procedures, then there will be an outbreak of witchcraft anxiety. These conditions are particularly likely to prevail in situations of rapid, enforced acculturation and can be interpreted functionally as an effort to restore an acceptable level of social control by invoking the sanction of witchcraft.

The interpretation of witchcraft as a function of the effectiveness of conflict-resolving mechanisms in the society is supported by two independent cross-cultural investigations. In these studies, the question of the relationship between witchcraft and social structure was investigated by statistical methods. Both Beatrice Whiting (1950) and Guy Swanson (1960) hypothesized that witchcraft would be most important in those societies in which secular authorities were unable to levy sanctions on, and thereby control, human behavior. Whiting, in the course of a study of witchcraft among the Paiute, surveyed materials from twenty-six societies. Each society was characterized on two binary dimensions: importance of witchcraft (important and unimportant) and prevalence of the principle of superordinate social punishment (absence of superordinate punishment and presence of superordinate punishment). Societies without superordinate punishment are those in which, in effect, irredeemable transgressions in human relations are not investigated and punished by secular authority, such as a council or a court of law, but are left to the offended person to avenge by whatever means are available to him. Societies with superordinate punishment require that "the authorities" punish at least major transgressions. Whiting's hypothesis was that disease, inflicted by witchcraft, would be an important sanction in non-superordinate societies, because it would be a method of retaliation, and fear of it would be a motive for conformity to accepted conventions, and because recourse to witchcraft is available to most injured parties, whatever their circumstances of age, sex, and kinship. The result of her investigation fully confirmed the hypothesis, as Table 3 shows.

Thus in a sample of twenty-six societies chosen from many parts of the world, witchcraft clearly occurred far more often in societies

TABLE 3

Witchcraft	*Authority*		
	No superordinate punishment	Superordinate punishment	Total
Witchcraft important	15	1	16
Witchcraft not important	2	8	10
Total	17	9	26

SOURCE: Adapted from Beatrice Whiting, *Paiute Sorcery*. New York: Viking Fund Publications in Anthropology, 1950, No. 15, p. 90.

without superordinate punishment than in societies with it, and indeed occurred almost exclusively in such societies. As one might expect, furthermore, because small societies are usually less well provided with the agencies of government, witchcraft was negatively associated with largeness of community.

Swanson's hypothesis was similar to Whiting's. He suggested that in those human relationships that are not legitimated or controlled by higher social authority, witchcraft is apt to be the recourse in situations of conflict of interest or transgression. Taking the twenty-eight societies from Swanson's data that score high or low in prevalence of witchcraft, and rating them as positive or negative for the occurrence of unlegitimated and/or uncontrolled relationships, we find the following situation in Table 4 (see p. 183).

Thus Swanson's data also show that witchcraft is highly prevalent—indeed, occurs almost exclusively—in those societies where social roles are not subject to effective control by secular authority. Swanson also found that prevalence of witchcraft is not related to the adequacy of the food supply; level of social organization, rather than economic deprivation, is the responsible factor.

The frequency of witchcraft allegations should also—other cultural things being equal—vary with the frequency of unresolved social conflicts in stable societies. LeVine has provided a clear-cut statistical demonstration of such a relationship in his study of the relation between witchcraft and family structure (LeVine [1962]).

TABLE 4

Witchcraft	*Unlegitimated or Uncontrolled Relationships*		
	Absent	Present	Total
High prevalence	1	17	18
Low prevalence	9	1	10
Total	10	18	28

SOURCE: Adapted from Guy E. Swanson, *The Birth of the Gods: The Origin of Primitive Beliefs*. Ann Arbor: University of Michigan Press, 1960, pp. 137–152 by permission of The University of Michigan Press. Copyright © by The University of Michigan Press 1960.

In a sample of sixty-two cultures, he found a very sharp positive association between polygyny and witchcraft accusations. The tabulation appears in Table 5.

TABLE 5

Witchcraft Accusations	*Household Type*			
	Polygyny, with plural wives in same house	Mother-child household (usually polygyny with wives in separate houses)	Extended family household	Nuclear family household
High	13	9	8	9
Low	1	4	8	10

SOURCE: Adapted from Robert A. LeVine, "Witchcraft and Co-Wife Proximity in Southwestern Kenya," *Ethnology* (1962), 1:39–45.

Furthermore, as both the tabulation and the qualitative analysis of African data show, the intensity of witchcraft fear in polygynous families is likely to be greater where co-wives live under the same roof than where they occupy separate domiciles, each with her own children.

The functional conclusions to be drawn from these very clear correlations are simple: (1) whenever and wherever there exist no effective secular means for resolving conflicts of interest and settling accusations of wrongdoing, and mythological and ritual materials are at hand, the parties will tend to believe that their opponents will turn to witchcraft if they are aggrieved; (2) the strength of this tendency will increase as the frequency and intensity of the conflicts increase. The fear of witchcraft, presumably, will serve not only as a deterrent to violence and other "rational" means of seeking revenge or otherwise advancing one's own interests; it will probably also serve to inhibit giving of offense in the first place. Thus the *fear* of witchcraft should be regarded, in primitive societies without courts of law, as a principal means for maintaining widespread conformity to conventional, nonexploitive standards of propriety in interpersonal relationships of all kinds—love, friendship, trade, hunting partnerships, and so on.

WITCHCRAFT, RITUAL MEDICINE, AND THEORY OF ILLNESS AS FUNCTIONS OF CHILD-REARING PRACTICES

As we saw earlier, certain psychoanalytic hypotheses view adult religious institutions as "projections" of emotional conflicts engendered by childhood experience. In an effort to test the validity of these hypotheses—and thus, more generally, the adequacy of psychoanalytic theory for the cross-cultural field of culture and personality—John W. M. Whiting, and various of his students and colleagues, have for many years been engaged in a systematic program of testing the functional dependence of adult behavior, including religious belief, upon childhood experience. In an early volume entitled *Child Training and Personality* (1953), and in a series of separate papers, this group has undertaken a study which is simultaneously of great significance for personality theory and for the study of religion.

The basic premise of the Whiting tradition is that if psychoanalytic theory (and, *pari passu,* learning theory) is true, then adults must in their beliefs about illness, in their religious life, and in other areas of customary activity, express attitudes that were built into them as children by punitive or rewarding training regimes in such critical processes of personality formation as eating, elimination of body wastes, sex, aggression, and independence strivings. The method is cross-cultural; that is to say, a number of societies are rated with respect to both child training and adult custom, and the results are tabulated in a four-celled (or larger) table, from which statistical estimates of the degree and probability of a valid functional connection can be computed. From the many findings reported, we shall present here those that are of relevance to functional explanations of witchcraft and ritual medicine.

In their original work (Whiting and Child [1953]), the Whiting group found that a strong tendency to explain illness as a result of witchcraft is most likely to occur in societies where socialization is accompanied by severe anxiety in the child. On the other hand, strength of the belief that illness is the result of the action of supernatural beings other than witches (such as high gods, animal spirits, or ghosts) seems to have little relation to severity of socialization anxiety, occurring without significantly different frequency in communities with high socialization anxiety and low socialization anxiety. A difference in importance of witchcraft explanations of illness is associated with variation in socialization anxiety in each of the five areas of child training mentioned above, although most markedly, and with statistical significance, only in relation to oral, sexual, and aggression training.

Inasmuch as most societies give some credence to both witchcraft and other explanations of illness, it would seem necessary to conclude that the witchcraft and spiritual theories of illness are not really mutual alternatives, the former occurring in high socialization-anxiety societies and the latter in low socialization-anxiety societies. Rather, as the lack of any substantial correlation in the data between witchcraft and other supernatural theories of disease indicates, they must be considered to be independent of one another, the intensity of spiritualistic (but non-witchcraft) theories of illness being significantly influenced neither by socialization nor by the intensity of witchcraft beliefs. The intensity of the belief in witchcraft as a cause of illness, however, is definitely related to severity of socialization anxiety.

Whiting and Child were also concerned about identifying the precise psychological mechanism involved in the functional relationship, and suggested two possibilities: that accusations of hostility in others are a simple projection of repressed hostility in oneself; and that, by a more complicated channeling of impulses, they are a distorted projection of repressed sexual strivings. The socialization data do not clearly favor either hypothesis: severe socialization anxiety in the realm of sex and in the realm of aggression are both strongly associated with witchcraft fear.

Thus, while it is evident that witchcraft is more likely to be a pervasive fear in societies with high anxiety surrounding socialization, mere belief in *some* supernatural agency as a cause of disease is not significantly related to the intensity of the anxieties attendant on childhood training. It is still possible, however, that beliefs in the process by which illness is acquired—and, by implication, how it must be treated—may be related to the nature of childhood discipline, and most particularly, to the realm of experience (oral, anal, sexual, aggression, and dependency) in which most anxiety is felt. Thus, for instance, a great deal of anxiety about oral experience in infancy might be associated with beliefs that illness is acquired by eating or drinking something containing magically poisonous substances. Whiting and Child do find, indeed, that in the oral, aggression, and dependency areas, there is a statistically significant correlation between the intensity of socialization anxiety and the strength of the tendency to explain illness in oral, aggression, or dependency terms, respectively. Thus, societies with high oral anxiety during socialization are likely to explain illness as a result of breaking food taboos, of eating or drinking poisonous substances, or of verbal spells and incantations (that is, witchcraft of certain kinds) performed by others. Societies with high aggression anxiety during socialization tend to explain illness as a result of aggression or disobedience to spirits, of aggressive thoughts, of magically introjected poison or other foreign bodies (such as bones and balls of hair). Societies with high dependency anxiety during socialization tend to explain illness as a matter of soul loss or spirit possession. Furthermore, from other tabulations it appears that initial satisfaction in dependency and aggression are significantly associated with the corresponding theories of illness. But there is little support for the hypothesis that the theory of ritual medicine would be clearly related to child training and consistent with the theory of illness.

In general, then, the conclusion to be drawn from the studies of Whiting and Child, insofar as they directly concern witchcraft, ritual medicine, and theory of illness, is twofold: first, that the importance of belief in witchcraft in a culture is strongly related to intensity of socialization anxiety, and that theory of disease is also positively related to the program of childhood training in the oral, aggression, and dependency spheres; second, that there is no clear relationship between socialization and either strength of belief in other, non-witchcraft, supernatural explanations of illness, or the nature of the ritual medicine (if any) believed to be appropriate for therapy. These would seem to be functions of other conditions than early socialization and its resultant personality configurations.

Functions of Ideological Rituals

Most statistical studies of the functional connections of religion have been directed at those practices that are ideological in intent; that is, at those conservative, equilibrium-maintaining myths and rituals which aim precisely at education and social control. Although some of the studies emphasize sociological and others emphasize personality factors, they all fall nicely into a general circular paradigm which charts the principal flow of influence in an idealized, stable, slowly changing sociocultural system (see figure, p. 188). Even in this oversimplified form, the figure indicates that religion is a function of both the basic kinship, economic, and political institutions of the society and the child-training practices, and that these systems in turn are functions of religion. Thus changing any one system will be very likely to lead, directly or indirectly, to a change in the others. Because this amounts to saying that they are all mixed together, and because the dependencies are likelihoods rather than certainties, determining the precise weight of each of the influences would be a nearly impossible task. Nevertheless, we can usefully demonstrate in statistical form that some of the interdependencies do exist.

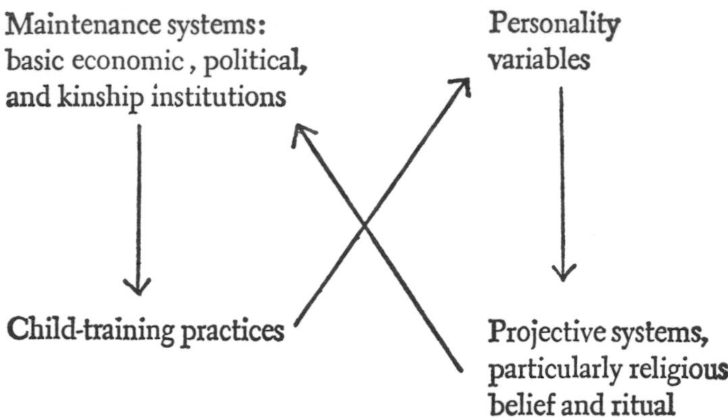

THE FUNCTIONS OF BELIEF SYSTEMS AND MYTHOLOGY

RELATIONSHIP TO THE SOCIAL STRUCTURE: SWANSON'S DATA

Max Weber, in his classic study *The Protestant Ethic and the Spirit of Capitalism* (1904), showed forcefully that an independent change in religious belief was intimately connected with a dependent change in economic and political institutions. His work in this vein has inspired later generations of sociologists and social anthropologists to pursue the topic. Weber's study of the Protestant ethic illustrated how a new system of ascetic religious values, evolving independently of economic changes, could lay the base for a subsequent transformation of other, nonreligious institutions. The Protestant ethic, emphasizing the virtues of sobriety, cleanliness, punctuality, hard work, saving, and so on, tended to produce the kind of businessmen and workers who could transform Europe from a feudal to capitalist economy and from medieval technology to industrialism. Thus the main thrust of Weber's work was to show that the maintenance system of society was a function of (among other things) the religious belief system.

Most of the subsequent work on relationships between maintenance and belief systems (except for that on revitalization movements, which we shall discuss later) has, however, in contrast to Weber, tended to emphasize the dependence of religion on economics and politics rather than the reverse. The extreme form of this tradition has been, of course, the vein of social criticism by both laymen and theologians of established religion as (in effect) "the opiate of the masses." This hostile phrase is principally intended as a recognition of religion's dependence upon, and service to, economic institutions of a capitalist variety. Although religion—even in the limited aspect of ideology under discussion here—cannot be summarily dismissed as an opiate, the data available from systematic research do show unequivocally that belief and mythology are intimately related to the maintenance systems and vary with them in predictable ways.

We reviewed evidence pointing in this direction in the previous section, in which witchcraft belief was shown to be related to political authority and polygyny. The most extensive, and elegant, demonstrations of the relationship between religion and social institutions are provided in Swanson's *The Birth of the Gods* (1960). Swanson systematically sought for associations between a set of specific theological beliefs and a set of economic, political, and kinship characteristics in a world sample of fifty societies from forty-seven culture areas (three culture areas had two representatives in the sample). The theological beliefs and the aspects of social structure chosen as variables were as follows:

Theological Beliefs Present	*Aspects of Social Structure Present*
Monotheism	Sovereign organizations
Polytheism	Nonsovereign organizations
Ancestral spirits	Specialists in communal activities
Reincarnation	Principal source of food
Immanence of soul in body	Amount of food
Witchcraft	Threat of armed attack
Supernatural morality	Amount of bride price
	Social classes
	Debt relationships
	Individual ownership of property
	Unit of settlement
	Size of population

Swanson, basing his theoretical considerations on Durkheim's study of *The Elementary Forms of the Religious Life* (1912), argued that the supernatural is the symbolic equivalent of society itself, or of some sovereign social institution with a "constitutional" structure within society, or of certain types of basic, but nonsovereign and unorganized, social relationships and interests. More specifically, spirits and gods are the equivalents of sovereign groups, which have purposes of their own, authority over members in some aspects of their behavior, and an identity that persists over time. *Mana*, on the other hand, is the equivalent of the unorganized "primordial links" among men.

Swanson points out that these equivalences between the supernatural and society are evident in four similarities: (1) respect for the moral authority of a society is like the respect for a god; (2) the control of society over the inner thoughts and feelings of men is like the control of human thoughts and feelings by a god; (3) people feel strong, confident, and at peace when obeying either society or a god; and (4) while man believes that he owes all he has to the gods, he does in fact owe all he has to his society. If these considerations are valid, Swanson argues, then the character of the gods of a society should be similar to, and a direct function of, the character of the social structure itself. And so he proceeds systematically to test, and in many particulars to verify, the general hypothesis. We have already reviewed his findings on witchcraft; let us turn to the other aspects of belief.

Swanson's data appear in the form of association tables which show the functional relationship between some aspect of theological belief and some aspect of social structure in a form susceptible to statistical tests of significance. We reproduce here, as an example, the table showing the relation between presence or absence of a belief in a high god (monotheism) and the number of types of sovereign (in effect, authority-bearing) groups in the society (see Table 6).

Swanson's principal significant findings from a large number of such tabulations can be conveniently summarized as follows:

Monotheism. The presence of a belief in a high god is strongly associated with social complexity. (This finding, as Swanson points

TABLE 6

NUMBER OF SOVEREIGN GROUPS AND PRESENCE OF HIGH GOD

Presence of High God	*Number of Sovereign Groups*		
	One or two	Three	Four or more
Present	2	7	10
Absent	17	2	1
Total	19	9	11
Per cent present	11	78	91

SOURCE: From Guy E. Swanson, *The Birth of the Gods: The Origin of Primitive Beliefs*. Ann Arbor: University of Michigan Press, 1960, p. 65 by permission of The University of Michigan Press. Copyright © by The University of Michigan Press 1960.

out, is contrary to the claim of the *Kulturkreis* school, which—without statistical procedure—saw monotheism as a primitive trait found particularly in very simple, unsophisticated societies.) The data given above in Table 6 may be seen even more forcefully in a simpler table (Table 7, below).

TABLE 7

High God	*Sovereign Groups*	
	One or two	Three or more
Present	2	17
Absent	17	3

SOURCE: Adapted from Guy E. Swanson, *The Birth of the Gods: The Origin of Primitive Beliefs*. Ann Arbor: University of Michigan Press, 1960, pp. 55–81 by permission of The University of Michigan Press. Copyright © by The University of Michigan Press 1960.

Polytheism. Belief in a number of superior gods (an Olympian pantheon) is significantly related to the presence of social classes. The data also suggest that the number of superior gods is related to the number of those occupational specialties in the society that are "compatible with" the nature of the society's "ultimately sovereign organization"; however, these data have been subjected to so much special handling that the meaning of the findings is obscure. The relationship of Olympian pantheon to social class is given in Table 8.

TABLE 8

Superior Gods	*Social Classes*	
	Present	Absent
Three or more	14	3
Two or less	12	19

SOURCE: Adapted from Guy E. Swanson, *The Birth of the Gods: The Origin of Primitive Beliefs*. Ann Arbor: University of Michigan Press, 1960, pp. 82–96 by permission of The University of Michigan Press. Copyright © 1960, by The University of Michigan Press, 1960.

Reincarnation. Belief in the reincarnation of the soul is significantly associated (see Table 9) with a settlement pattern in which the units of settlement are neither widely separated nuclear households nor villages, towns, or cities, but small, relatively isolated groups, larger than the nuclear family but smaller than the village. Types of such groups are small hamlets, extended family compounds, and small hunting bands. The rationale for such a pattern would seem to be that the survival of an individual, with all his unique capacities and interests, is most important to groups of this size and life expectancy. Nuclear households are by definition one generation in duration; larger units, while longer-lived, can because of their size afford to regard individuals as expendable.

TABLE 9

Reincarnation	*Grouping*	
	Small neighborhood	Nuclear household, or village, town, or city
Belief present	9	4
Belief absent	8	29

SOURCE: Adapted from Guy E. Swanson, *The Birth of the Gods: The Origin of Primitive Beliefs*. Ann Arbor: University of Michigan Press, 1960, pp. 109–120 by permission of The University of Michigan Press. Copyright © by The University of Michigan Press, 1960.

Immanence of the soul. The belief that the soul is a substance inherent in the human body, lodged in its flesh and infusing all of its parts with spiritual qualities, is significantly associated (see Table 10) with a pattern of social characteristics that can best be called "primitive." In other words, the likelihood of belief in the immanence of the soul is highest where the following social conditions are present: there are no sovereign kin groups larger than the nuclear family, the total number of types of sovereign groups is less than three, the settlement pattern is one of small hamlets or hunting bands, and there are important social relationships unlegitimated by sovereign organizations.

TABLE 10

Belief in Immanence	*"Primitive" Pattern*	
	Present	Absent
Present	6	4
Absent	3	14

SOURCE: Adapted from Guy E. Swanson, *The Birth of the Gods: The Origin of Primitive Beliefs*. Ann Arbor: University of Michigan Press, 1960, pp. 121–136 by permission of The University of Michigan Press. Copyright © by The University of Michigan Press 1960.

The supernatural and morality. Contrary to some popular impressions and to Tylor's early summary of observations (1871), even the most primitive peoples often regard violation of the moral code as entailing the threat of supernatural punishment. But there is, nonetheless, a significant association (see Table 11) between economic advancement and the supernatural rationalization of morality. Supernatural sanctions for morality are more likely to be invoked in societies where there are, between persons, considerable social differences derived from differences in wealth. The presence of social classes, of widely prevalent debt relationships, of private ownership of important property, of primogeniture, and of the raising of grain crops—each is significantly associated with the belief in supernatural sanctions for morality. The most significant relationship of all is between social classes and supernatural morality.

TABLE 11

Supernatural Morality	*Social Classes*	
	Present	Absent
Present	25	2
Absent	8	12

SOURCE: Adapted from Guy E. Swanson, *The Birth of the Gods: The Origin of Primitive Beliefs*. Ann Arbor: University of Michigan Press, 1960, p. 166 by permission of The University of Michigan Press. Copyright © by The University of Michigan Press 1960.

RELATIONSHIP TO CHILD-TRAINING PRACTICES AND THE MODAL ADULT PERSONALITY

Other scholars in the Whiting tradition have investigated the functional relations between secular culture and religious beliefs, emphasizing particularly the socialization process and family structure. Simmons, who explored the use of large samples of comparative data from different cultures in a pioneering paper that anticipated the exploitation of the Human Relations Area files in both Murdock's classic *Social Structure* (1949) and Whiting's more precise investigations, found several interesting correlations. The couvade—a widely distributed type of ritual in which the husband of a parturient woman simulates various aspects of childbirth himself and observes taboos on contact with the child—was found to be highly and significantly associated with three aspects of matrilateral kinship organization: matrilocal residence, matrilineal descent, and matripotestal family authority. Simmons also demonstrated a high degree of association between the existence of priesthoods (as opposed particularly to shamanism) and other aspects of the maintenance system. Priesthood was found to be positively associated with both agriculture and herding, and negatively with hunting, fishing, and gathering; it was associated with communal as opposed to private property in land; and with patrilateral as opposed to matrilateral kinship (Simmons [1937]).

Spiro and D'Andrade, investigating the relationship between supernatural belief and socialization practice, hypothesized that the sequential patterning of satisfactions and anxieties would be related to whether the gods were rewarding or punitive. They demonstrated (in a very small sample) a significant association between high socialization anxiety and the punitiveness of the gods when divine demands were not fulfilled. Where socialization anxiety was less severe, however, and where initial satisfaction was high, the gods were conceived as rewarding rather than punitive. The socialization of dependency strivings proved to be an especially sensitive indicator: where anxiety was generally low in dependency training, the gods were seen as unconditionally indulgent; where initial satisfaction was high, the people felt that they could compel the gods by ritual to provide nurture; and even where an initial period of high satisfaction of dependency was followed by high socialization anxiety, ritual of some sort, either coercive or propitiatory, was usually regarded as efficacious (Spiro and D'Andrade [1958]).

In a small sample of coyote myths from American Indian tribes, McClelland and Friedman (1952) found that there was also a significant relationship between a pattern of high initial indulgence, followed by early and severe independence training, and a high degree of need for achievement. Interestingly enough, no relationship was apparent between need for achievement and the severity of socialization of oral, anal, and aggressive behavior. Lambert, Triandis, and Wolf (1959) found, similarly, that absence of pain inflicted by the parents or their surrogates in infancy was significantly associated with a benevolent image of the gods, whereas a pattern of intense and severe training for self-reliance and independence was significantly associated with an aggressive image of the supernatural. They also demonstrated a very close association between the personality trait of rigidity and an aggressive image of the gods.

Although these studies are scattered and their results not strictly comparable, because the concepts, the measures, and the samples vary from one author to the next, nevertheless they add up to a very consistent functional pattern. The nature of the gods and the relationship of the gods to man are clearly related to the economic, kinship, and political structure of the society; they are related to the child-training practices; and they are related to the modal personality.

In regard to the relationship between social structure and religion, as revealed in the witchcraft studies and in Swanson's and Simmons' works, it is apparent that theology tends to mirror social structure while ritual tends to complement it. Thus, belief in high gods mirrors the existence of great differences in rank among living people; belief in malevolent witches mirrors the existence of interpersonal conflicts in an unorganized social group; belief in a morally concerned pantheon mirrors a social structure in which private ownership and personal debts are an important consideration in human relationships. Ritual complements the social structure by providing additional procedures that are necessary to make the whole system work, but which are unavailable in interpersonal relationships. Thus the rituals in honor of the high gods require a public acceptance of differences in rank in human society because the high gods themselves are ranked and because they are believed to endorse human ranking; the practice of witchcraft, and the fear of it, tend to curb precisely those trespasses that the social structure fails to prevent; and rituals of salvation, directed toward a morally concerned god, entail the settling of debts as a condition of grace.

Insofar as socialization practices are concerned, their relationship to myth and ritual seems to be particularly clear in regard to the training of the child for self-reliance and independence. It would seem that those transformations of personal identity that have to do with the abandonment of a generalized infantile dependence on the parents and the assumption of a responsible autonomous adult role are the area of socialization within which the nature of religion is most precisely fitted to the needs of the society. An explanation of this relationship may be suggested. It would appear that the general function of a belief in gods of a particular character is to provide a screen upon which to project those images of people and those styles of behavior, surviving from infancy and childhood, that would be most inconvenient if brought into the arena of real-life, day-to-day behavior. Thus, lingering feelings of infantile helplessness and longings for an all-indulgent mother would be an awkward intrusion into the daily round of hunting, warfare, and political negotiation; but they may with relative safety be expressed in a dependent, trusting relationship to a god, since here they entail little consequence in human relations, are sanctioned by the society, and may be admitted to consciousness without shame or guilt. Similarly, it would be inconvenient if malevolent, aggressive, and hateful images of adults and of all persons with power or authority were admitted to consciousness and the hostility felt toward these images directed toward neighbors, public officials, and kinsmen in daily life. These feelings, and strivings for their expression, can be more comfortably directed toward a supernatural realm. In most general form then, we can say that the supernatural beings in whom the members of a society believe will have precisely those personality (not social-structural) characteristics that people cannot afford, and do not dare, to attribute as adults to their fellow men. The function of the beliefs, and of the rituals that the beliefs rationalize, will be to reduce the likelihood of these motives erupting into consciousness in relation to real people, causing guilt and shame, and into action in social contexts, causing disruption of efficient, cooperative effort.

The general cultural cause of both the complementary and projective processes, in distinction to the mirroring process, must evidently be some inconsistency in the culture. If a function of religion is to make people want to do what they have to do, then there must be something in most societies that would make people, without religion, want to do things other than what they have to do. Two sorts of cultural inconsistencies have been suggested that could, in the absence of religion, lead to this effect: first, any sort of internal cultural contradiction in values, or in the roles that adults must play, resulting either from the vicissitudes of incomplete cultural change or intracultural differences in custom or status, as between men and women or ethnic groups or classes and castes; second, any sort of discontinuity in the behavior that is expected of people at different ages. Lévi-Strauss, in his structural analysis of mythology (Lévi-Strauss [1955]; Leach [1961]), has suggested that the plot of myths involving supernatural beings portrays the prevailing contradictions in the culture, and their symbolic resolution. Ruth Benedict (1938) in her concept of discontinuities in cultural conditioning, Spiro (1952) in his notion of teleological functionalism, and Hallowell (1955) in his discussions of the role of supernatural anxiety in ensuring conforming behavior, all suggest that the role of religion is to take up the slack, as it were, between infantile or childhood patterns of behavior and adult expectation.

Examples of the function of religion in patching up chronological discontinuities in the life cycle, by facilitating projection, are easy to find. Hallowell points out that anxiety about witchcraft ensures a characteristic style of decorous and polite adult conversation among Ojibwa people, who fear retaliation by witchcraft from insulted partners in dialogue, and that anxiety about supernaturally sent illness motivates conformity to incest taboos. The dream cult among the Iroquois (Wallace [1958b]) provides an even more patent example. The conservative Iroquois believe that an unconscious part of the soul cherishes arbitrary wishes and desires, some of them inborn and instinctive, and inherited by the adult from his infancy. These wishes express themselves in dreams. If not gratified, these wishes are believed to prompt the soul to punish the body with illness and even death. In order to avoid such a suicidal degree of frustration, the individual is encouraged to discover in his dreams the wishes of his soul, and society not merely permits, but requires him, in the course of certain rituals, to have these wishes gratified. In the discontinuity formulation, the role of religion is thus that of an escape valve, diverting personally and socially inconvenient feelings and impulses left over from childhood into settings least likely to disrupt the normal course of economic, kinship, and political behavior.

In the schismatic formulation, the complementary role of religion appears to be more that of a lubricant which minimizes friction between groups, or between persons, or even between the roles of individual persons. Examples that demonstrate this function are also easy to come by. The literature of social criticism in our own Western civilization over the past hundred years is rife with the accusation that Christianity, insofar as it teaches the poor and the disadvantaged to obey authority, be patient under deprivation, and seek happiness in heaven, has been a made-to-order lubricant for the abrasive friction between economically higher and lower classes. The practical discomforts of economic inequality are made less painful for the poor, and less guilt-inspiring for the rich, by the myth of individual salvation through faith, hope, and charity.

In non-Western cultures, internal schisms are apt to involve other group conflicts than economic class. The rituals of couvade in matrilateral societies, for example, can be interpreted as a resolution of male resentment of female prerogatives by permitting male identification with females and, simultaneously, as a segregation of the male from a context in which his jealousy of the newborn is felt, intuitively, to present a danger. Even the Oedipus myth, as interpreted by Bachofen and later by Fromm, has been seen as an effort to resolve a conflict of values in early Greek cultures between an older, matrilateral system and a newer, patrilateral one. The crime of incest in the myth symbolizes an illicit striving to return to the older, matriarchal order. And among the Iroquois, the Dekanawidah myth, which we described earlier, clearly spells out the cultural contradiction between a revenge code for the redress of personal grievances and the maintenance of an intertribal political order. While on the one hand the myth sanctions external aggression (rationalized as justifiable revenge) against alien offenders, on the other hand it specifies a new set of supernatural beings, and a new collection of rituals (the Condolence Ceremony) to preclude a socially disruptive outbreak of internal conflict.

But it is ritual, and not myth, which does the actual work of conflict resolution, and perhaps the most dramatic examples of both the ritual resolution of discontinuities and of contradictions are provided by the widespread customs of puberty rituals and other rites of passage. Let us turn our attention now to these.

The Functions of Rites of Passage

The manifest intention of rites of passage is to introduce to each other the two parties to a new relationship, and to prepare them for, and launch them into, their new roles. Just what such rituals actually accomplish, and how efficiently, is perhaps best investigated in that class of rites that has attracted most attention from sociologists and anthropologists—puberty initiation ceremonies. Here we have, in addition to the anecdotal evidence of individual ethnographers, two major efforts to determine function by cross-cultural statistical research. These two efforts have approached the problem from different theoretical positions. John Whiting and his associates have pursued the culture-and-personality nexus by way of early socialization practices; Young has attempted to demonstrate a sociological hypothesis which, he asserts, contradicts the culture-and-personality approach.

Whiting theorized that the function of male initiation ceremonies was to resolve, in the interest of adult behavioral efficiency, unconscious and potentially disruptive psychological conflicts aroused in the male infant by too close association with his mother. The extreme of mother-son intimacy was considered to be reached when the mother and her son slept together, with the father absent, and when there was a post partum taboo on sex between the mother and father. At first, Whiting and his associates suggested a simple Oedipal situation: The youth approached the age of puberty with a strong unconscious hatred and envy of his father and, by extension, of all older males; he still maintained, unconsciously, a strong incestuous bond with his mother. In these circumstances, the function of the initiation rite should be to require the abandonment of these unconscious strivings as a condition for admission to adult society. In later papers, Whiting and his co-workers amplified the Oedipal theory to take account of the punitive function of initiation ceremonies as a means for counteracting any tendency for little boys who slept exclusively with their mothers to identify with their mothers (perceived by the little boy as having high status) rather than with their absent fathers. The initiation ceremony for males, then, could be seen as serving multiple functions: reducing young males' hostility to older, fatherlike males; reducing young males' incestuous, dependent attachment to older, motherlike females; and reducing status-envious young males' cross-sex identification with females. In support of this interpretation, Whiting and his co-workers showed that the presence of initiation ritual (that is, of any one, or any combination, of genital operations, hazing, seclusion from women, and tests of manliness) was positively and significantly associated with the pattern of exclusive sleeping and post partum sex taboo. Furthermore, to give further support to the cross-sex identification hypothesis, it has been pointed out that the custom of the couvade (in which the male displays a ritual identification with the female) has a distribution complementary to that of male initiation among exclusive-sleeping and post-partum taboo societies, initiation occurring with patrilocal residence, and the couvade with matrilocal (Whiting, Kluckhohn, and Anthony [1958]; Whiting [1961]). Also, with particular reference to Australian initiation ceremonies involving sub-incision, Bettelheim (1954) has independently suggested that genital mutilation may satisfy, and thus reduce conflict about, an unconscious but powerful cross-sexual envy of men for women, by giving them an analogue of female genitalia.

Young, however, in a paper critical of the Whiting hypothesis, presents evidence to show that an even stronger association exists between male initiation and certain features of the maintenance system; he concludes that early socialization and personality are not required as intervening variables (1962). Young shows that the trait of "male solidarity"—indicated by the presence of at least one community-wide organization of adult males, controlling male behavior in such matters as war, hunting, and politics—is very closely associated with male initiation, and also with polygyny and the resultant absent-father pattern. The function of male initiation from this point of view is to complete the identification of the immature (but not necessarily cross-sexually identifying) male with the responsible organization of mature adult males. The pertinent tabulation (Table 12) from Young's paper does show this association clearly.

But, although Whiting and Young debate fiercely the different assumptions of a "Freudian," "culture-and-personality," "disruptive emotion" hypothesis and a "functionalist," "symbolic interactionist," "male solidarity" hypothesis, it remains in the end unclear just where the difference lies, for both approaches con-

TABLE 12

Exclusive Male Organization	*Male Initiation Rites*	
	Present	Absent
Present	16	2
Absent	4	32

SOURCE: Adapted from Frank W. Young, "The Function of Male Initiation Ceremonies: A Cross-Cultural Test of an Alternative Hypothesis," *American Journal of Sociology*, Vol. 67, 1962, p. 383 by permission of The University of Chicago Press. Copyright ©, 1962, by The University of Chicago Press.

verge on the same functional assertion: that initiation ceremonies probably do effectively promote the identification of the young man with the group of mature males because the ceremonies are to be found most frequently in those societies (in particular, polygynous societies with high male solidarity) where this identification is presumably delayed in early childhood because of the fathers' limited association with their sons. And, after all, this is exactly what the participants in initiation ceremonies say that they are trying to do: to make men out of boys.

In a parallel series of investigations, Yehudi Cohen (1964) reports on the relationship of initiation ceremonies and other social behavior. He finds, in the lack of association between the practice of initiation and the prohibition of premarital sexual relationships, evidence that initiation ceremonies do not, and are not intended to, prepare immature persons for heterosexual intercourse; but he does find systematic relationships between the presence or absence of initiation ceremonies and the systems of descent and of responsibility. Initiation ceremonies are confined almost entirely to societies with unilinear descent groups (see Table 13, p. 203). And initiation ceremonies tend to occur only in societies in which social responsibility ("joint liability") is shared by the members of an extended kin group, such as a sib (see Table 14, p. 203).

Similar, if not as detailed, studies have been made of the functions of other rites of passage, such as female initiation rites,

TABLE 13

Unilinear Descent Groups	*Initiation Ceremonies*	
	Present	Absent
Present	18	26
Absent	1	20

SOURCE: Adapted from Yehudi Cohen, *The Transition from Childhood to Adolescence*. Chicago: Aldine Publishing Co., 1964, p. 114.

mourning behavior, menstrual taboos, and pregnancy taboos. There is no need to review these studies in detail here, for they simply confirm what by now we already know: that the presence and character of the rites of passage are related to, among other things, the ecological and sociological circumstances of the society. But, in view of the multitude of forces at work in this processual field, it would seem still unreasonable to pick on any single variable—sleeping arrangements or type of economy or severity of independence training or social structure—as *the* prime determinant. Rather, one must conclude generally that rites of passage are a type of ritual which educates participants for, announces publicly, and initiates a new social relationship.

TABLE 14

Joint Liability	*Initiation Ceremonies*	
	Present	Absent
Present	17	11
Absent	2	35

SOURCE: Adapted from Yehudi Cohen, *The Transition from Childhood to Adolescence*. Chicago: Aldine Publishing Co., 1964, pp. 131–143.

THE FUNCTIONS OF RITUALS OF REBELLION

There is a class of religiously sanctioned ritual that has the characteristics of catharsis; the most conspicuous and best analyzed of these rituals have an anti-authoritarian cast and have been called "rituals of rebellion" (Gluckman [1954]). In rituals of rebellion—or, as Norbeck (1963) calls them, rituals of conflict—hostility is expressed, temporarily and moderately, by subordinates to their social superiors. Rulers may be assaulted, verbally at least, by the ruled; men may dress and act as women; the majority may be reviled by the minority. But other cathartic rituals may express little hostility toward authority per se and merely constitute a temporary abrogation of normal rules of propriety, permitting the ceremonial participants to indulge appetites that must otherwise be held in check. Sexual license (even to the permission of incest, in some cases), violation of food taboos, the interruption of working and sleeping schedules, and similar aspects of saturnalia would seem to be aimed at least as much at the enjoyment of the pleasures of the flesh as at the gratification of hostility. Furthermore, the possible cathartic function of folklore and mythology must be recognized. The Rabelaisian content of trickster and other culture hero myths; the sado-masochistic content of the medieval biographies of martyred saints and of the religious art that depicted the agonies of the pious; even the fantasies of witch fear in primitive societies—all these may have served as spiritual purgatives, draining the souls of the faithful of accumulations of emotional debris.

Unfortunately, however, there is less hard evidence to show the functional efficacy of these rituals than there is for rites of passage and of theological belief, which we discussed earlier. The most systematic body of thought has been applied to those rituals that have a distinct flavor of hostility. As Norbeck (1963) points out, these may be most usefully considered in the context of conflict-resolution theory. Certain social groups are, in a given society, always trembling on the edge of an open and socially disruptive conflict, and giving such conflicts an opportunity for ritualized expression before they develop into "real" fights would appear to be a sensible procedure. Norbeck identifies five major social relationships that are apt to generate tension and for which rituals of conflict may be prophylactic: between the kin groups of bride and groom, between the sexes, between superiors and inferiors, between any persons (or groups) holding grievances, between formally defined social and political groups.

Unfortunately, however, a controlled statistical study is needed to demonstrate that more socially divisive conflict occurs, in regard to a given type of relationship, in societies without a relevant conflict ritual than in those with such ritual. Such a study has not, to my knowledge, been carried out. It is possible to assemble a good deal of anecdotal evidence to show that unconventional behavior is found in this ritual or that; however, its function as catharsis or as merely solemnizing remains uncertain. Furthermore, whatever the motives and whatever the positive functions, it is possible with these as with other rituals whose aim is conservative, for some actual consequences to be socially revolutionary or even destructive.

An interesting example of the apparently changing function of ritual is afforded by the Iroquois rituals of revenge. A bereaved Iroquois adult who knew, or believed, that her kinsman had been killed by another person traditionally urged her male relatives to calm her sorrow by bringing her a substitute. The substitute might be a scalp or a live prisoner; and the live prisoner, at her discretion, could be tortured and killed or taken into her sib; in all cases, however, the transaction was regarded as an "adoption" of an equivalent to the dead person. One may speculate that this custom served to abbreviate a socially undesirable mourning process in the grieving survivor and to reinforce the solidarity of the kin group. But, according to the Iroquois themselves, it also made impossible any effective political cooperation among the several Iroquois tribes, because there were always too many unsettled scores between (and within) the tribes. Hence (again according to the Iroquois) came the innovation of the Condolence Ceremony on the death of a chief; the function of the ceremony was to stop revenge before it started, in the interest of political amity. But a consequence of this, it would seem, was the displacement of revenge-seeking tendencies outward onto non-Iroquois tribes. This, in conjunction with a high degree of internal amity, made it possible for Iroquois revenge seekers to assemble very large war parties to assault neighboring tribes. This, in turn, led to retaliation by culturally similar Indian groups seeking their own revenge, and quickly embroiled the Iroquois in such protracted and continuous warfare that their villages were half depopulated and the survivors were plagued by nightmares of torture and death. Furthermore, because the mechanism for the war party was primarily familial rather than political, it was extremely difficult for the Iroquois to terminate an intertribal feud once begun. The intransigence of feuding Indian families led Europeans to condemn Iroquois diplomats for double-dealing.

The point is that, over a time span of centuries rather than a couple of years, some of the actual functional consequences of a ritual custom may be very different from, and far less positive than, either the intentions of its practitioners or the impression of an ethnographer whose perspective is limited both geographically and temporally. This negative aspect of the function of ritual would seem to be especially likely to emerge in connection with rituals of catharsis that assuage but do not remove the frustrations and grievances which presumably led to their original acceptance.

Functions of Salvation Rituals

TREATMENT OF THE MENTALLY ILL

In the preceding chapter, we introduced four types of rituals whose object was to effect a desirable change in the identity of the subject: possession (or its converse, exorcism); becoming a shaman; mystical experience; and expiation. These rituals of salvation are, in a sense, similar to rites of passage because they seek to effect a change in the career line of their subject; conversely, rites of passage, such as the Plains Indian vision quest, may involve mystical phenomena in the course of identity changes. The justification for setting aside a special category of salvation rituals lies in the fact that some identity crises are not universally anticipated in a society and are not treated with universally applied rites of passage, but rather are more or less ad hoc ceremonies performed by and upon only those persons who "spontaneously" enter into the experience for the sake of spiritual enrichment or salvation. The line between the voluntary search for a fuller and more complete spiritual life and the desperate quest for an experience that knits together the raveled aspects of an identity into a new, coherent synthesis is hard to draw. However, the extreme cases are clear enough; these are to be found in individually experienced episodes of possession, shamanic initiation, and mysticism.

The function of ritual, in these cases, is undoubtedly to provide a pattern for a process of remission of psychopathology which will bring the victim of a severe mental illness out "on the other side," so to speak; if the ritual is effective, he will arrive at a condition that will permit him to take care of himself and perform useful services (often ritual services) for the other members of the community. In other words, rituals of salvation are a means by which a community can treat both acute psychotic episodes and cases of chronic mental disorder without extruding the victim from the community. But the evidence in support of this assertion is, unfortunately, largely ancedotal, being based on case histories and autobiographical accounts. While these show that religious salvation was, for given individuals, the means to salvation, they do not demonstrate how effective as a public health measure salvation rituals may be in one society, much less generally. The social anthropologist Nadel (1946), who attempted to relate the incidence (as estimated by himself) of "insanity" and "epilepsy" in several African Negro tribal groups to the presence or absence of shamanism, found no clear relationship to report. Nevertheless he was impelled, as other anthropologists have been, to conclude that shamanism molds (even if it does not prevent or cure) nervous disorders into socially acceptable syndromes. Similar remarks may apply to the function of both possession and mysticism: that although they can hardly be said to prevent or cure hysteria, depression, epilepsy, or other emotional and neurological ills, they may provide a program for the course of the condition that will render it predictable, acceptable, and even useful to both the victim and his community.

Training of Religious Professionals

To the extent that the program of salvation produces religious professionals who are motivated to construct myths and to perform rituals on behalf of their fellow men, the rituals of salvation may also have another function: to recruit and train personnel for the performance of ritual tasks that are not only of therapeutic value to the sick, but also of value in various other functional ways to the normal members of the community. In shamanic societies, indeed, this may be a social function more important than any public health value of the salvation process. And in societies under stress, as we shall indicate in the next section, these salvation experiences provide the medium by which prophets generate the new codes of behavior which are the focus of revitalization movements.

In the light of these considerations, it would appear that rituals of salvation are as much exploitative as therapeutic. In the sections on the ritual process, we shall discuss the ways in which these rituals make use of psychopathological processes of dissociation, depression, and paranoid ideation to cultivate devoted ritual practitioners, dependent for their mental stability upon the traditional rituals which they perform and upon religious and social innovations which they generate. Although there seems to be nothing to suggest that the rituals of salvation produce, indirectly through the distorted socialization of children by "saved" persons, the very illnesses they "cure," the possibility cannot be ignored that there may be a circular process within certain family lines by which these charismatic religious specialists are developed.

Providing a Scapegoat

The "saved" person—be he shaman, mystic, or enthusiastic convert—has still another service to perform in many communities. These persons are surrounded by a kind of ambivalent glamor; they are both valuable and dangerous. As Coleridge put it, in "Xanadu," the impulse is to:

> Beware! Beware!
> His flashing eyes, his floating hair!
> Weave a circle round him thrice,
> And shut thine eyes in holy dread,
> For he on honey dew hath fed,
> And drunk the milk of paradise.

The shaman is also apt to be witch; the mystic may be identified both with Christ and anti-Christ; the possessed may be mounted by god or devil. The product of salvation, in other words, plays some of the role of the pantheon itself, being potentially good and evil at the same time and a fit scapegoat for the sins of the community as well as its potential savior.

In our own relatively secular society, the shaman's role has been taken on by the scientist, who sees himself and is seen as a dual being, capable of transfiguring the world for both good and ill. This role is celebrated every day and every night in movies, television plays, and comic strips, which show the "mad scientist" at work, a being of dual nature, a Jekyll-and-Hyde hero of noble powers and base weakness, infinitely beneficent and infinitely corrupt. And, not unexpectedly, some persons enter science as the result of an identity crisis and a salvation experience which ushers them into the special world of the laboratory or the clinic or the computer room, complete with white coat, nervous tic, and a psychopathic urge to do the rituals of science for a fee in money, honor, or special privilege.

The technical value of the shaman, whether religious or scientific, is perhaps less important than his value as a kind of psychological lightning rod, a channel for the displacement of the ambivalences of his public. In the role of savior-and-scapegoat, indeed, he finds both his own principal satisfaction and one of his principal uses to the community.

Functions of Revitalization Rituals

Cultural Innovation

Just as it is difficult to do more than suggest plausible hypotheses concerning the function of rituals of salvation, so it is difficult to demonstrate the actual, functional consequences of revitalization movements. As we have seen, the structural (rather than functional) classification of the varieties of revitalization movements has proved to be a difficult task; and without such a classification, it is not possible to use the cross-cultural method to establish associations between movement varieties and other dimensions of culture. One is left with a collection of case histories by historians and ethnologists from which to glean whatever common threads of function such movements may have. Useful case history accounts are available for such movements as the Handsome Lake religion, the Ghost Dance, and the peyote cult among North American Indians; the *terre sans mal* movements in South America; the Vailala Madness and the Paliau movement in Melanesia; the Mahdi in the Anglo-Egyptian Sudan and the Xosa rebellion in South Africa; the nativistic movement among the Nangiomiri in Australia; the nineteenth-century Taiping Rebellion and the more recent Communist revolution in China; Sikhism in India; the Protestant Reformation, and later John Wesley's Methodism, in Europe; and Mohammedanism in the Near East.

An understanding of the cultural function of these movements can conveniently be approached by means of a simple analogical model. There are a variety of chemical reactions that do not occur except under certain conditions. The substances in whose interaction one is interested may be placed in solution, where they mingle freely, but preserve their own identity. However, if the temperature of the solution is increased and a small amount of another substance known as a catalyst is added, the hitherto indifferent materials may be induced suddenly to "react," forming new chemical combinations, releasing energy, and often also producing "waste" products which can be driven off as gaseous residues. The new product, a synthesis of elements previously present in the solution, may perhaps be precipitated as a crystalline structure as the temperature falls and the watery matrix evaporates.

If we adapt this model to our uses, we may compare the new compound to the new culture that the revitalization movement recommends and, to some extent, brings into reality. The new culture is invariably composed of more or less incompatible traits which have been "in solution," as it were, in the society for some time. The new culture thus is a synthesis of elements which had hitherto existed independently and with minimal articulation; brought together, they form a new, unique, and more or less permanent combination with its own structure and with new functions being played by the old elements. The "waste" products, disposed of during and after the critical reaction of the chemicals, are comparable to those cultural traits and trait complexes that are disallowed or destroyed. The increase in temperature in the solution may be compared with the increase in the disorder in the society, wherein frustrated, stress-laden people behave less and less predictably and reliably. And, of course, the "catalyst" in the revitalization movement is to be found in the role of the prophet himself. By the agency of a "charismatic" authority, the prophet is able to effect—in his code and in the ritual he recommends—the welding of the old elements into a synthesis hitherto rejected.

Analogies of this sort, of course, cannot be driven too far, lest their service as general models be lost in the task of sorting out detailed correspondences and contradictions. The main value of this analogy is to emphasize that, from the standpoint of its cultural function, a revitalization movement is the process by which cultural materials which have hitherto appeared to the members of a society as dissonant are analyzed and combined into a new structure. Prolonged contact between two different cultures is a frequent source of these dissonant materials, but the condition of chronic cultural dissonance could be arrived at, presumably, by other, if less frequent, routes, such as adaptations to war or natural catastrophe, uncontrolled innovation, segmentation resulting from factionalism, class and caste differentiation, age and sex distinctions, regionalism, or even individual differences. In any case, the stabilized coexistence of mutually contradictory beliefs and customs in a society is the prior condition for a revitalization movement, which—with more or less success—breaks up existing structures, conserving some of their component elements and rejecting others, and combines the materials selected for preservation into a new structure. The function of revitalization movements, then, with regard to culture, is to bring organization into a rich but disorderly field by eliminating some of the materials (thus reducing the cultural repertoire to more manageable size) and combining what is left into a more orderly structure. In the interplay of destructive and conservative forces in revitalization movements, one is observing a thermodynamic (or information) process comparable to other natural processes commonly studied by natural scientists.

An example for illustrative analysis is, again, the new religion of Handsome Lake. The Iroquois Indians had, between their first contacts with Europeans in the sixteenth century and 1799, when the movement began, been holding "in solution" an increasingly varied combination of cultural materials from Indian and European sources. In addition to their own base line culture dating from, let us say, 1550, they had been incorporating cultural materials from a large number of other Indian tribes in the course of trade, diplomacy, the capture of war prisoners who were adopted into Iroquoian families, and the incorporation of alien tribes into the League (some of them, indeed, by moving whole villages into the Iroquois homeland). Furthermore, they had been acquiring not only the material apparatus, and the liquor, but also a knowledge of the social organization, economic system, religion, and language, of not one but several more or less distinct European nations—French, English, Dutch, and Swedish. Still further, their belief in dreams had permitted a kind of cumulative piling up of instances of a certain kind of institution, the medicine societies. Witchcraft, an ancient concern, had become a more persistent fear with the breakdown of traditional means for conflict resolution.

Handsome Lake, in his "new" religion, suddenly presented a dogmatic synthesis of some of the elements of this potpourri, and an equally dogmatic rejection of others. Alcohol, witchcraft, the medicine societies, and the traditional influence of the mother-in-law in the matricentered lineage were rejected; white models of farming, literacy, and technology, and various Indian customs including religious beliefs, were combined into a "new way"; the Creator was given a more important role in the pantheon, and public confession as a device for promoting self-control was made the core of ritual in place of the old, cathartic, therapeutic ceremonies of the medicine societies. None of the elements of the new way was really new, and the customs rejected were not being criticized for the first time. What was happening was a sudden effort to crystallize old notions into a new pattern and an equally sudden effort to reject others that did not fit into this pattern.

THE RESOLUTION OF GROUP IDENTITY DILEMMAS

Very commonly revitalization movements occur in societies, or groups within societies, which perceive themselves to be locked in a peculiar identity dilemma. Such dilemmas are apt to occur in acculturation situations, in international politics, and in situations of factionalism within a single society. The structure of the dilemma is as follows: the group in question sees itself as surrounded by two other threatening or competing groups, with one of which, whom it admires in some respects, it would like to identify and with which it would also like to form a political alliance against the third, the "enemy." But it is rejected by its "natural ally," both identity-wise and politically, who may even ally itself with the "enemy." The group cannot, however, identify itself with the "enemy," whom it despises or affects to despise, and therefore cannot accept an alliance with it. This dilemma can only be solved, as long as the identity preferences of the group preclude its alliance with the third group, by a revitalization movement which redefines the situation. This redefinition must include a new image of the group which is so satisfying, in a nativistic sense, that the group is confident of its ability to "go it alone," without identification or alliances with either of the other two groups.

Such triangular alliance-and-identity dilemmas present themselves, as we have observed, in acculturation situations; Handsome Lake's post-revolutionary Seneca, for instance, had been rejected both for identification and for alliance by their natural allies, the other tribes of the Confederacy and their erstwhile satellites; but they could not fully ally themselves with the enemy—the white Americans—because they could not accept the implied identification with white culture. Handsome Lake's movement resolved the dilemma by postulating a new, neutralist, culture under the sponsorship of God and the Four Angels. One may look at the situation of international Communist China, vis-à-vis the United States, also in these terms: unable to secure adequate identification and alliance with her "natural ally," the Soviet Union, the Chinese are unable to form an alliance with the other great power, her enemy the United States, because to do so would require adopting an unacceptable identity. In China's case, one must predict an imminent revitalization movement which will redefine the situation for the Chinese, so that they can see themselves as a third force, a unique culture with a unique destiny independent of either the Soviet Union or the United States. And in the domain of intra-societal factionalism, one can see the situation of the poor white southerner as being similarly structured: rejected and deserted by his "natural ally," the (white) federal establishment, he is unable to ally himself with the ever more insistently competing Negro population because such an alliance would challenge his identity. Here too one can predict some sort of revitalization movement in which he finds a fantasy ally with whom identification is possible.

The social function of revitalization movements for groups caught in such triangular identity-and-alliance dilemmas is, thus, to redefine them in such a way that the group no longer feels a need to identify, or ally itself, with either surrounding group. The code does this by postulating a fantasy group—the ancestors with cargo, a new or old pantheon, a *terre sans mal,* even an impersonal historical process—with which identification is possible and in alliance with which the group believes (rightly or wrongly) that it will be able to survive without allying or identifying itself with either of the two parties to the original dilemma.

Social Reorganization

But there is still another, and more general, way to regard the function of revitalization movements. They are concerned with the dialectic of organization and disorganization; if one regards societies as varying over time in their level of organization, then the revitalization movement is the process by which an extremely disorganized society accomplishes the task of reorganization. When there are too many elements present in the cultural "solution," when behavior is minimally predictable and approaches randomness, then to increase order it is necessary to eliminate some behavioral elements and to codify the residue in such a way that when one event occurs, it is possible to predict the next with reasonable confidence. This is, in fact, what organization means, and societies strive to maximize it by maximizing both order and complexity. But when too many possibilities are already in the field, and when the orderliness of events diminishes, the only possibility for improvement lies in simultaneously simplifying the repertoire and insisting on regularity of performance. Such a procedure, often carried out under the auspices of religion, constitutes a revitalization movement.

In the largest sense of the word, therefore, one can say that revitalization movements reduce the stress level prevalent in a system by increasing its internal organization. The rigorous ritualism, puritanical morality, austerity, and fanatical determination of such movements rapidly dissipate after the reorganization has been accomplished and the movement is no longer utopian but ideological, no longer radical but conservative. Its legacy—and this, too, is a functional consequence—is a body of ritual and myth which preserves, in more or less distorted form, the memory of past inspiration as a guide for the training of youth and the reinspiration of the mature.

V

The Processes of Religion: Origins, the Ritual Process, History, and Evolution

WE HAVE NOW REACHED a point in our study of religion where consideration of processes is appropriate. Structures, goals, and functions have been analyzed in some detail; but the dynamics of religion—how religion originates, how it works, and how it changes—have been only briefly reviewed. In this chapter we shall discuss process in religion from these several standpoints, recognizing that all such processes are interrelated, but assuming also that categorical distinctions among them are justified for analytical purposes. First we shall take up the problem of origins, under two heads: ritual among animals and ritual among Paleolithic peoples, particularly the Neanderthals and the Cro-Magnons. Considerations advanced here, in conjunction with the material in the foregoing chapters, suggest the next topic: the nature of the ritual process itself. Then problems of the general evolution of religion, and the special evolution, or history, of particular religions, are considered. And finally, we shall speculate about the future of religion as a human institution.

The Origins of Religion

It is always hazardous to set forth in search of the headwaters of human institutions. The unwary scholar is all too apt to find himself soon mired in a noisome bog of speculations, unable to extricate himself with dignity and subject to stoning by his more prudent colleagues on the bank. Nonetheless, in this section we shall, in as gingerly a fashion as possible, consider the problem of the origins of religion. We shall seek the beginnings, not of any particular religion, but of religious behavior *sui generis.* We do this, not merely from antiquarian interest, but because a consideration of origins is prerequisite to a theory of ritual process.

Our approach will be restricted to two kinds of phenomena, which, considered together, may afford some information about the origin of religion. These phenomena are, first, the "ritual" behavior of certain animals below man in the evolutionary scale, and second, the religious remains of forms of "early man," the Neanderthals and the Cro-Magnon people of Europe.

But before saying anything about "religious," pseudoreligious, or protoreligious behavior in animals or early man, we must clarify certain concepts. The situation of inquiry is like that with regard to mating behavior. One does not so much seek to find the "origin" of some particular human form of marriage, or family structure, or kinship system in a lower animal; rather, one searches for whatever general statements can be made about the mating behavior of humans, of primates, of mammals, or of vertebrates, all together; hopefully, then, one can regard human mating behavior as a special case—with its special features clearly definable—of a more widespread pattern. Thus, the human pattern of mating is a special form of the biparental family group, common to the primates, in which adults of both sexes and their offspring maintain a year-round association. There is no implication in such a statement that any particular form of the biparental family is ancestral to the rest; in fact, among the lower primates, as among men, many mating arrangements are found in the various taxonomic groups. Nor does one need to attribute mating behavior, or marriage, to an instinct. As students of animal behavior, like students of human behavior, have found, the concept of instinct is difficult to apply to particular behaviors because it is extremely awkward to distinguish between the innate and the learned components of the complete action.

Animal Ritual

We do not seek to find any particular religious custom among animals that can be defined as ancestral, nor do we wish to define a religious instinct. We ask, rather, whether there are any generalized forms of behavior among both animals and men which serve some common function and which, in man, are additionally invested with such characteristically and peculiarly human aspects of religion as a mythology and a pantheon of gods. We are looking, in other words, for forms with functions; we assume that if we find a formal-functional property of animal behavior that is intrinsic to religious behavior in man, we have defined a behavioral nucleus around which at least some of the elaborate symbolisms and multiple functions of human religion have arranged themselves like a pearl around its central grain of sand.

SOCIAL (ALLO-COMMUNICATIVE) RITUAL

The most obvious candidate for such a role is the phenomenon of ritual. "Rituals" or "ceremonies" among many different kinds of animals have been extensively described by ethologists. Mammals and birds characteristically engage in behavior that has the twofold qualities of mechanical, stereotyped repetitiveness and separation from such obviously necessary activities as fighting, flight, the seizing of food, copulation, the building of nests, and the tolerance of proximity. Such rituals seem rather to serve as primitive communication devices, their performance acting both to stimulate in the actor a psychophysiological readiness to engage in certain necessary behavior and (where a partner is concerned) to arouse a complementary state in the partner which will enable both parties to behave cooperatively.

Such rituals are particularly evident in fighting and courting behavior. Among timber wolves, for instance, an elaborate and standardized ritual combat precedes the practical denouement of actual fighting and submission. Lorenz describes a typical instance:

> An enormous old timber wolf and a rather weaker, obviously younger one are the opposing champions and they are moving in circles round each other, exhibiting admirable "footwork." At the same time, the bared fangs flash in such a rapid exchange of snaps that the eye can scarcely follow them. So far, nothing has really happened. The jaws of one wolf close on the gleaming white teeth of the other who is on the alert and wards off the attack. Only the lips have received one or

two minor injuries. The younger wolf is gradually being forced backwards. It dawns upon us that the older one is purposely manoeuvring him towards the fence. We wait with breathless anticipation what will happen when he "goes to the wall." Now he strikes the wire netting, stumbles . . . and the old one is upon him. And now the incredible happens, just the opposite of what you would expect. The furious whirling of the grey bodies has come to a sudden standstill. Shoulder to shoulder they stand, pressed against each other in a stiff and strained attitude, both heads now facing in the same direction. Both wolves are growling angrily, the elder in a deep bass, the younger in higher tones, suggestive of the fear that underlies his threat. But notice carefully the position of the two opponents; the older wolf has his muzzle close, very close against the neck of the younger and the latter holds away his head, offering unprotected to his enemy the bend of his neck, the most vulnerable part of his whole body! Less than an inch from the tensed neck-muscles, where the jugular vein lies immediately beneath the skin, gleam the fangs of his antagonist from beneath the wickedly retracted lips. Whereas, during the thick of the fight, both wolves were intent on keeping only their teeth, the one invulnerable part of the body, in opposition to each other, it now appears that the discomfited fighter proffers intentionally that part of his anatomy to which a bite must assuredly prove fatal. Appearances are notoriously deceptive, but in his case, surprisingly, they are not! . . .

. . . the strained situation may continue for a great length of time which is minutes to the observer, but very probably seem hours to the losing wolf. Every second you expect violence and await with bated breath the moment when the winner's teeth will rip the jugular vein of the loser. But your fears are groundless, for it will not happen. In this particular situation, the victor will definitely not close on his less fortunate rival. You can see that he would like to, but he just cannot! A dog or wolf that offers its neck to its adversary in this way will never be bitten seriously. The other growls and grumbles, snaps with his teeth in the empty air and even carries out, without delivering so much as a bite, the movement of shaking something to death in the empty air. However, this strange inhibition from biting persists only so long as the defeated dog or wolf maintains his attitude of humility. Since the fight is stopped so suddenly by this action, the victor frequently finds himself straddling his vanquished foe in anything but a comfortable position. So to remain, with his muzzle applied to the neck of the "under-dog" soon becomes tedious for the champion, and, seeing that he cannot bite anyway, he soon withdraws. Upon this, the under-dog may hastily attempt to put distance between himself and his superior. But he is not usually successful in this, for, as soon as he abandons his rigid attitude of submission, the other again falls upon him like a thunderbolt and the victim must again freeze into his former posture. It seems as if the victor is only waiting for the moment when the other will relinquish his submissive attitude, thereby enabling him to give vent to his urgent desire to bite. But, luckily for the "under-dog," the top-dog at the close of the fight is overcome by the pressing need to leave his trade-mark on the battlefield, to designate it as his personal property—in other words, he must lift his leg against the nearest upright object. This right-of-possession ceremony is usually taken advantage of by the under-dog to make himself scarce. [Lorenz, 1952, pp. 186–189.] *

Such a mock battle evidently is a communication ritual whose most usual function is to arouse complementary attitudes of dominant rage and submissive fear in two animals, and thereby to substitute for a destructive combat, a mutually acceptable, nonfighting, tolerance-of-proximity relationship. Comparable struggles among birds have been described; and, of course, among both birds and mammals, there are rituals between prospective mates that serve to establish in both the moods appropriate for initiating sexual, reproductive, and nurturant relationships.

SOLITARY (AUTO-COMMUNICATIVE) RITUAL

The foregoing rituals may be termed social or allo-communicative because they involve an exchange of meaningful signs between two (or more) partners. But the parties to the interaction seem to respond not only to their partner's messages but also to their own; the ritual, in other words, has an auto-communicative function as well as a social one. We may expect, therefore, that some ritual behavior among animals requires no partner or is solitary. And we are not mistaken. Portmann, for instance, describes ritualized activity in response to intense but ambiguous stimulation:

* Reprinted from Konrad Z. Lorenz, *King Solomon's Ring*. New York and London: Thomas Y. Crowell Co. and Methuen & Co. by permission of the publishers. Copyright © 1952 by Thomas Y. Crowell Company, New York.

The over-excitement induced in animals by a plane roaring above can release mating actions, as Lack (1941) saw from a low-flying plane in the Kenya National Park: when this monster in the sky appeared, one male ostrich after another sank into the ground and spread his wings as if worshipping it. In such cases cats suddenly begin washing their fur; birds abruptly start singing or pecking on the ground without picking anything up; a turkey may go to a spring and make drinking movements without swallowing any water. [Portmann, 1961, p. 153.]

The tendency of pigeons to engage in apparently irrelevant ritual responses to an arbitrary feeding schedule unrelated to any particular action on the part of the bird ("adventitious reinforcement") has even led the psychologist Skinner to write papers on "superstition" in the pigeon (Skinner [1948]; Skinner and Morse [1957]). This work has been discussed by Bachrach, who classifies the "superstitious" responses of pigeons into two types, heuristically labeled "prayer" and "propitiation." The responses consist of pecking rates. "Prayer" responses are adventitiously reinforced pecking rates, in which the bird seems to peck, as it were, "hopefully," in response to some irrelevant cue in an ambiguous stimulus field. "Propitiation" responses are the continuation of these useless behaviors even after a more reliable relation between pecking, cue, and reinforcement has been learned (Bachrach [1962]). These experiments suggest to Bachrach those theories of human magic and divination in which stereotyped responses to irrelevant stimuli are considered to be anxiety-reducing in situations (such as agricultural planning and hunting strategy) where many of the important variables, such as weather and the movement of game, are not only uncontrolled but unpredictable. They also suggest, to the writer, the more general point revealed by information-theory experimentation, that when human subjects are presented with data containing high statistical information (that is, as the stimulus pattern approaches randomness) they will tend to develop a stereotyped response. In his efforts to test the psychoanalytic concepts of fixation and regression, Sears (1943) made similar findings in experimental work with rats, who developed fixed and stereotyped responses to ambiguous learning problems.

Finally, one is reminded of the "experimental neuroses" produced in laboratory animals by systematically presenting them with discrimination tasks that exceed their capacities; here too, one finds a tendency toward fixed, stereotyped, and irrelevant behavior. In all of this material on auto-communicative ritual, one can observe that in the face of ambiguous stimuli, the subject responds with highly stereotyped patterns of action which have no functional value, insofar as an observer can determine, beyond the control of some internal state ("mood," "emotion," or "anxiety level") in the affected animal.

One further feature of at least some ritual behavior in lower animals is its regressive quality (in an ontogenetic sense). Portmann notes:

> Another important similarity is the use of symbolic actions. Childish patterns of behavior are often to be found in sexual ritual: e.g. in many bird species the young bird's humble begging, with wing quivering and slightly drooping, has been incorporated into their mating rites as part of the female's ceremonial. Movements and attitudes which have been co-ordinated from earliest childhood have now become adapted to new nervous and hormonal activities. The same applies to food and feeding as symbolic in animal rituals. Common terns arrive in their brooding territory unmated and mating is preceded by courting play in which the male (presumably, for the sexes look exactly alike) will offer the female a small fish. Sometimes, carrying the fish in his bill, he will fly around with a mate in a special "fish-flight," and the fish is never eaten but is used on many such flights. With other species the same "fish-play" occurs instead in the actual sexual ceremonies. This is the case with sandwich terns, where unions are formed for years, perhaps sometimes for life, so that the birds arrive in the territory already in pairs. [Portmann, 1961, p. 215.]

Here again one is reminded of the common negative commentary on human religious behavior by the anticlerical philosopher: that religion simply reduces the devout to an infantile dependence upon the divine parent.

There is an extraordinary gap, only now being filled in, in studies of animal rituals—the absence of more than a few accounts of ritual, in the sense in which we have been using that term, among nonhuman primates. One study using rhesus monkeys approximately replicates Skinner's work on "superstitious" learning among pigeons; but this kind of "superstitious" response is a property of individual rather than social learning (Sidman [1960]). The best examples of primate social ritual observed in nature are those by Schaller (1963) among gorillas, DeVore (1962) among baboons, and Goodall (1963) among chimpanzees. The gorilla "chest-beating" ritual, which includes the simulation of feeding as well as thumping the chest, is a complex and stereotyped response to threat whose function, presumably, is a complementary arousal of fear in the intruder and of confidence in the gorilla. The "mounting" ritual of baboons, as among other primates, is a perfunctory simulation of copulation and seems to constitute a complementary assertion of their relative positions by two animals in an already established dominance hierarchy. And some chimpanzees appear to perform a stereotyped dance on occasions where the sun changes after rain. But no systematic attention has been paid to the possibility that, in large-brained animals capable of making tools and maintaining elaborate and learned social structure, there may be ritual phenomena analogous to rites of passage on such occasions as puberty and other life crises affecting the group. It may be expected that research will show ritual systems of considerable complexity among the nonhuman primates.

In summary, then, we can say that among many of the lower mammals and birds, evolutionary processes have produced patterns of behavior that can fairly be denoted by the term "ritual." In common with human ritual, these behaviors are repetitive, stereotyped, and complex; they can be either solitary or social; and they function to arouse or reduce drive, not by direct mechanical interaction with the environment, but by auto- and allo-communication. Social rituals (allo-communicative) arouse in the participants a state of readiness and an intention to perform the consummatory action, whether it be sexual or aggressive or the establishment of a relationship such as dominance-submission or mutual territorial rights. Solitary rituals (auto-communicative) seem useful principally in reducing anxiety in situations of ambiguity with respect to learning or discrimination. And, frequently, ritual behavior in animals incorporates regressive features, in the sense that one component or another is ontogenetically early, having been appropriate in the immature state as a signal for nurturance.

Now we are not arguing, in this presentation of evidence, that human religion is *nothing but* an archaic primate, or mammalian, or vertebrate, behavioral characteristic which survives in man by virtue of some sort of evolutionary lag. Rather, we are saying that ritual is a common form of animal behavior, which serves a necessary function even in lower orders, and that comparable rituals (both religious and secular) can be observed in man, serving him in the same way. What has presumably happened is that, in the course of human cultural development, much ritual has *become* religious as it has been rationalized and explained in language by reference to beliefs about supernatural beings. And, further, ritual has to a considerable degree remained the fulcrum by which the communicational energy of these more elaborate linguistic formulations is applied to the work of psychophysiological state transformation, and social coordination, in man. In other words, from the evolutionary vantage point, religion can be defined as the use of language to increase the effectiveness of ritual.

PALEOLITHIC RELIGIONS [1]

NEANDERTHAL (LOWER PALEOLITHIC) RITUAL

As we have seen, there is little information available as yet about ritual among nonhuman primates. However, the earliest evidences of ritual of a "religious" kind among humans are of considerable antiquity. These evidences come from the Middle Pleistocene and are on the order of 50,000 to 100,000 years old. They were created by an extinct species (technically, genus) of man, *Homo neanderthalensis*, and were associated with a Lower Paleolithic culture, the Mousterian. These religious remains are the burials of the bodies, or parts of the bodies, of men and of cave bears.

The phylogenetic origin of Neanderthal men is obscure and so is their fate. These people flourished during a period of roughly 100,000 years (from the Riss to the Würm glacial epochs, roughly spanning the epoch from 150,000 to 50,000 years ago), in Europe, the Near East, and possibly Africa. The skeletal remains of dozens

[1] *Vide* Maringer, 1960.

of Neanderthals, male and female, of various ages, have been uncovered and studied; and along with them, in the caves where they lived, have been found their stone tools and the hearths of their fires. The typical Neanderthal man, by our aesthetic standard, was a "primitive"—a burly, beetle-browed creature with a broad and brutish face. But these external disadvantages must be evaluated in the light of the fact that his brain was large—even larger than ours—averaging about 1450 cc. Before the Neanderthals appeared, there were high-browed men like us. Such men lived alongside the Neanderthals, in some places, and may well have intermarried with them; and they watched the extinction of the Neanderthals, who survived only in the chromosomes of men of another, more durable breed. Conceivably, it was a combination of the bigger Neanderthal brain in the more limber non-Neanderthal body which produced at least some strains of modern man. In any case, the archaeological data demonstrate that the Neanderthal people practiced what can only be called religious observances. These observances are of two kinds: the burial, or other ritual handling, of the human body; and the burial, and ritual handling, of the remains of the cave bear.

The Neanderthal people buried at least some of their own dead in caves. They dug graves in the cave floor, deposited the body carefully, and sometimes covered the grave with heavy flat stones. The graves were located near the cave mouth, where the living quarters were. It is, of course, not possible to say whether the living and dead stayed thus together, or whether graves were dug in abandoned cave dwellings, or whether dwellings were abandoned by the bereaved after the burial and reoccupied later. The care with which the dead body was deposited is indicated by the fact that the legs are usually found flexed or even contracted tightly against the body; the head may be pillowed upon the arm. The practice of burial was, apparently, not confined to some special group within the society; the remains include both men and women, ranging in age up to forty or fifty, and youths and children of both sexes, including at least one infant so small that it may have been a fetus. With some of the bodies grave-goods were left: a child's body was surrounded by a circle of ibex horns; a young man was left with a hand ax, a flint scraper, and miscellaneous other tools and animal bones; an old man was buried with a whole bison leg, tools, and lumps of red paint (ocher); an old woman was left with animal remains, flint tools, and fiber threads. In some cases, the grave had been lined with stones; in others, fires had been lit over the grave. The burials, in some instances, are found in groups, suggesting that certain caves, unsuitable for dwellings for such reasons as low roofs, were used for cemeteries.

There is also slight, and rarer, evidence of another type of ritual treatment of human remains. In one cave, a Neanderthal skull was found in a solitary crypt, raised on a platform of earth and stones and ringed by a circle of stones. From its position one might suppose that the skull had, perhaps, been set on a stick, which eventually rotted away. The right temple was fractured, probably by the blow that had caused death; the two cervical vertebrae had been excised and the foramen magnum enlarged either to remove the brain or to facilitate mounting the skull upon its stake. No trace of the rest of the skeleton was found. These remains suggest either a ceremonial cannibalism or, more likely, a cult of which this dark chamber was the holy of holies and its skull the sacred ark. The cannibalism of the Neanderthals remains, in fact, a moot point. In other sites, skulls crushed by heavy blows (and with the foramina enlarged) and, occasionally, fragments of other bones have been found in circumstances that suggest to some observers that the victims had been killed and eaten, with or without benefit of ritual. On the other hand, skull fractures are not prima facie evidence of some other human being's protein hunger, and the removal of the cervical vertebrae may just as easily be evidence of a ritual disposition of the skull as of a cannibalistic taste for brain. Some of the "cannibal feast" remains suggest rather the scattering of recent interments by animal scavengers than anthropophagous orgies by Neanderthal headhunters. In sum, the evidence for ritual cannibalism among the Neanderthals is inconclusive.

The burial rituals of the Neanderthals were not confined to human remains. Cave bears, with whom they competed for domiciles and upon whom they fed, were also the object of a cult whose principal feature was the interment of the skull. In the interior chambers of several Alpine caves occupied by Neanderthals there have been found, carefully arranged and protected, the skulls and occasional other bones of numerous cave bears. In some cases, the skulls were carefully packed in stone chests, constructed of limestone slabs; in other cases, the skulls were mounted on niches in the wall, sometimes protected by flat stones. The skulls were often oriented east to west, and sometimes were intact, indicating that they had not been used for food; in some cases, long bones, unsplit for marrow, accompanied the skull. In two instances a fertility symbol—a penis-shaped bone—was found with the skulls. While it would be hazardous to associate these bear remains with the bear cults of more recent primitives, it is unquestionable that *a* bear cult, involving the ritual interment of bear skulls in the interior chambers of caves, was practiced by the Neanderthals.

CRO-MAGNON (UPPER PALEOLITHIC) RITUAL

The Neanderthals in Europe were contemporaneous with and were eventually succeeded by a different and more modern breed of man, the species *Homo sapiens*. One race of such men, probably ancestral to some living European populations, was the so-called Cro-Magnon people. The Cro-Magnons occupied southern Europe and the Mediterranean littoral from about 50,000 years ago to perhaps 10,000 years ago. Their cultures were in fundamentals very similar to the Mousterian: they hunted for their food and knew no agriculture; they frequently made their dwellings in caves and rock shelters and possibly also constructed huts with pole frames and coverings of brush, skins, or turf. Their stone tools were more finely and precisely made, perhaps as a technological response to the changing climatic conditions which the last great glaciation, occurring in their time, imposed on the regions south of the ice sheets.

The Cro-Magnons, like the Neanderthals, buried their dead in the mouths of caves. The bodies were carefully arranged in the grave; frequently they were flexed and sometimes they were deposited in a sleeping position. Occasionally a fire was kindled in a grave and the body deposited in the thick layer of ashes and covered with more ashes. The graves were often sealed with a layer of stones, presumably to protect the corpse from animal scavengers. More commonly and more lavishly than among the Neanderthals, the bodies were heavily smeared with red paint (red ocher) and were provided with grave-goods and personal ornaments. Ornamental shells, deer teeth, fish vertebrae, and bone disks surrounded head and neck, upper arms, elbows, wrists, waist, thighs, knees, and feet. Skulls and other bones of various animals —mammoth and reindeer in particular—found near the graves suggest food offerings or the remains of a funeral feast. Cro-Magnon customs with regard to the dead also had another aspect: the manufacture, from parts of the human skeleton, of objects that probably had a ceremonial or ritual use. Shallow cups have been found fashioned from human skulls; some of them had been lined with red ocher. Human teeth, pierced for threading on a cord and incised with ornamental designs, have also been discovered. Although we cannot now, of course, know the beliefs connected with these practices, they are suggestive of a magical use of human remains to control, to secure the good will of, or to acquire the virtues of the departed, whether he had been kinsman or enemy.

As with the Neanderthals, so also among the Cro-Magnons the ritual disposition of human remains was paralleled by the ritual disposition of animal bones. The skull and long bones and sometimes entire skeletons of certain animals—cave bear, mammoth, reindeer, arctic fox, and rhinoceros—were on occasion carefully disposed of by their hunters without any evidence of the animals' having been used for food (the long bones, for instance, had not been cracked to extract the marrow). In connection with certain of these practices (those occurring at summer hunting stations in Germany) a ritual offering must be inferred—some sort of first-fruits ceremony. The ritual involved the slitting of the abdomen of a dead reindeer, slain in May or June, the insertion of one or more heavy stones (weighing up to eighteen pounds) into the thoracic cavity, and the submerging of the animal in an ancient lake. Here again, although the details of the ritual and its rationale can never be reconstructed with certainty, the fact of hunting ritual is unmistakable. One can almost begin to see the outlines of a "reindeer cult." With even more probability, one can infer a "bear cult" from a single find: the fossilized skull of a young brown bear, in a cave, with scarcely worn molars, but with incisors and canines worn down to the pulp and then partially re-covered with new dentine. Such wear is impossible under natural conditions; this bear's front teeth had been filed down during its lifetime and even show the file marks. The filing of the teeth of a young bear is a diagnostic trait of a particular bear cult, widely distributed in recent times among circumboreal hunters living under climatic and hunting conditions not dissimilar to those confronting the Upper Paleolithic hunters.

But the most dramatic evidences of religion among the Upper Paleolithic hunters are not burial customs or animal sacrifices but sculpture and painting. The cave art of the Upper Paleolithic is undoubtedly religious art; and, so far as is known, it is the earliest formal artistic tradition of mankind. Upper Paleolithic artists used a variety of media: mural paintings, in color and in line drawings, painted on the walls of caves; engravings in ivory, bone, and stone; carvings in ivory, bone, and stone; and models in clay both in relief and in the round. The most famous and most informative creations are the murals which lavishly decorate the walls of dozens (and probably of hundreds) of limestone caverns and rock shelters in France and Spain. The principal subject of the murals is animals, particularly the large game animals: mammoth, bison, deer, boar, horse, reindeer, ibex, wild ox, chamois, hyena, and bear. Outlined in strong, flowing, black strokes, and colored in soft shades of brown, gray, and red, the animals are depicted in a series of stereotyped attitudes, running, leaping, mounting, gravid with young; not infrequently the animal is portrayed as the victim of a human hunter, caught in a trap or pierced with arrows or spears, and bleeding. Man himself is seldom shown, although there are a few paintings of hunters and shamans. Curiously, the dog appears rarely, if ever, in the rock paintings, perhaps because this animal was regarded as a domestic companion (or pest) rather than as game or as hunting assistant.

Engravings in stone and bone comprise a second category of ritual art. Such engravings, found both upon cave walls and on smaller pieces of stone and bone or ivory, are done with the same fluid grace, presumably developed by long practice in a well-defined tradition, as the large polychrome paintings. Like the paintings, the engravings represent for the most part the large game animals.

The third category, carvings in the round, in addition to representations of animals includes a special set of carvings of the female human figure, the so-called "Venuses." These objects, generally less than a foot in height, were carved from stone, bone, or ivory, and have been found over a wide area in the Eurasia land mass from the Atlantic Coast to Siberia. They show the female form (only one male statuette has been found), usually nude, with carefully dressed hair, massive breasts, buttocks, and thighs, and frequently with the protuberant abdomen of pregnancy. The arms and hands are weakly modeled or missing, and the legs taper into a point; it has been suggested that the figurines were made to be stuck upright into earth or clay. Traces of paint have been found on some of them. In later developmental stages, the lifelike figurines seem to have evolved into geometric forms representing the female figure in a highly stylized and schematic way.

The fourth category of Upper Paleolithic art, found in the inner recesses of several of the major caves, comprises the occasional large models in clay of major game animals. These clay models of bears and lions were, at least in some cases, completed by attaching to them by wooden dowels the head of a recently killed bear; and, while the clay was still soft, the model was attacked by men wielding spears. The round holes left by spear thrusts remained as the clay dried and hardened.

In all of the media mentioned above, except the clay models, there were, in addition to more or less realistic representations of human beings and animals, also geometrical figures: patterns of dots, grids, broken circles, and so forth, which may have represented in some cases traps, pounds or corrals, and drive lanes, as well as mere ornament or arbitrary magical symbols.

The modern viewer of these art products of the Upper Paleolithic may, quite properly, be principally impressed by their aesthetic qualities. Our interest, however, is in the nature of the religious beliefs and practices of which this art, along with the human and animal burials, is the remains. It must be observed, first, that the religious behavior of the peoples characterized as Upper Paleolithic was not a monolithic and unchanging thing, uniform in all times and places. There is evidence of considerable regional differentiation: the cave art, for instance, is pre-eminently French and Spanish; the rock shelter art is Spanish; the Venuses do not occur in Spain; and the deer cult is centered in Germany. Furthermore, styles changed markedly over time, with a general tendency, most marked perhaps in the treatment of the Venuses, toward abstraction of the living form into geometric elements; and, one must suppose, the mature representational style of the murals and the Venuses must itself have been the product of a long period of formalization which made it possible at the height of the tradition for practitioners to be trained in the technique of both observation and representation in a particular medium. Because, after all, so little information is available concerning particular communities during short periods of time, there is a tendency to telescope the finds and to treat them as if they were *a* culture assignable to a particular community within a specifiable generation. In point of fact, we have the remains of hundreds of separate communities, widely scattered in space and deriving from a span of time that must be measured in tens of thousands of years. The task of defining the regional and temporal dimensions of cultural variability in the Upper Paleolithic and classifying particular communities in the resulting taxonomy, only with respect to the religious aspect of culture, necessarily exceeds the scope of this chapter.

At best, we can here distinguish several prominent ritual foci which may or may not always have coexisted in individual communities, or even in any one community, but which in sum can be attributed to the Upper Paleolithic. These four ritual foci in the Upper Paleolithic are *human burials, animal burials, hunting ceremonies,* and *human fertility ceremonies.*

Human burial with grave-goods, as we have indicated, began in the Lower Paleolithic, at least as early as the Neanderthal cultures, and thus is not a unique property of Upper Paleolithic cultures.

Uniqueness cannot be claimed for Upper Paleolithic customs in the disposal of animal remains, either; in this ritual category, too, the Neanderthals anticipated the Upper Paleolithic peoples. But the later cultures added to the Lower Paleolithic repertory, continuing the so-called "bear cult" but developing in addition, in some regions at least, the custom of water-burial of deer and similar herd animals, perhaps as a kind of first-fruits offering to a supernatural "Keeper of the Game."

The Upper Paleolithic peoples, however, were the first, so far as we know, to develop elaborate rituals involving the manipulation of symbolic representations of game animals. These rituals themselves are depicted graphically in the cave art—as for instance in the paintings of men and women dressed in animal skins, engaging in some sort of ceremonial play. Hunting rituals have also left material remains in the caves, for the bulk of the cave art was not just a picture of ceremonies but was part of the ritual paraphernalia of the ceremonies. Just what the nature of the rituals was must remain uncertain. Some of the scenes suggest that puberty rituals, involving instruction in the mysteries associated with the hunt and with human and animal mating and reproduction, were being communicated to youths in the dark recesses of the cave. An alternative hypothesis is that the caves were the workshops of ancient magicians, attempting magically to control the behavior of the game animals by imitative magic.

Finally, the "mother-goddess," represented in the figurines of the human female head and torso, is new in the Upper Paleolithic and incidentally would appear to be the first realistic and mature portrayal of the human figure (for in the cave art the human figure is, except when dressed in animal skins, not shown with a skill comparable to that lavished on the animals).

As we look back then, over the eons of physical and cultural evolution that began with man's early vertebrate precursors and cousins, and culminated in the Upper Paleolithic, we can observe, with regard to the elements of "religious" behavior, a single but massive continuity—ritual. Originally developed and maintained by little-understood mechanisms of learning and instinct, ritual served to prepare the lower animals for efficient execution of the intricate individual and social behaviors involved in combat, food-getting, and reproduction. Ritual continued to serve these same functions in early man; for, in the first human cultures, those rituals that have left material remains suggesting a belief in the soul (of men and animals alike) still center about the problems of death, birth, combat with other animals, and the getting of food. What seems to differentiate human and animal ritual is the self-consciousness of ritual action in man. As technology improved, and as causal connections were considered, ritual required rationalization in order to inspire confidence; and the religious rationale was the idea of the soul and, by extension, of other supernatural beings.

The Ritual Process

The Essential Nature of the Ritual Process: Stereotyped Communication

It is now time for us to formalize the implications of foregoing discussions of ritual, supernatural belief, and their relationship. In approaching a consideration of the essential nature of the ritual process, we are confronted by a seeming paradox: although ritual is the primary phenomenon of religion, the ritual process itself requires no supernatural belief. It can be worked by anyone—cleric or layman, devotee or atheist, Christian or Marxist—who knows the rules. Ritual may, perhaps, most succinctly be classified as communication without information: that is to say, each ritual is a particular sequence of signals which, once announced, allows no uncertainty, no choice, and hence, in the statistical sense of information theory, conveys no information from sender to receiver. It is, ideally, a system of perfect order and any deviation from this order is a mistake.

But to say that ritual is communication without information is merely to state that ritual behavior is stereotyped; this criterion differentiates it from such action sequences as conversation, games, and play, in all of which the course and outcome of the behavior is uncertain, but does not distinguish it from equally stereotyped technical procedures like setting a trap, grinding corn, or working on an assembly line. The difference between ritual and mere stereotyped physical labor lies in the distinction between the functions of the two kinds of action: the primary function of ritual is the use of energy to communicate; the primary function of physical labor is the use of energy to manipulate matter. (In a thermodynamic sense, of course, both communication and physical labor involve work—the transformation of energy—but the communication process per se requires far less energy than those manipulations of matter which both ultimately aim to effect.) The particular function of ritual communication is quickly to prepare an individual or individuals to execute an action with maximum efficiency. Where only one organism is involved, the ritual may accomplish its preparatory function by resolving motivational conflict, reducing fear and anxiety, increasing confidence, focusing attention on the task at hand, and mobilizing appropriate psychophysiological systems for the execution of the act. Such solitary rituals as the sick patient's praying for strength to endure pain, the foxhole-bound soldier's praying for divine protection during a prolonged bombardment, or the warrior's handling of his talisman before going into battle are examples of solitary, but institutionalized, religious rituals.

Such solitary but institutionalized rituals are also prone to develop in persons suffering from anxiety arising from unconscious motivational conflict; the famous hand-washing ritual of obsessive-compulsive neurotics, for instance, has the function of reducing the guilt-anxiety resulting from a conflict between hostility and conscience. Theoretically, at least, such solitary rituals, whether conventional or bizarrely regressive, are effective in preserving the individual from disablement brought on by prolonged and excessive anxiety. While the cost of the ritual is waste of time and energy in mechanically ineffectual activity, on the other hand the cost of not removing the anxiety may be complete disablement or even death. One could point out, of course, that the best way of eliminating the anxiety is to remove its roots in neurotic conflict, ignorance, or the threatening aspect of the real environment; but unconscious conflict is difficult to treat, knowledge is slow to replace ignorance, and many real dangers cannot be immediately removed. Ritual that maintains the organism in some sort of shape to cope with reality by keeping anxiety low and confidence high certainly has survival value.

The communication involved in solitary ritual is auto-communication, whether it be talking to oneself, or hearing one's prayers to a god, or whistling in the dark, or reminding oneself of one's power by fingering beads. The person's anxiety is reduced by his perception of concepts, relationships, or things that mean that he is adequate, secure, worthy, or loved. To be sure, other observers —and even, to some extent, the solitary ritualist himself—may construe these rituals as evidence of weakness or fear, inferring from their practice a vulnerability to the very anxiety that the ritual is meant to reduce. Thus Pontius Pilate's guilt, although presumably lessened in his own awareness by the hand-washing ritual, is also made manifest by the ritual; and Captain Queeg's guilty fear of a cross-examination which might reveal his rigid panic in the face of a storm (the event that prompted the Caine Mutiny) is displayed for all the court to see in his personally reassuring ritual of grinding together the steel ball bearings in his pocket.

The communicational aspects of ritual are more manifest, however, in social ceremonies. Here, as the parties respond rhythmically to each other's performances, one can readily recognize that what is being observed is an exchange of signals. In social rituals, in addition to any anxiety-reduction function which may be present, one sees clearly also a mobilizing and coordinating function: the parties to a social action are brought more rapidly to the state of readiness for the cooperative execution of the act than is likely if mobilization and coordination were to depend upon less stereotyped communication. In the courting rituals of birds, for example, the exchange of signals is accompanied by a rapid, coordinated series of complementary psychophysiological changes in male and female which readies both for the mating itself much more rapidly and reliably than would dependence upon a random coincidence of time and place in birds independently varying in cycles of mating readiness.

Let us now, in summary, define ritual and then go on to con

sider how ritual works. Ritual may be defined as stereotyped communication, solitary or interpersonal, which reduces anxiety, prepares the organism to act, and (in social rituals) coordinates the preparation for action among several organisms, and which does all this more quickly and reliably than can be accomplished (given the characteristics of the organisms and the circumstance) by nonstereotyped, informational communication.

How Ritual Works

THE CONTENT OF RITUAL COMMUNICATION

First, we must recognize a difference between sets of signals (both communicational) that are meaningful and informational. Not all meaningful messages are informational; not all informational messages are meaningful. In other words, a sequence of meaningful signals whose order is fixed, so that the receiver always knows what signal will follow the preceding one, will have no information value because there is no uncertainty to be reduced by the outcome of each successive event. Conversely, a message may be meaningless either because its information value is too high or because the component signals are arbitrary.

Meaningfulness, then, does not depend on whether or not the message is informational. Meaningfulness has to do with the receiver's ability to respond to a message—that is, to respond to a small stimulus with a relatively large response. The simplest level of meaning would, therefore, be represented by the simple *unconditioned reflex*. The next level of meaning is the relation between a response and *conditioned stimulus*; the buzzer, to the Pavlovian dog, is meaningful in this sense because it elicits the salivation reflex. The third level of meaning would be that described as *instrumental learning*, in which the organism learns to perform a complex, instrumental action "in order" to secure reinforcement. The most complex level of meaning, presumably, is the *semantic response*, wherein the receiver translates the signal into a set of equivalent other signals (which can be substituted for the original signal). From this set of defining, substitutable, alternative signals he is able to infer the properties of the class of events referred to by the original signal and to infer relationships to still other classes of events by chains of logical relationship. Thus, when we say that ritual is meaningful (and therefore communicational) we do not imply that the meaning is necessarily learned or conscious or verbalizable, or even that language is necessarily involved at all (although it often is, of course, in human rituals both sacred and profane). Ritual functions can, as we have seen in the case of lower animals, be accomplished without either learning or the use of language; but learning and language, as we shall see, serve as powerful tools for extending the range of ritual's usefulness to a species.

Thus the effectiveness of ritual depends not only on the stereotypy but also on the content of its communication. The content of human ritual communication is a twofold message: first, it is a statement of an intention; second, it is a statement of the nature of the world in which the intention is to be realized. The conscious intentions of human rituals, as we have seen, can be broadly categorized as transformations of state in the technological, therapeutic (and anti-therapeutic), ideological, salvational, and revitalizational senses. But it must be recognized that several intentions can be expressed in the same act of communication, often on different levels of awareness. It has been the principal contribution of the psychoanalytic approach to ritual to emphasize that multiple intentions, sometimes congruent and sometimes contradictory, can be expressed by the same ritual act, and in the same ritual sequence. Furthermore, the "language" of ritual is, in a sense, extremely abstract; the rather simple signals of which it is composed refer to extensive and complex ideas of value, structure, and transformation, whose verbal statement requires considerable time. Consequently, the symbolism of ritual is often obscure, since it refers to intentions and beliefs that are complex and, in part, unconscious. Thus the simple ritual act of crossing oneself, in Catholic custom, by touching the fingers to the forehead and chest in four places, can be understood, depending on the context, as a statement of intent to secure divine power as a protection against danger, spiritual or physical, or as an assertion of spiritual sincerity and respect for the sacred at a time of prayer and commitment. The "sign of the Cross," the extremities of which are indicated by the points touched, invokes the whole story of Christ and its complex meanings; the accompanying litany invokes a particular theological conception—the Trinity—and constitutes both a prayer and a primitive magical conception of power inherent in naming. The points of the body chosen may be believed to be seats of particular spiritual functions in man; and the nature of the danger to be warded off, or of the prayer or commitment being presented, is obviously likely to be a complex combination of conscious and unconscious fears and wishes. Thus this simple act may be a statement of extremely complex intentions and is an assertion of a world view which is embodied in an extraordinarily elaborate set of beliefs based both on ancient Christian mythology and on even more ancient conceptions of magic.

In some rituals, the connection between the signal and that to which it refers is more easily recognizable. One thinks particularly of rituals involving sexual and aggressive symbolism construable by the kind of logic implied in Freudian dream interpretation. Thus, for instance, the analyst may interpret the Australian sub-incision ceremony as a statement of intent by men to secure female sexual parts and to achieve certain generative powers associated with femininity; and this interpretation has some support from native informants. But it is also a test, and a sign, of manhood, of admission to a social status that involves the acceptance of both rights and obligations; and these rights and obligations are defined, in part, in an extensive mythology. In general, then, we must recognize that "the" meaning of any ritual act is apt to be multiple rather than singular, and that explanations of ritual that claim a simple singularity are almost invariably over-simplifications.

But, even though the intentional meaning of a rite is both highly particular and highly complex, it has always one other message, which is implicit rather than explicit. This is the message of organization. The stereotypy of ritual is orderliness raised to an extraordinary degree; rituals are predictable, the contingent probabilities in chains of ritual events are near unity; the myth upon which the ritual is based describes a world in which chaos is being, or is to be, replaced by order. Furthermore, the content of ritual reduces the complex heterogeneity of the reality to which the ritual refers to a simpler homogeneity and explains the mystic unity which lies behind the phenomenological diversity. Thus ritual, and its supporting belief system, constitute a world of symbols that is simple and orderly. This is hardly unexpected, for, as we have seen, one of the principal functions of religion is to reduce anxiety and enlarge confidence, and if this is to be accomplished, the human —or nonhuman—organism must view life and circumstances as a system so well organized as to permit quick decision and confident action. An organism overwhelmed by information overload is incapable of discriminating response; ritual, by reducing the information content of experience below the often bewildering level of complexity and disorder with which reality confronts him, permits adaptive response. In this sense, the goal of science and the goal of ritual and myth are the same: to create the image of a simple and orderly world.

THE RITUAL LEARNING PROCESS

The accomplishment of the ritual reorganization of experience thus is a kind of learning, sometimes done once by a given individual and not again, as in many rites of passage, and sometimes done repeatedly, as in those calendrically scheduled communal ceremonies which readjust values and perceptions and refocus attention. But the psychological mechanisms upon which ritual learning depends are not confined to the practice-and-reinforcement schedule which has been so carefully investigated by experimental psychologists. The ritual learning process, whether its effects be measured in years, as in the case of puberty rituals, or in hours or minutes, as in the case of certain technological rituals, seems to involve a special five-stage process, which invokes not so much the law of effect (as in conditioning and instrumental learning) nor the law of repetition (as in imprinting) but what might be called the law of dissociation. This is the principle that any given set of cognitive and affective elements can be restructured more rapidly and more extensively the more of the perceptual cues from the environment associated with miscellaneous previous learning of other matters are excluded from conscious awareness, and the more of those new cues which are immediately relevant to the elements to be reorganized are presented. How permanent such a new cognitive synthesis will prove to be depends, presumably, in part on the maintenance of the dissociation (by such devices as actual isolation from prior contacts and the continued presentation of the selected matrix of new cues, including direct suggestions) and in part on reinforcement in the conventional learning sense.

The stages of the ritual process of cognitive-and-affective restructuring are as follows:

Pre-learning. At least some of the several elements to be reorganized in the new cognitive synthesis must already be present as a result of previous learning. For instance, novitiates usually have some knowledge of the standardized rights and obligations of the new role even before a rite of passage; persons about to become possessed are aware of the possessing being's interests and characteristics; persons hopeful of salvation know something of what the new identity would be like; the incipient prophet is already well stocked with criticisms of the status quo and with recommendations for reform. But the cognitive content of relevant prelearning is internally contradictory and not sorted out from other cognitive material.

Separation. The ritualist separates himself, and/or is separated by others, from conscious awareness of irrelevant environmental information. This can be accomplished in several ways:

a. by deprivation of sensory contact with previously significant features of the environment, by such devices as physical isolation, darkness, and distracting noise;

b. by the use of desemanticating drugs, such as mescaline and lysergic acid dyethylamide, which interfere with the ability to assign meaning to previously familiar data;

c. by the imposition of extreme physical stress, through pain, fatigue, sleeplessness, hunger and thirst, or even actual trauma or illness, in order to restrict attention;

d. by the presentation of monotonous and repetitive stimuli, such as drumming, flashing lights, and dancing, which (as in hypnosis) help to induce trance.

While the degree of separation of attention achieved by these methods can vary greatly—from the probably minor effect of simple withdrawal to a quiet "sacred" place to the profoundly dissociative effect of drugs, complete sensory deprivation, extreme stress, or prolonged drumming—all these procedures seem to have the effect of facilitating the process of cognitive restructuring.

Suggestion. Once the state of separation or dissociation (sometimes called "trance") has been achieved, the cognitive material relevant to resynthesis can be readily recombined under the influence of direct suggestion from others or from one's self (the general instructions for resynthesis having been prelearned, as for instance in the case of the Plains Indian vision quest). But even in the absence of any specific suggestion, a spontaneous sorting out of dissociated elements is apparently possible, if one can judge from the reported experience of prophets like Handsome Lake and the reports of experimental subjects in drug and sensory deprivation experiments. Such a resynthesis may take the form of transient changes in mood, as in most technological rituals. Or it may take the form of an alternate but only temporarily manifest personality, as in those cases of temporary multiple personality which are interpreted by a theory of possession; Haitian voodoo would be an example. But resynthesis may also take the form of an enduring and sometimes irreversible restructuring of beliefs and values, as in the radical mazeway resynthesis of the religious prophet or the identity transformations of rites of passage and of salvation.

Execution. After the achievement of resynthesis, the ritual subject will be expected, sooner or later, to act in accordance with the new cognitive structure. If "sooner," it may mean immediately, even during the dissociated state, as it does in ritual possession; but if the new role is to be a permanent one played out in a secular context, its execution may be delayed until after the dissociated state is over, and the expectation may be for a lifelong change of personality.

Maintenance. In cases of ritual possession, the resynthesis is implemented during the dissociated state and is terminated with the end of those procedures that maintain the dissociation. The once-possessed individual apparently retains a lower threshold for dissociation and personality alternation, however. In some instances, the maintenance of the new structure depends on posthypnotic suggestion; but this, by itself, does not usually remain effective for more than several weeks or months at most. Therefore, for "permanent" change, it is necessary either to renew, periodically, the ritual itself, or to provide the subject with tangible cues from the ritual experience that will serve to maintain the new structure, or both. The necessity for repetition of the ritual, even in attenuated form, has been recognized by evangelists (like John Wesley) who insisted on their converts' joining cells, congregations, or study groups to hold periodic meetings. As for tangible reminders, they are of course provided by such devices as amulets, talismans, and medicine bundles, by special ornaments and uniforms, and by public symbols (like the Cross). By such means as these, the survival of a resynthesis achieved under dissociation can be extended for a long period of time, perhaps indefinitely, even with minimal reinforcement (in the sense of a schedule of rewards or punishments).

The anthropologist should recognize that, although the process of ritual learning invokes a specialized and quasi-pathological mechanism for the achievement of cognitive changes, it is nonetheless closely dependent upon culture. The necessary prelearning, of course, will in large measure be the learning of traditional culture and of various personal attitudes toward it; and the techniques of separation, and both the techniques and content of the suggestions, are similarly closely related to culture. Thus, despite the connotations of individualistic spontaneity, of pathology, or of radical innovation which these mechanisms of resynthesis have for team-minded Western readers, they should be viewed as neither extraordinary nor noncultural. The ritual process, as described above, is a universal human phenomenon, and indeed is not restricted to man. What man has done has been to rationalize this process and to institutionalize it in particular forms which are different in detail in each society. One—but only one—way of rationalizing the ritual process is to interpret it and apply it within the context of a belief in supernatural beings.

The Relation of Belief to Ritual

In our treatment of religion so far, we have asserted the primacy of ritual and have devoted most of our attention to it rather than to systems of belief. But we have also generally observed that belief, codified in linguistic structures, rationalizes ritual and renders it more effective than it would be by itself. Furthermore, in the preceding section, we have suggested that the meaning of ritual is, at least in part, determined by the beliefs with which it is associated. We shall now take up the issue of the relationship of belief to ritual in more detail.

Belief systems may, at the outset, be divided into two groups of statements: first, theology per se; and second, mythology and folklore. By "theology" we mean the formal description of the pantheon and of the cosmos. Theology can range in style from a loose, encyclopedic abstraction of material from origin myths and other stories, which describes the gods, the human soul, and the nature of the universe, to a metaphysics, ethics, and cosmology which is almost as deliberate and impersonal as physics, astronomy, sociology, and other sciences. The structure of theology is dependent upon its postulates and upon logical deduction.

Mythology and folklore, by contrast, are stories which have a plot of some sort in which anthropomorphic beings strive toward and achieve with more or less difficulty, or fail to achieve, anthropomorphic goals. Mythology and folklore imply theology, but at a certain point in evolution theology, which stems from mythology, assumes autonomy and can, in the course of its further development, outgrow mythology or even contradict it. Theology in advanced societies tends to become science; mythology tends to become literature. But in primitive societies the two are nearly indistinguishable.

According to the principles laid down in this book, neither theology nor mythology can be adequately understood apart from ritual. Therefore any analysis of mythology and folklore that does not recognize that their function is to rationalize ritual must be incomplete at best and, at worst, profoundly misleading. This stricture applies to contemporary "structural" studies of mythology and folklore no less than to such traditional approaches as the liberal theological itself, the Tylorean, and the psychoanalytic. The recent studies of myth and folk tale, inspired by Lévi-Strauss, are thus merely the last in a long line of efforts to interpret myth as a form of primitive philosophy which rationalizes, not ritual, but the sociocultural system as a whole. (*Vide* Lévi-Strauss [1955]; Propp [1958]; Leach [1961]; and Dundes [1964]). While it would be fruitless to argue that theology, myth, and folklore do not express general beliefs about the nature of the world and institutions of society, thereby serving to rationalize the entire system, it must be pointed out that all general beliefs, whether religious or not, also serve the same purpose. Furthermore, this somewhat aseptic viewpoint, congenial to scientists who have little use for religious ritual, fails to deal at all with the fact that theology and myth, in living religious systems, are in practice intimately connected with ritual by being, at the very least, recited in the course of ritual.

But structural analysis has a virtue as well as a fault and we may do well to follow the practice of the structuralists in this regard. This virtue resides in a willingness to divide a text into a sequence of events, each component event of which can be classified under a small number of -etic or -emic headings. What we shall do, rather than theorize about primitive speculation on such riddles as life versus death, is to carry the virtue of structural analysis of myth into the structural analysis of ritual. We shall show that the same sort of analysis, using the same headings, can be performed on ritual as on myth; and we shall suggest that, in the last analysis, a myth can be defined as a transformation of a ritual.

STRUCTURAL ANALYSIS OF RITUAL: THE OEDIPUS MYTH

As a basis for discussion, let us consider the Oedipus myth, which has proved to be a useful basis for all sorts of theories, from Bachofen, to Freud, to Fromm, to Lévi-Strauss. Lévi-Strauss, in particular, argued that the Cadmus–Oedipus–Antigone myth could be understood, on the basis of internal evidence alone, as a resolution of a combined social-structural and theological dilemma. The Greeks worried over the problem of whether man had an autochthonous or a chthonous origin; and Lévi-Strauss solved this riddle, in the Oedipus myth, by asserting the equation: "The overrating of blood relations is to the underrating of blood relations as the attempt to escape autochthony is to the impossibility to succeed in it." This resolution, he further asserted, follows a logical model which is true of *all* myths, of all peoples, at all times.

Whether or nor the logical structure of the beliefs expressed in all myths follows a single formula we may doubt; in any case, that is not the problem to which we shall address ourselves. Rather, we ask, to what ritual or rituals is the Cadmus–Oedipus–Antigone trilogy relevant, and what is the nature of the relationship?

First, we observe that the Cadmus–Oedipus–Antigone trilogy is, in sum, a story told by Athenians of the tragic fate of the lineage of Cadmus and of the city of Thebes which he founded. Thebes was ruled over successively by Cadmus, his son Polydorus, his grandson Labdacus, his great-grandson Laius, his great-great-grandson Oedipus, and his fratricidal great-great-great-grandsons Eteocles and Polynices; it was finally (in the myth) destroyed by *their* sons, the great-great-great-great-grandsons of Cadmus. (In actuality, Thebes remained to war against Athens as an ally of Sparta.) But the doomed lineage of Cadmus had a divine branch. Cadmus' daughter Semele conceived the god Dionysus, male deity of fertility, by Zeus; and to Dionysus, and his female counterpart, Demeter, the Athenians were religiously devoted. The cult of Dionysus was celebrated on an annual calendar whose focal point, at Athens, was the great annual spring intensification festival at which the Dionysian rituals of possession were celebrated and, most importantly, tragic plays were performed as rituals in honor of the god. The plays of Sophocles, including the Oedipus tragedies, were among those written for and performed at this annual ceremony. The mysteries at Eleusis, furthermore, were performed in the name of Demeter and Dionysus on another occasion as an initiation rite for Athenian citizens, both men and women.

Second, each segment of the myth is, in effect, the social-maturational history of an individual; and each segment describes an abortive maturation. This feature in itself would seem to connect the myths with those rites of passage that accompany, and effect, the social transformations. But the myths do not describe a normal or successful process of maturation; rather, they each display a catastrophic failure of normal social development. Thus, if we divide each segment of the myth into three parts, corresponding to the ritual stages of separation from the old group, mystical experience of transformation, and reaggregation to the new group, we find a standard pattern. Let us see how it works.

CADMUS

Separation. Cadmus leaves home, accompanied by his mother, in order to seek and recover his sister, who has been ravished by the great god Zeus. On the journey his mother dies.

Mystical Experience. Cadmus fails to sacrifice a cow who has joined him after his mother's death, and instead kills a dangerous serpent sacred to Zeus. He sows the dragon's teeth in a field, and armed men spring up, engage in combat, and kill one another off, leaving only five survivors. Zeus, enraged by the death of the dragon, sentences Cadmus to eight years of atonement.

Reaggregation. Cadmus joins the Spartoi (the five survivors of the dragon-born men), marries a wife provided by Zeus, founds Thebes, and brings the alphabet to Greece. But he is unhappy, plagued by thoughts of doom, and he abandons Thebes. Finally, Zeus transforms him into a serpent and takes him away to Elysium.

OEDIPUS

Separation. Oedipus leaves home, but not by his own will, being exposed to die by his father Laius on the advice of an oracle who has predicted that Laius will be killed by his own son. But Oedipus is saved and brought up, ignorant of his lineage, by another family.

Mystical Experience. Oedipus, unable to identify himself, seeks advice from an oracle, who advises him to shun his native country lest he kill his father and lie with his mother. He flees his adopted country by mistake, and on the way meets and unknowingly kills his own father. He guesses the riddle of the Sphinx "What walks first on four legs, then on two, and at last on three?" by giving the answer "Man, who crawls, then walks upright, and at last leans on a cane," thereby delivering the country from this monster, which dies.

Reaggregation. Oedipus marries the widowed queen of the land that he has saved by guessing the riddle of the Sphinx; but this widow is, unknown to him at first, his own mother Jocasta, and thus his children are at once his own half-siblings. His sin discovered, he blinds himself, his mother commits suicide, and Oedipus leaves Thebes.

ANTIGONE

Separation. Antigone leaves her brothers and her home in Thebes with her father (who is also her half-brother), whom she nurses in his exile until his death.

Mystical Experience. After her brothers kill one another in fratricidal strife over the rulership of Thebes, Antigone violates the king's prohibition and buries her brother Polynices.

Reaggregation. Antigone is immured in a cavern, where she dies, along with her lover, whom she joins only in death.

As one examines these myths, a uniform pattern becomes evident. This pattern is, in effect, the negative of the normal ritual pattern. In each case, the protagonist apparently leaves home and family at the beginning, but not really: Cadmus takes his mother along, and seeks to find his sister; Oedipus doesn't even know that he has left home, and thus cannot distinguish between strangers and relatives; and Antigone takes her father along, and remains attached to her brothers. In each case, the protagonist fails to perform the proper rituals, or performs a ritual that is directly proscribed, or misunderstands the ritual: thus, Cadmus fails to sacrifice the cow, kills the sacred serpent, and sows dragon's teeth instead of grain; Oedipus misunderstands the oracle and improperly accepts the challenge of the Sphinx; and Antigone buries her brother in spite of the prohibition. In each case, the protagonist apparently joins a new group, but discovers no satisfaction in it: Cadmus allies himself with the Spartoi, marries and has children, but remains unhappy; Oedipus thinks to marry and have a family, and finds only disaster because he marries his mother after killing his father and is forced into shame, blindness, and exile; Antigone and her lover join each other only in death.

Thus, one can say that each component of the Oedipus myth is a precise negative transformation of the general program of a rite of passage. In mathematical terms, a negative identity matrix transforms the ritual sequence into the mythic sequence and myth back again into ritual:

$$(S, M, R)\begin{bmatrix} -1 & 0 & 0 \\ 0 & -1 & 0 \\ 0 & 0 & -1 \end{bmatrix} = (-S, -M, -R), \text{ and}$$

$$(-S, -M, -R)\begin{bmatrix} -1 & 0 & 0 \\ 0 & -1 & 0 \\ 0 & 0 & -1 \end{bmatrix} = (S, M, R).$$

Using the idea of positive and negative permutations from matrix algebra, we can generalize the relationship of ritual and myth in the following definition: every myth describes a sequence of events that corresponds, item for item, with a sequence of events in some ritual and is the product of a permutation matrix which may contain negative elements and a vector representing the ritual sequence.

A classification of myths springs immediately from this definition. There are, first of all, myths that *mirror the ritual sequences* and have a happy ending (they show the goal achieved). Such myths are produced by the identity operator. An example of such a mirroring of ritual by myth is the relation between the Christian Mass, or Holy Communion, and the story of the Last Supper of the eleven true disciples with Christ. Second, there are myths that are the *perfect negative of the ritual;* these myths are produced by what we may call a negative identity operator, which preserves sequence but transforms each set of acceptable ritual variants (or its behavioral referents) into the complementary set of unacceptable variants. The Oedipus trilogy, which we have just analyzed, is an example of this variety; so is the story of Judas, the false disciple, at the Last Supper. Third, there are myths that are *partial negatives,* produced by an identity operator which contains both positive and negative terms. The myth of the Great World Rim

Dweller, in relation to the curing rituals of the Iroquois False Faces, is such a partial negative, in that the central terms are negatives (repairing things transforms into damaging things, and being fed transforms into injury to the mouth and nose) but the initial and final terms are the same. Fourth, there are myths that are *true permutations*, produced by a nonidentity matrix operator with a negative element in the lower right-hand corner. In these, the proper order of ritual events is juggled, and the final term is negative. Some segments of the Trickster myth of the Winnebago illustrate this type and display the dire consequences of performing actions in the wrong order.

The instructional function of such myths, in relation to their rituals, is patent. They assert that the goal of ritual is achieved only if the proper rituals are performed in the proper order and that disaster (the negative of the goal) will occur if order is reversed or if improper elements (the negatives of the preceding terms) are introduced. It is not difficult to recognize, then, that—apart from the theological assumptions they convey—myths serve to rationalize rituals even—and perhaps especially—when they do not contain explicit descriptions of them.

The History of Religions

So far in the book we have presented a largely functional analysis of religion as it works in society. Our discussions of revitalization movements have, indeed, introduced some historical perspective, and the review of considerations of animal ritual and Paleolithic cults has laid the basis for a treatment of the evolution of religion. But the history of particular religious traits and cult institutions has been largely neglected. In the present section we shall consider some of the processes of diffusion and change, of combination and recombination, which account for the peregrinations of ritual practices and mythological themes over time and space.

Documentary Historical Approach

There are several traditional approaches to this problem. One such approach may be characterized as directly historical rather than comparative, since it is concerned with tracing the fate of particular religious manifestations from their points of origin; each such study confines itself to a specific form and follows it through its varying social and cultural contexts. Such histories of particular religions, and of particular cult institutions, symbols, or beliefs, have been the object of prodigious scholarly investigation and have evoked an awesomely large literature. Christianity and Islam, for instance, have been studied by religious historians in great detail; in consequence, the various sects and denominations of these faiths have also been chronicled extensively. Furthermore, in addition to purely historical studies of these great religions, there have been a multitude of approaches—theological, metaphysical, philosophical, and comparative—whose aim has been to explicate underlying assumptions and principles, and to interpret the great faiths' essential meaning or identity.

Apart from their contributions to the archives of religion, such studies tend to show that the *forms* of religion—the particular signs and symbols, the particular ritual acts, the particular institutional structures, the particular metaphysical propositions, the particular value assertions—have an extraordinary constancy. The Roman Catholic Church, for instance, has been able to preserve much of its formal structure intact through a span of nearly 1500 years; and these millennia of its life have been, indeed, the most changeable in the history of mankind. Evidently religious ritual and belief can survive over extraordinarily long periods of time, in the face of extensive changes in technology, political structure, and other aspects of culture. Evidently, also, the forms of religion are extraordinarily diffusible: the symbols and customs of a great religion, such as the Church of Rome, are used across the world by millions of persons of the most diverse racial and cultural backgrounds. Thus, from the example of Christian religious history alone, the anthropologist can infer that the forms of religious ritual and belief can spread, and endure, over vast expanses of time and space. It is not necessary to subscribe to the more extreme varieties of direct historicism (such as the heliocentric school of Perry, which attempts to trace the fate of Egyptian religious ideas) in order to be convinced by direct historical evidence.

Comparative Historical Approach

The historical approach to religion has generally been dominated by this insight into religion's ability to spread and to endure, but not all scholars have pursued religion in a direct historiographic way. Several scholarly traditions, individually divergent in interest, unite in a concern with the demonstration by means of comparative ethnological, rather than documentary historical, evidence of this apparent tendency of religious forms, both Christian and non-Christian, to spread geographically and to survive chronologically. Early works of this kind in England, by Frazer, Lang, Tylor, and Marett, contributed importantly to the formulation of evolutionary theories of culture. Perhaps the most celebrated of these comparative historical traditions is that of the *Kulturkreislehre*, and its successors of the German historical school, which has attempted to trace the history of the idea of a high god from an era of primeval revelation, through various phases of degeneration and distortion, and across continents and oceans by processes of diffusion. We have already alluded in Chapter I to this tradition of comparative historical scholarship. Although the notion of culture circles as a set of successively superimposed complexes of extraordinarily wide distribution has been pretty much abandoned, even by the German historical school, and although the thesis of primeval monotheism and degeneration has been of greater interest perhaps to theologians than to the anthropological profession, a legacy remains. This is a respect for the diffusibility of culture traits, for the philosophical sophistication of technologically simple peoples, and for the role of processes of cultural fatigue (conceived as a degeneration, or as an increasingly sterile formalization, of originally vital concepts whose "true" meaning becomes lost in the course of time and with distance from their origin).

The difficulty with this kind of comparative historical scholarship, for most American readers, is that too often it is neither good history nor useful comparison. The same criticism that was once leveled at the comparative method used by nineteenth-century evolutionists must be applied to the European historical comparative treatment of religion. Bits and pieces of custom are taken from a variety of cultures, scattered all over the world; a similarity, or complementarity, of concept is pointed out; and then either some common origin, or some universal psychological principle that explains their common inner meaning is manufactured. Vague notions of archaic mentality are invoked to explain apparently similar rituals and myths. Thus the interesting work of Mircea Eliade, which seeks to find the meaning of similar customs in all parts of the world, contains such exercises as the following attempt to explain the significance of New Year ceremonials among early Babylonians, Hittites, Egyptians, Christians, Persians, Jews, Chinese, and Hindu Indians:

> In the primitive mind, the old time consisted of the profane succession of all the events without meaning, events, that is, with no archetypal models; "history" is the remembrance of those events, of what can only really be called "unmeanings" or even sins (inasmuch as they are divergences from the archetypal norms). As we saw, to primitives, true history is not that, but myth; all that true history records are the archetypal actions displayed by the gods, the ancestors or the culture heroes, during the mythical time, *in illo tempore;* to the primitive, all repetitions of archetypes take place outside profane time; it follows then, that, on the one hand, such actions cannot be "sins," divergences from the norm, and on the other, they have no connection with ordinary succession, the "old time" that is periodically abolished. The driving out of demons and spirits, the confession of sins, the purifications and, specially, the symbolic return of the primeval chaos—all this indicates the abolition of profane time, of the old time during which occurred all the meaningless events and all the deviations. [Eliade, 1949b, p. 401.]

Such interpretation methodologically goes beyond the observation of the manifest similarity of some religious forms and functions in more or less diverse cultures, to postulate a single and specific "inner meaning" or historical connection. When a special type of mythopoeic, or pre-logical, or sacral mentality is invented to account for this inner meaning, and some sort of simple degenerative process from an *Ur*-form (for example, desacralization or formalization) is posited to account for the cross-cultural differences, then interpretation becomes mystical. Similar criticisms must be made of certain European psychoanalytic approaches to the comparative history of religion (Jung [1938], Jung and Kerényi [1949], and so on). Campbell, in his summaries (1949, 1959) of the confluent traditions of the European cultural historical school and the European (and primarily Jungian) psychological historical school, displays both the virtues and the vices of the approach. Speculation about inner meaning is, as a matter of fact, useful as a way of phrasing hypotheses concerning the goals and functions of religious ritual, and about the world view that rationalizes the myth that rationalizes the ritual. But to take speculations about inner meaning as facts to be explained by still further historical and comparative speculations, with no more evidence available than a rich miscellany of illustrations, is less than convincing.

Where the aims are less global, however, and attention is directly focused on temporal and geographical continuities demonstrable by detailed evidence—historical, archaeological, or ethnographic—then the comparative historical approach is useful. Thus, for example, Hallowell's (1926) treatment of bear ceremonialism in the Northern Hemisphere, Maringer's (1960) review of the archaeological distribution of the bear cult in the Paleolithic, and Frazer's (1911) and Levy's (1946) treatments of the cult of the mother goddess in the circum-Mediterranean area are convincing demonstrations of historical continuity that do not require allusion to psychic universals and vague notions of diffusion and degeneration for support. In more recent times, likewise, it has been possible to show the historical development of individual beliefs, rituals, or cult institutions. Thus, for instance, Löwith's *Meaning in History* (1949), Bury's classic *The Idea of Progress* (1921), and Lovejoy's (1936) treatment of the ideas of the Great Chain of Being trace the evolution of a particular religious world view. The old circum-Mediterranean theory of secular cycles (for example, the Gold, Silver, Bronze, and Iron Age sequences) is transformed into the Christian notion of a singular episode of creation, degeneration, and apocalypse, and that in turn into the more modern ideas of progress and evolution through divine guidance. In like manner, the forms and functions of particular cult institutions can be followed historiographically through various transformations in time and space to show both constancy and change. Thus the transformations of Christianity from a millenarian, apocalyptic, Jewish sect led by the fanatical Messiah Jesus, into a Gentile Graeco-Roman sect led by Paul, and eventually into the giant institutions of the Roman church and its offshoots are chronicled in detail by a host of scholars (including, for the first two transformations, Schweitzer [1910, 1958]; and R. Goodenough [1954]).

Thus one may conclude that, when a particular cult institution or individual belief or ritual is considered over time within a specifically delimited geographical area, it is possible by the use of archaeological, ethnological, and historical data to show processes of diffusion, of change in form, and of adaptive variations in meaning and function. Furthermore, such studies do demonstrate an impressive durability of religious forms over time and space. But this approach is not promising where nearly universal forms are involved, such as shamanism or the idea of an imitative magic or belief in some high god, however otiose, or the conception of rites of passage as, metaphorically, processes of death and rebirth or the notion of supernatural power itself. With respect to such fundamental forms of religious experience, the comparative historical approach can do little more than demonstrate their ubiquity. The explanation of the origin and "inner meaning" of these broad categories of religious experience would seem to demand frankly psychological and functional research approaches which seek to isolate and describe those general psychosocial processes in man and society from which religious experience of one type or another may be deduced. Thus, for example, the idea of the Keeper of the Game is a widespread concept, as Jensen (1951) points out. But the comparativist culture historian who would essay to explain the distribution of this particular mythological belief by diffusion from some ancient *Ur*-cultural center must engage in too much speculation if he tries to trace the details of the process, even though the general argument is plausible. The field of comparative folklore and mythology is filled with problems of this kind. The myth of the world-destroying flood, the concept of the world tree, the mandala symbol, the Trickster myth, and many other specific combinations of forms may very well have originated in a particular place, diffused broadly, and survived for an extraordinarily long time, with multitudinous changes in both form and function as the form was adapted to different settings. What began in one cultural setting as a shamanic trait may, in different times and places, become an individualistic practice, or an element of an elaborate ecclesiastical institution.

Thus historical and comparative treatments cannot be considered to be alternative to functional ones; rather, they show the survival of formal structures in a diversity of functional settings. No doubt this durability of arbitrary ritual and mythological form is possible because of a plasticity of function, and this plasticity of function, in turn, is perhaps the result, not so much of the universality of certain archetypal "ideas" or "themes" which are indissolubly linked to form, as of the very ambiguity of their meaning. Like inkblots, inherently ambiguous symbols can be given new meanings appropriate to the perceptual needs of widely varying individuals and cultures.

The Evolution of Religion

Stages in the Evolution and Goals of Religion

Apart from the combination of functional and historical processes, which account for many of the variations in religious behavior from society to society and in one society over time, are there any grand evolutionary processes in religion comparable to those postulated for technology and social organization? The older efforts to outline evolutionary stages of religion, as we have seen, have not survived scholarly criticism. Tylor's celebrated scheme of a progressive simplification of theology, from animism through polytheism to monotheism, is vulnerable at both ends of the continuum. At the animistic level, concepts of a high god are already present as well as the pre-animistic notion of *mana*; and modern monotheisms, as careful study clearly shows, are rarely devoid of an elaborate pantheon of lesser spirits. Frazer's familiar argument that the evolutionary sequence begins with magicians (conceived as prescientists), proceeds through divine magicians and divine kings, and eventuates in priesthoods dedicated to true gods (while science and technology diverge to deal with empirical reality) has little evidence to support it as a general scheme because of the difficulties inherent in making a sharp distinction between magic (that is, control of *mana*) and religion (that is, control of supernatural beings).

But these views, although they are not acceptable as a general theory of the evolution of religious social structures, contain the germ of a valid model. They propose a beginning in what we have called shamanic cult institutions and a culmination in ecclesiastical cult institutions; this simple sequence is implied in the scale of cult institutions and of societies ranked along this scale which we introduced for taxonomic purposes in Chapter II. We may, indeed, use an adaptation of the scalar taxonomy as the nucleus for an evolutionary statement of religion: That religion began with (1) societies that possessed both individualistic and shamanic cults; proceeded to (2) societies with individualistic, shamanic, and communal cults; then went to (3) societies with individual, shamanic, and communal cults, plus ecclesiastical cults devoted to a pantheon of Olympian deities; and finally produced (4) societies with individualistic, shamanic, and communal cults, plus ecclesiastical cults devoted to a singular monotheistic conception of deity —that is, a high god who, while not usually the sole supernatural entity or manifestation, nevertheless has unquestioned sovereignty and ultimate power over both man and all other supernatural entities.

Along with this sequence, each stage defined by the presence of cults characterized by a particular combination of theological belief and social organization, there have occurred certain broad changes in the attention paid to the goals of religion. These changes would seem to be at least four in number: (1) The importance of technological ritual and of therapeutic and nontherapeutic rituals, in which the goal is the direct manipulation of physical nature, both human and nonhuman, progressively declines as technology and socioeconomic institutions become increasingly effective; (2) there is increasing conscious concern with formulating religious belief as a system of metaphysical thought, internally consistent and capable of explaining all phenomena observable in the world; (3) as religion accumulates an ever larger establishment of material apparatus and personnel, and as it develops its relationships to increasingly hierarchical social, political, and economic institutions, it becomes more and more concerned with resolving problems of human morality—that is, with defining good and bad behavior in relations between peers and between persons in positions of relative super- and subordination; and (4) as cultural change accelerates, as population expands, and as social density rises, the problems of individual and social welfare become more challenging to religion.

The Effect of Technological Development upon Religion

These postulated evolutionary changes in religion are, theoretically, related to certain evolutionary changes in technology and social organization. In regard to the first process, one may observe that as capability of technological control advances over a phenomenon that religious ritual has traditionally attempted to govern, religious cult institutions first attempt to deny the adequacy and/or propriety of the new technology; then, as demonstration of its value becomes unimpeachable, they attempt to take control of the technology itself; and finally, they abandon it to secular interests and concentrate on the moral implications of the accomplished technological change for social organization. Thus, for example, in the areas where the so-called "hydraulic societies" developed, with elaborate irrigation works administered by political bureaucracies, one must assume that before the irrigation technology was developed, communal or ecclesiastical cult institutions performed rituals intended to control rainfall; that, as the effectiveness of irrigation methods became apparent, after questioning the impiety of human intervention in a divinely controlled process the religious cult institutions joined forces with secular organization to ritualize and administer the new technology; and that finally, of course, the political and economic institutions assumed complete control over the technology, while religion concerned itself with metaphysics and the morality of human behavior.

One can observe religious bodies taking a similar role in a more recent, and still proceeding, process of this kind—namely, birth control. At first, the religious institutions attempt to handle the fertility problems of individual families and to deal with the social problems resulting from over- or under-population, by prayer and other ritual devices. Then, as the capability of effective birth control by contraceptive means is developed by secular persons, the ecclesiastical bodies question its religious propriety. As they perceive that the innovation is nevertheless gaining acceptance, however, and that their own ritual control is comparatively weak, they attempt to take over the technology or to develop a technical modification that is not inconsistent with existing ritual and belief. Finally, they abandon the issue, giving up to other institutions all technological and administrative questions and confining themselves to metaphysical and moral considerations. The Roman Catholic Church, at present, is at the point where it can no longer effectively question the desirability of some sort of birth control technology on religious grounds. It is currently attempting to control the practice of contraception by recommending one particular form; and one can expect that the Church will soon find it expedient to abandon the technological issue altogether and to concentrate on developing a metaphysical rationale, and a morality, which will justify the effective and responsible administration of the contraceptive solution for a problem that once could be approached only by ritual or by abstinence.

If one considers the fact that technology, developed by an increasingly wide and profound body of scientific knowledge, has for tens of thousands of years been finding workable solutions for the problems to which technological and therapeutic rituals have traditionally been the only human recourse, one need not find it surprising that there has been a continuing segregation of religion from technological issues and a continuing diversion of religious attention to the social and psychological transformations necessary to exploit new technology. This process has resulted in a transformation of religion itself. The accumulation of technological successes in human culture has been forcing religion to give up its technological pretensions and to concern itself with metaphysics, with morality, with the welfare of the human personality and of human society.

Thus the increasing bigness of technology has been, over the millennia, continuously redirecting the attention of ritual and myth from technology to man himself as a thinking and feeling social being. The balance of attention has been moving away from technological and therapeutic goals and toward ideological, salvational, and revitalization goals. In situations where religious cult institutions compete for human allegiance, whether of the masses or of the managerial class, those cults are chosen to survive which do not interfere with rational secular control of technology and which offer aid in solving psychological and social problems. The category of psychological and social problems is divided into two classes. In one category are those perennial and universal human problems or processes, either immune to technological change or at least not yet effectively touched by technology, for which religious ritual as a means of inducing transformations of state is for most people more effective than any other procedure. Such individually experienced problems as death itself (which can be postponed but not prevented by technology), birth (which also can be postponed and made less frequent for individual parents but which cannot be completely prevented without societal suicide), life-cycle crises such as puberty and retirement—all these remain subject to effective ritual influence.

In the second category are those psychological and social problems that are, at least in part, the result of the very technological changes that have diverted religious attention: population increase, urbanization, industrialization, technological unemployment, war, conquest, social inequalities, and the like. In this arena one typically observes a considerable lag in the development and dissemination of world views, ethical or moral codes, and rites of passage that would be optimally fitted to the effective use of the new technology. The complex arrangements of human attitude and behavior necessary to living in large cities, for instance, are not discovered along with brick-making, the wheel, iron, massive architecture, and surplus-producing agriculture. A whole assemblage of new social roles is implied; further technological innovations—for bringing in water, getting rid of wastes, controlling fire, and so on—must be invented as the city grows. These in turn will involve more new roles; and the process of escalation between technical and social innovation will continue for generations, for centuries, or indefinitely. In this process, new codes of behavior must be introduced that will make moral issues out of actions that once were matters of individual option, such as waste disposal or the quarantining of sick persons or the contribution of labor, produce, or money to public enterprises or discrimination against minorities. And these issues, in turn, need to be incorporated by ritual practitioners into *rites de passage*, communal ceremonies, in exercises of spiritual salvation, in order to ensure the survival of the social system. Furthermore, if serious social disorganization occurs, whole new patterns of society must be rapidly conceived and rapidly introduced, not merely by authoritative fiat, but with maximum public support. In enterprises of this kind, religious institutions, as we have seen, often serve as a kind of center for evaluating the feedback information from cultural change and for proposing minor or major corrections in the aims and performance of the system. Religion, in other words, by reason of its interest in over-all levels of organization in the individual and in society, is frequently in a position to diagnose and treat not only old but also new disorders.

THE COMPETITION FROM SCIENCE AND GOVERNMENT

But, along with religion, two other institutions have been developing capabilities along these same lines; they are science and government. Thus, even while religion has, over the millennia, been responding to the successes of technology by increasingly concentrating its attention on problems of human behavior, these two other institutions have been becoming ever more serious competitors. They compete with religion in different spheres, to be sure, and are themselves not fully allied. But the competition is mounting. Science competes with religious mythology, with its metaphysics, with its belief system; government competes with religious ritual by introducing ritual of its own.

The simple, primitive relationship of science and religion, described by Malinowski (1925) as being the relationship between two complementary systems of thought, dealing, respectively, with the knowable and controllable, on the one hand, and with the unknowable and uncontrollable, on the other, has not been valid for thousands of years in areas of urban civilization. Here, in a process that can be historically documented at least from the age of Pericles, religious belief has been repeatedly challenged by scientific knowledge and the rational habits of scientific thought. In these contests, whenever the battle is fully joined, and both parties commit themselves to the struggle, science *always* wins. This, indeed, can be stated as a cultural law: that, because of science's reliance upon demonstrable proof, perceptible by any normal human being, and religion's reliance upon the fit between belief and ritual, any serious intellectual conflict between science and religion must always end either in a victory for science or in a draw (for if a religious assertion happens to be true, science will sooner or later assert it, too).

The conflict between religion and government probably began, as a serious issue, only when large secular bureaucracies became necessary for the administration of human behavior in urban living and in large technological enterprises such as the creation and operation of irrigation systems. In pre-bureaucratic societies, there is no occasion for competition to arise. Political decisions are made by the same persons who perform religious rituals; religious ritual and belief are applied to so wide a range of human concerns and activities that the boundary between secular and sacred separates different actions rather than different people and places. Although it is something of an overstatement to characterize all activities of a primitive community as sacred, the diffusion of ritual and myth into many areas of behavior precludes the development of competition between religious and secular ritualists. Even in the early urban states, the ecclesiastical bureaucracy tended to overlap extensively with the secular bureaucracy: royal roles were usually rationalized as divine—or, at least, priestly—roles, and priests performed many of the political and bureaucratic functions of the state. But, as time went on, an increasingly marked separation of church and state developed, *de facto* if not *de jure*, and this separation in most nations has now reached a point where only minimal *religious* ritual and rationale are employed to facilitate the business of government and the processes of mobilizing political power.

This does not mean, however, that secular politicians and bureaucrats are not concerned with ritual or myth. To the contrary, they eagerly turn to ritual and to myth-making to achieve some of the very same kinds of goals—ideological, salvational, and revitalizational—at which religion has aimed. In states administered by Communist politicians and bureaucrats, there is conscious and deliberate competition for control of ritual and mythic access to the population. There are secular (that is, non-supernaturally rationalized) rites of passage marking events in the life cycle (such as marriage and the achievement of adult status); there are massive communal ceremonies (such as May Day); there is a kind of ecclesia (the Communist Party apparatus itself); there are "sacred" figures (such as Marx and Lenin), "sacred" places (the tombs of Party leaders), "sacred" symbols (the hammer and sickle), and "sacred" texts (the works of Marx, Engels, and Lenin); there are elaborate myth construction and metaphysical speculation (dialectic materialism); there is forced conversion (by the rituals of "brainwashing"). In Nazi Germany and Fascist Italy, and in fact in all totalitarian states, there is the same kind of political exploitation of secular ritual—charismatic leader, sacred symbolism, mass revival meetings, texts, myth-making, the sacred party, and so on—again, in direct competition with at least some of the religious ecclesiastical cult institutions and their congregations (very frequently the Jews). Even in the United States, where church and state are theoretically noncompetitive, there is an extensive and powerful group of secular cult institutions—in the schools, in medical institutions, in clubs, in neighborhoods—which administer ritual and maintain myth with little or no supernatural rationale.

A convenient example of a type of secular cult institution commonly found in the United States is the Greek-letter college fraternity and sorority. These organizations, elaborately organized on a national basis, with "chapters" on individual campuses, serve the obvious function of providing board and lodging to college students. But their principal function is to accomplish an identity change in their members, transforming them from boys and girls into college men and women who can claim membership in an elite group. They conduct, in other words, the principal puberty rituals for many thousands of members of our society. Furthermore, they do so by using the same essential ritual process that has been described for similar rituals in tribal societies such as those of Australian aborigines and West African Negroes. Typically, the pledge is isolated from parents and other adults and from less-favored peers and is subjected to a gradually intensifying series of stresses (fear and anxiety, fatigue, sleeplessness, physical torture, and cognitve disorientation). Then, with dissociation accomplished, the suggestion of the new status, with its rights and duties, is made to the pledge in a group setting. Finally, the novitiate is admitted to membership in the adult group of society members (Leemon [1965]). What is particularly interesting about these rites of passage is the jealousy they arouse, not so much in nonfraternity members (although this may exist), but in the administrators of other rites of passage for freshmen on college campuses—guidance counselors, deans, personnel officers, and religious officials. These administrators correctly (and painfully) perceive that he who controls the rites of passage controls the society and that, since they cannot offer membership in their own group to those whom they wish to mold, they cannot conduct adequate rituals.

Another kind of secular ritual in American society is that whose function is to maintain caste boundaries—and ritual gaps—in Negro-white relationships. Many conventional rituals, particularly in the South, are intended to serve as constant reminders to both whites and Negroes of their superiority-inferiority relationship: customs of mutual address (Negroes being addressed by first name by whites, and whites by title and last name by Negroes), seating in public conveyances, white priority in competitive encounters (such as meetings on narrow sidewalks), and so forth and so on all serve the same purpose. They are boundary-maintaining ideological rituals par excellence. Furthermore, Negroes have been traditionally excluded from many of those rites of passage—religious and secular—by which the immature white is initiated into adult society: coming-out parties, Greek-letter societies, dances, and graduation ceremonies in all-white schools and churches. From this viewpoint, the recent Negro civil rights demonstrations have been, in addition to their realistic function in securing access to various services, also rites of passage for their Negro participants. By participating in a demonstration, being beaten, fined, and jailed, the demonstrator is in effect initiated into a Negro adult group whose identity is very different from that of the traditional Uncle Tom, who was socialized into an identity that overtly accepted (and only covertly condemned) his subordinate social status.

It should be evident, then, that in contemporary industrial societies secular organizations can and do make use of the same ritual processes for inducing the same kinds of transformations of state as religion traditionally has done. The challenge to religion is a ubiquitous one and is raised even by persons who in their own lives are devout Sunday churchgoers. They may come to feel that certain transformations of state, such as the development and maintenance of efficient performance of such secular tasks as equalitarianism, good citizenship, patriotism, personal hygiene, and studiousness are too important to be left to the vagaries of denominational differences and therefore demand coordinated secular attention.

The Future of Religion

We have seen that religion, under the combined assault of science and politics, has been more and more restricted in its field of application. We may very well ask, therefore, what the future course of this evolutionary process is likely to be.

In answering this question, it must be kept in mind that the definition of religion employed in this work includes explicit supernaturalism (including *mana*) as an indispensable element. As we have pointed out, secular faiths exploit the same ritual process as religions; they differ in that their system of belief (the mythology, ethics, and metaphysics) that gives meaning to ritual is explicitly nontheological. There does not appear to be much likelihood that secular cult institutions will disappear, abandoning their fields of application to religion once again. Indeed, they can be expected to enlarge their scope of influence and coordinate their belief systems ever more effectively, and to become, perhaps, more and more "religious" in all respects save supernatural belief. Thus, in starkest form, the question about the evolutionary fate of religion is a question about the fate of supernaturalism.

To the question put in this way, the answer must be that the evolutionary future of religion is extinction. Belief in supernatural beings and in supernatural forces that affect nature without obeying nature's laws will erode and become only an interesting historical memory. To be sure, this event is not likely to occur in the next generation; the process will very likely take several hundred years, and there will probably always remain individuals, or even occasional small cult groups, who respond to hallucination, trance, and obsession with a supernaturalist interpretation. But as a cultural trait, belief in supernatural powers is doomed to die out, all over the world, as a result of the increasing adequacy and diffusion of scientific knowledge and of the realization by secular faiths that supernatural belief is not necessary to the effective use of ritual. The question of whether such a denouement will be good or bad for humanity is irrelevant to the prediction; the process is inevitable.

But the functional consequences, desirable and undesirable, of such an event as the elimination of supernaturalism from the human cultural repertoire, are very much worth considering. Under some circumstances, the disappearance of supernaturalism would have very unfortunate consequences. The secular faiths which move into the field left by religion may permit the same attitudes to develop toward the state, and toward political figures, as commonly have been directed toward supernaturals (and this substitution of state and leader for supernatural force and person can, indeed, be predicted from the concepts of Durkheim and his followers as being just as inevitable as the demise of supernaturalism itself). To the extent that this substitution does occur, some very undesirable things will happen. The intense ambivalences of love and hate, the devouring dependencies, the masochistic longings, and other emotional debris which in religious systems are displaced in part from human objects onto supernatural ones, and are there reorganized and resolved in symbolic compromises, will when confined to the society itself intensify rather than reduce social problems. As critics of religion have often pointed out, many crimes have been committed in the name of God; but even more crimes are likely to be committed if the same people have no God. The religious person who reveres the Divine Being is left intellectually free to criticize the state and the political leader, to see them as "only human," liable to error and deserving of sympathy or in need of restraint. But if this same person were to place upon the state and its officials the reverence he once bestowed upon God, he would be unable either to sympathize or to criticize; the political process, in other words, would be contaminated with precisely those attitudes that critics, in misplaced antipathy, have found so unsavory in religion itself. The "cult of personality" replaces the cults of the gods. Thus, given the same spectrum of human nature with which we work today, the decline of supernaturalism would, in purging mankind of a benign cognitive error, only afflict his social relationships with matter which in the tissues of society is malignant.

There are several possible ways of forestalling this undesirable turn of events. One, of course, is to establish an ideal society, of the sort that Freud (1928) envisaged in *The Future of an Illusion:* a society in which, by virtue of an optimal growth-environment for children, belief in supernaturals would not be necessary for a non-neurotic humanity. But Freud's was a counsel of perfection: mankind must become mature before he can abandon the support of the gods; and it can be taken as axiomatic that any proposal for social or cultural change that requires, for its workability, a perfect humanity, is in fact unworkable. Thus, to plan to prepare man for the demise of the gods by establishing in advance the perfect system of child-rearing is futile. To be sure, all possible improvement in the way of maturation must be sought; but the gods will die before mankind grows up.

Another alternative is for the existing theistic religions gradually to desupernaturalize. The simplest method is to change, gradually and undramatically, the meaning of the terms for supernaturals and thus to become, without abandoning their rituals or their texts, in effect secular. This process is already visible in many progressive religious groups, like the Unitarians, who seek a metaphysical union with science and an ethical union with wise and practical secular institutions. And it is this course which the recent "God is dead" movement among liberal theologians would seem to foreshadow. A more radical approach to desupernaturalization is to delete both theistic terms and theistic concepts. An "atheistic theology" must anticipate both a greater attention to improving man's lot on earth and also a rapprochement with science and technology. Some scientists and engineers foresee a time nearly upon us when the curve of technological progress will level off. When travel time to any point on the globe is reduced to a few hours, further increases in speed are of little importance; when computers process information at nearly the speed of light, there will be little advantage in approaching the universal constant. Thus both science and religion, in this view, will need to meld metaphysically and join in the resolution of those human social problems that will remain after the ultimate technology is reached (*vide* Platt [n.d.]).

But whether the process be one of desupernaturalizing a traditional theology, leaving its terms intact, or of introducing a whole new atheistic vocabulary, the metaphysical merging of science and religion requires the invention of what may be called—with due recognition of its apparent absurdity—a nontheistic theology. The properties of such a theology must be: (1) that it postulate no supernatural being or force; (2) that it not contradict scientific knowledge in any particular (although, of course, it may—along with any other body of thought—raise questions for scientific investigation); (3) that the entities that are the elements of its pantheon be such that they can be (in psychoanalytic terminology) cathected; (4) that these entities not be any recognizable human person, group, or institution; (5) that the belief system, including its theology, mythology, and ethics, by its emphasis on an organization of relevant motives and roles be an effective rationale for particular rituals, including secular rituals, which are designed to induce socially and culturally desirable transformations of state; and (6) that this belief system also rationalize an appropriate ecclesiastical organization (which must be independent of secular cult institutions).

Now this is, indeed, a formidable assignment, and my own theological imagination is hardly equal to the task of presenting such a pantheon, let alone the associated mythology and ethics, in the next few pages. Various efforts in this direction, of course, have been made by distinguished thinkers. One recalls, for instance, the anthropologist Margaret Lantis' suggestion that "friendship" be established as "the symbol of a new religion" (Lantis [1950b]);

the existential ethical philosophies; Julian Huxley's *Religion Without Revelation* (1941), which invokes evolution as a theological concept; the humanistic idea of emergent godliness; the notion of increasing organization; and so on. It would seem, however, that whatever theological entity is chosen, it must include a teleological aspect; a notion of purpose in this sense must be invoked in the rationalization of ritual. Perhaps, indeed, it matters far less what the metaphysical definition of this entity should be than what its inherent purposes are. A certain flexibility of meaning, a friendly ambiguity in the positive characteristics of the entity, will permit its cathexis more readily than would a sharp and precise definition.

But, with respect to the purpose of the entity, there can be far less ambiguity. The purposes must include the accomplishment of those ideological, salvational, and revitalizational transformations that are considered essential for the creation and maintenance of healthy personalities in a healthy society. Thus there is required a fairly specific theory of what constitutes a healthy personality in our society, what are the desired roles of an adult, what sort of society it is or should be. Indeed, a study of man and society, and of the values that ritual is intended to serve, must in a sense precede, or at least be conducted *pari passu* with, any theological formulation; otherwise, the new "deity" might prove irrelevant.

Finally, the nontheistic theology must at all times be aware that ritual is the cutting edge of faith. Without ritual not only supernatural religion and secular faith but also our new nontheistic cult are sterile. Therefore, if it is not to abandon the field entirely to secular faiths, the new theology must actively embrace the essential ritual process, not merely admit it intellectually. The new religion must provide rites of passage, particularly for the adolescent-to-adult transformation; it must provide rituals of salvation for those adults who, feeling alienated from the processes of their society, have grown depressed and cynical; and it may need to mount a vigorous revitalization movement.

At the present time it would seem that there is little space for such a nontheistic religion, and that it would be quickly ground to pieces or elbowed into obscurity by competing supernaturally religious and politically secular cult institutions. Nevertheless, it is conceivable that both of these types of system may fail to cope with certain major social problems of our time and of the future, thereby leaving the way open for a new religion to solve them.

These major social problems are obvious enough: population control, technological unemployment, intergroup conflict (both intra- and international), the dialectic between bureaucratic administration and individual initiative, and personality development (particularly with respect to identity structure). The production and distribution of goods and services and the provision of medical care, which once were major social issues, are now, in principle at least, amenable to adequate technological control, and there have been developed, over centuries, more or less satisfactory principles of social behavior relevant to the operation of these technologies. These principles, indeed, do not vary much even between Communist and Free World societies; the issues being fought over have more to do with the aforementioned regions of uncertainty than with the social structure or technology.

It would seem, then, that the new faith which we are imagining should concentrate its attention on the nature of the optimal solution of these social problems, and on the associated ethical principles, rather than on those matters relating to technology and technological education, which are already relatively well in hand and for which secular rituals of various kinds are readily available. Furthermore, such a faith should be truly international in reference, a catholic faith in the generic sense, raising a standard to which the righteous of all nations can repair, attending to issues that are of universal concern while eschewing partisan involvement with the particular tactical choices that divide mankind.

To a degree, therefore, we are talking about a revitalization movement. I have discussed the process of revitalization movements elsewhere and need not repeat that discussion here. But one tactical point might be added. Although revitalization movements proselytize, they are not indiscriminate in their recruitment of disciples and followers, at least in their early phases. On the contrary, the successful movement is an elite group, requiring that new members undergo a strenuous and transforming rite of passage, excluding insofar as possible the pure opportunist, the compulsive joiner, the lazy and cowardly, and seeking only the true believer who will commit his life to the cause. Thus the new faith at first must be open to all except the uncommitted; membership must be a prize; the aspirant must reach out for the way of salvation. Otherwise the faith will be diluted by desultory believers who continuously consume the energies of the devout without change in themselves or contribution to others. The organization must not become dependent for its self-respect, as some traditional religious organizations now are, upon feeling righteous for performing unsolicited favors for those who do not believe in it, and upon securing half-minded attention to evangelical pleas and half-hearted expressions of agreement from those who out of courtesy have been persuaded to listen to its message.

In conclusion of this discussion of the nontheistic religion which evolutionary processes are generating, we must reiterate several points, which are in effect a recapitulation of the argument of this book:

1. Ritual is instrumentally primary and belief system is secondary.

2. Ritual aims at accomplishing five types of transformation of state: technological, therapeutic, ideological, salvational, and revitalizational.

3. The function of ritual is to prepare a human being for the efficient performance of a task by communicating an image of a highly organized world system, already described in the belief system, and by suggesting a role during a ritual learning process which follows the law of dissociation.

4. In a viable religion, appropriately fitted rituals and belief systems accomplish those transformations of state that are functionally necessary to the development and maintenance of the kind of society that exists or that the ritual practitioners want.

5. Scientific belief and secular ritual, in a long-continuing evolutionary process, are restricting the application of religious belief and ritual, both theistic and nontheistic, to the ideological, salvational, and revitalizational spheres, and are increasingly replacing religious ritual and belief even in these areas.

6. Viable faiths of the future will be nontheistic and will not "deify" either person or state.

Bibliography

ACKERKNECHT, E. H

1942a "Problems of Primitive Medicine," *Bulletin of the History of Medicine*, 11:503–521.

1942b "Psychopathology, Primitive Medicine and Culture," *Bulletin of the History of Medicine*, 12:545–574.

ALLPORT, GORDON

1950 *The Individual and His Religion*. New York: Macmillan, 1953.

ARIETI, S.

1956 "Some Basic Problems Common to Anthropology and Modern Psychiatry," *American Anthropologist*, 58:26–39.

BACHOFEN, J. J.

1861 *Das Mutterrecht*. Stuttgart: Krais & Hoffman.

BACHRACH, ARTHUR J.

1962 "An Experimental Approach to Superstitious Behavior," *Journal of American Folklore*, 75:1–9.

BARLOW, NORA (ed.)

1945 *Charles Darwin and the Voyage of the Beagle*. London: Pilot Press.

BEALS, RALPH, and SIEGEL, BERNARD

1960 "Pervasive Factionalism," *American Anthropologist*, 62:394–417.

BENEDICT, RUTH FULTON

1922 "The Vision in Plains Culture," *American Anthropologist*, 24:1–23.

1923 *The Concept of the Guardian Spirit in Native North America.* American Anthropological Association, Memoir No. 29.

1934 *Patterns of Culture.* New York: Pelican Books, 1946.

1938 "Continuities and Discontinuities in Cultural Conditioning," *Psychiatry,* 1:161–167.

Bettelheim, Bruno

1954 *Symbolic Wounds, Puberty Rites, and the Envious Male.* New York: Free Press of Glencoe.

Boas, Franz

1911 *The Mind of Primitive Man.* New York: Macmillan, 1938.

Bohannon, Paul

1958 "Extra-processual Events in Tiv Political Institutions," *American Anthropologist,* 60:1–12.

Boisen, Anton J.

1936 *The Exploration of the Inner World.* New York: Harper & Bros.

Burridge, Kenelm

1960 *Mambu.* New York: Humanities Press.

Bury, J. B.

1921 *The Idea of Progress.* London: Macmillan.

Callaway, Henry

1870 *The Religious System of the Amazulu.* London: The Folk-Lore Society, 1884.

Campbell, Joseph

1949 *The Hero with a Thousand Faces.* New York: Pantheon Books.

1959 *The Masks of God, Primitive Mythology,* Vol. 1. New York: Viking Press (2 vols.).

Cannon, Walter B.

1942 "The 'Voodoo' Death," *American Anthropologist,* 44:169–181.

Cantril, Hadley

1941 *The Psychology of Social Movements.* New York: John Wiley.

CARPENTER, EDMUND S.

1959 "Alcohol in the Iroquois Dream Quest," *American Journal of Psychiatry*, 116:2.

CASSIRER, ERNST

1946 *Language and Myth*. New York: Harper & Bros.

CHAMBERS, ROBERT

1845 *Vestiges of the Natural History of Creation*. London: Churchill.

CHAPPLE, ELIOT D., and COON, CARLETON S.

1942 *Principles of Anthropology*. New York: Holt.

CLEMENTS, FOREST E.

1932 *Primitive Concepts of Disease*. Berkeley: University of California Publications in American Archaeology and Ethnology, Vol. 32, No. 2.

CLODD, EDWARD

1905 *Animism: The Seed of Religion*. London: Archibald Constable.

COHEN, YEHUDI

1964 *The Transition from Childhood to Adolescence*. Chicago: Aldine.

CZAPLICKA, M. A.

1914 *Aboriginal Siberia: A Study in Social Anthropology*. Oxford: Clarendon Press.

DARWIN, CHARLES

1846 *Journal of Researches into the Natural History and Geology of the Countries Visited During the Voyage of* H.M.S. Beagle *Round the World*. New York: Harper & Bros. (2 vols.).

1859 *The Origin of Species by Means of Natural Selection; or, The Preservation of Favored Races in the Struggle for Life*. New York: Modern Library, 1936.

1863 *The Descent of Man and Selection in Relation to Sex*. New York: Modern Library, 1936.

DARWIN, FRANCIS (ed.)

1863 *The Life and Letters of Charles Darwin, Including an Autobiographical Chapter*. New York: D. Appleton.

DARWIN, FRANCIS, and SEWARD, A. C. (eds.)
1903 *More Letters of Charles Darwin*. New York: D. Appleton.

DAWSON, CHRISTOPHER
1958 *Religion and Culture*. New York: World, Meridian Books.

DEARDORFF, MERLE
1951 "The Religion of Handsome Lake," in W. N. Fenton (ed.), *Symposium on Local Diversity in Iroquois Culture*. Washington: Bureau of American Ethnology, Bulletin 149.

DEREN, MAYA
1953 *Divine Horsemen: The Living Gods of Haiti*. London and New York: Thames and Hudson.

DEVORE, IRVEN
1962 *Social Behavior and Organization of Baboons*. Unpublished doctoral dissertation, University of Chicago.

Dictionary of National Biography. Oxford University Press. London: Humphrey Milford.

DU BOIS, CORA
1944 *The People of Alor*. Minneapolis: University of Minnesota Press.

DUNDES, ALAN
1964 *The Morphology of North American Indian Folktales*. Helsinki: FF Communications, Academica Scientarum Fennica, Vol. 81, No. 195.

DURKHEIM, ÉMILE
1912 *The Elementary Forms of the Religious Life*. New York: Collier Books, 1961.

EISELEY, LOREN
1959 "Charles Darwin, Edward Blyth and the Theory of Natural Selection," *Proceedings of the American Philosophical Society*, 103:94–158.

ELIADE, MIRCEA
1949a *The Myth of the Eternal Return*. Trans. by Willard R. Trask. New York: Pantheon Books, 1954.

1949b *Patterns in Comparative Religion.* Trans. by Rosemary Sheet. New York: Sheed and Ward, 1958.

1950 "Shamanism," in Ferm Vergilius (ed.), *Ancient Religions.* New York: Philosophical Library.

1958 *Birth and Rebirth; The Religious Meanings of Initiation in Human Culture.* Trans. by Willard R. Trask. New York: Harper & Row.

FABER, GEOFFREY

1933 *Oxford Apostles.* London: Penguin Books, 1954.

FENTON, WILLIAM N.

1936 "An Outline of Seneca Ceremonies at Coldspring Longhouse," *Yale University Publications in Anthropology,* No. 9.

1940 "Masked Medicine Societies of the Iroquois," in Smithsonian Report for 1940, pp. 397–430. Washington, D.C.: Smithsonian Institution.

1946 "An Iroquois Condolence Council for Installing Cayuga Chiefs in 1945," *Journal of the Washington Academy of Sciences,* 36:110–127.

FERM, VERGILIUS (ed.)

1945 *An Encyclopedia of Religion.* New York: Philosophical Library.

1950 *Ancient Religions.* New York: Philosophical Library.

FESTINGER, LEON

1957 *A Theory of Cognitive Dissonance.* Evanston, Ill.: Row, Peterson.

FESTINGER, LEON, RIECKEN, H. W., and SCHACHTER, H.

1956 *When Prophecy Fails.* Minneapolis: University of Minnesota Press.

FRAZER, JAMES

1911–1915 *The Golden Bough.* London: Macmillan (12 vols.); New York: Macmillan, 1922 (abridged one vol. ed.).

FREUD, SIGMUND

1907 "Obsessive Acts and Religious Practices," in Ernest Jones (ed.), *Collected Papers,* Vol. 2. Trans. under supervision of Joan Riviere. London: Hogarth Press and Institute of Psycho-analysis, 1924 (5 vols.).

1911 "Psycho-analytic Notes upon an Autobiographical Account of a Case of Paranoia (Dementia Paranoides)," in Ernest Jones (ed.), *Collected Papers*, Vol. 3. Trans. by Alix and James Strachey. London: Hogarth Press and Institute of Psycho-analysis, 1925.

1913 *Totem and Taboo*. New York: Norton, 1952.

1928 *The Future of an Illusion*. London: Hogarth Press, 1949.

1939 *Moses and Monotheism*. New York: Vintage Books, 1955.

1947 *Freud on War, Sex, and Neurosis*. Sander Katz (ed.) Trans. by Joan Riviere. New York: Garden City Publishing Co., 1949.

FROMM, ERICH

1950 *Psychoanalysis and Religion*. New Haven: Yale University Press.

1951 *The Forgotten Language*. New York: Rinehart.

GEARING, FRED

1958 "The Structural Poses of 18th Century Cherokee Villages," *American Anthropologist*, 60:1148–1157.

GILLIN, JOHN

1948 "Magical Fright," *Psychiatry*, 11:387–400.

GLUCKMAN, MAX

1954 *Rituals of Rebellion in South-East Africa*. Manchester: Manchester University Press.

GOFFMAN, ERVING

1956 "The Nature of Deference and Demeanor," *American Anthropologist*, 58:473–502.

1959 *The Presentation of Self in Everyday Life*. Garden City, N.Y.: Anchor Books.

1961 *Asylums: Essays on the Social Situation of Mental Patients and Other Inmates*. Garden City, N.Y.: Anchor Books.

GOODALL, JANE M.

1963 "My Life among Wild Chimpanzees," *National Geographic*, Vol. 124, No. 2.

GOODE, WILLIAM J.

1951 *Religion in Primitive Society*. New York: Free Press of Glencoe.

GOODENOUGH, ERWIN R.

1931 *The Church in the Roman Empire*. New York: Holt.

1965 *Psychology of Religious Experiences*. New York: Basic Books.

GOODENOUGH, RUTH

1954 *The Development of Christianity*, ms.

GOODENOUGH, WARD H.

1963a "Some Applications of Guttman Scale Analysis to Ethnography and Culture Theory," *Southwestern Journal of Anthropology*, 19:235–250.

1963b *Cooperation in Change*. New York: Russell Sage Foundation.

1964 (Ed.), *Explorations in Cultural Anthropology*. New York: McGraw-Hill.

1965 "Rethinking 'Status' and 'Role': Toward a General Model of the Cultural Organization of Social Relationships," No. 1 *The Relevance of Models for Social Anthropology*, Association of Social Anthropologists Monographs. London: Tavistock Publications.

HALLOWELL, A. I.

1926 "Bear Ceremonialism in the Northern Hemisphere," *American Anthropologist*, 28:1–175.

1942 *The Role of Conjuring in Salteaux Society*. Vol. 2, Philadelphia: University of Pennsylvania Press.

1955 *Culture and Experience*. Philadelphia: University of Pennsylvania Press.

HAMMOND, PETER B. (ed.)

1964 *Cultural and Social Anthropology*. New York: Macmillan.

HARING, DOUGLAS G.

1948 *Personal Character and Cultural Milieu: A Collection of Readings*. Syracuse: Syracuse University Press.

Harper, Edward B. (ed.)
1965 *Religion in South Asia.* Seattle: University of Washington Press.

Harris, Marvin
1964 *The Nature of Cultural Things.* New York: Random House.

Harrison, Jane
1903 *Prolegomena to the Study of Greek Religion.* New York: World, Meridian Books, 1955.

Heine-Geldern, Robert
1964 "One Hundred Years of Ethnological Theory in the German-Speaking Countries: Some Milestones," *Current Anthropology,* 5:407–418.

Herskovits, Melville J.
1938 *Dahomey.* New York: J. J. Augustin.

Hoffer, Eric
1951 *The True Believer: Thoughts on the Nature of Mass Movements.* New York: Harper.

Homans, George C.
1941 "Anxiety and Ritual: The Theories of Malinowski and Radcliffe-Brown," *American Anthropologist,* 43: 163–172.

Honigmann, John J.
1959 *The World of Man.* New York: Harper.

Howells, William
1948 *The Heathens: Primitive Man and His Religions.* Garden City, N.Y.: Doubleday.

Hsu, Francis L. K.
1952 *Religion, Science and Human Crises.* London: Routledge & Kegan Paul.
1961 (Ed.), *Psychological Anthropology: Approaches to Culture and Personality.* Homewood, Ill.: Dorsey Press.

Huxley, Aldous
1952 *The Devils of Loudun.* New York: Harper & Bros.

Huxley, Julian
1941 *Religion Without Revelation.* New York: Harper & Bros., 1957; London: Watts, Thinkers Library, 1941.

Hyman, Stanley E.

1955 "The Ritual View of Myth and the Mystic," *Journal of American Folklore,* 68:462–472.

James, William

1902 *The Varieties of Religious Experience.* New York: Longmans Green.

Jensen, Adolf E.

1951 *Myth and Cult Among Primitive Peoples.* Trans. from the German by Marianna Tax Choldin and Wolfgang Weissleder. Chicago: University of Chicago Press, 1963.

Jung, Carl G.

1938 *Psychology and Religion.* New Haven: Yale University Press.

Jung, Carl G., and Kerényi, Karl

1949 *Essays on a Science of Mythology.* New York: Pantheon Books, Bollingen Series XXII, 1949.

Kaplan, Bert (ed.)

1961 *Studying Personality Cross-Culturally.* Evanston, Ill.: Row, Peterson.

Kardiner, Abram, and Linton, Ralph

1939 *The Individual and His Society.* New York: Columbia University Press.

1945 *The Psychological Frontiers of Society.* New York: Columbia University Press.

Kenton, Edna (ed.)

1927 *The Indians of North America.* New York: Harcourt, Brace (2 vols.).

Kilpatrick, J. F., and Kilpatrick, A. G.

1964 "Cherokee Burn Conjurations," *Journal of the Graduate Research Center,* 33:17–21.

Kluckhohn, Clyde

1936 "Some Reflections on the Method and Theory of the Kulturkreislehre," *American Anthropologist,* 38: 157–196.

1942 "Myths and Rituals: A General Theory," *Harvard Theological Review,* Vol. 35, No. 1.

1944 *Navaho Witchcraft*. Cambridge: Peabody Museum Papers, No. 22.

KOPYTOFF, IGOR

1964 "Classifications of Religious Movements: Analytical and Synthetic," in Melford E. Spiro (ed.), *Symposium on New Approaches to the Study of Religion*. American Ethnological Society Proceedings.

KRAMER, SAMUEL NOAH

1956 *From The Tablets of Sumer*. Indian Hills, Colo.: Falcon Wing Press.

LACK, D.

1943 *The Life of the Robin*. London: Penguin Books, 1946 (4th rev. ed. 1953).

1959 "Some Correlates of Beliefs in the Malevolence and Benevolence of Super-natural Beings: A Cross-societal Study," *Journal of Abnormal and Social Psychology*, 58:162–169.

LANG, ANDREW

1898 *The Making of Religion*. London: Longmans Green.

LANTERNARI, VITTORIO

1960 *The Religions of the Oppressed: A Study of Modern Messianic Cults*. New York: Knopf.

LANTIS, MARGARET

1950a "The Religion of the Eskimos," in V. Ferm (ed.), *Ancient Religions*. New York: Philosophical Library.

1950b "The Symbol of a New Religion," *Psychiatry*, 13: 101–113.

LEACH, EDMUND R.

1961 "Lévi-Strauss in the Garden of Eden: An Examination of Some Recent Developments in the Analysis of Myth," *Transactions of the New York Academy of Sciences*, Series 2, 23:386–396.

LEEMON, THOMAS

1965 "Fraternity Initiation as a Rite of Passage: a Description of a Study in Progress." Ms.

LESLIE, CHARLES (ed.)
1960 *Anthropology of Folk Religion.* New York: Vintage Books.

LESSA, WILLIAM A., and VOGT, EVON Z.
1958 *Reader in Comparative Religion.* Evanston, Ill.: Row, Peterson, 1965 (2nd ed.).

LÉVI-STRAUSS, CLAUDE
1955 "The Structural Study of Myth," *Journal of American Folklore,* 68:428–444.

LEVINE, ROBERT A.
1962 "Witchcraft and Co-Wife Proximity in Southwestern Kenya," *Ethnology,* 1:39–45.

LEVY, GERTRUDE
1946 *The Gate of Horn.* London: Faber & Faber.

LÉVY-BRUHL, LUCIEN
1910 *Primitive Mentality.* Trans. by Lilian A. Clare. New York: Macmillan, 1923.

LINTON, RALPH
1943 "Nativistic Movements," *American Anthropologist,* 45:230–240.

LITCHFIELD, HENRIETTA (ed.)
1915 *Emma Darwin, A Century of Family Letters, 1792–1896.* London: Murray (2 vols.).

LORENZ, KONRAD
1903 *King Solomon's Ring.* Trans. by M. Wilson. New York: Crowell, 1952.

LOVEJOY, ARTHUR
1936 *The Great Chain of Being.* Cambridge: Harvard University Press, 1948.

LOWIE, ROBERT H.
1924 *Primitive Religion.* New York: Liveright Publishing Corp., 1948 (new ed.).

LÖWITH, KARL
1949 *Meaning in History.* Chicago: University of Chicago Press.

LYELL, CHARLES
1830–1833 *The Principles of Geology*. London: Murray (3 vols.).

LYELL, MRS.
1881 *Life, Letters and Journals of Sir Charles Lyell, Bart.* London: Murray.

MALINOWSKI, BRONISLAW
1925 *Magic, Science, and Religion*. Garden City, N.Y.: Doubleday, 1955 (new ed.).
1926 *Myth in Primitive Psychology*. New York: Norton.
1927 *Coral Gardens and Their Magic*. London: Routledge and Kegan Paul.

MALTHUS, T. R.
1798 *An Essay on the Principle of Population*. Georgetown, D.C.: C. Cruikshank.

MANNHEIM, KARL
1929 *Ideology and Utopia*. New York: Harvest Books, 1936 (new ed.).

MARETT, R. R.
1909 *The Threshold of Religion*. London: Methuen.

MARINGER, J.
1960 *The Gods of Prehistoric Man*. Trans. from the German by Mary Ilford. London: Weidenfeld & Nicholson.

MARRIOTT, MCKIM (ed.)
1955 *Village India: Studies in the Little Community*. Chicago: University of Chicago Press.

MCCLELLAND, DAVID G., and FRIEDMAN, G. A.
1952 "A Cross-Cultural Study of the Relationship Between Child-Training Practices and Achievement Motivation Appearing in Folk Tales," in E. Maccoby, T. M. Newcomb, and E. L. Hartley (eds.), *Readings in Social Psychology*. New York: Holt.

MEAD, MARGARET
1956 *New Lives for Old*. New York: Morrow.
1960 "A New Framework for Studies of Folklore & Survivals," in Anthony F. C. Wallace (ed.), *Men and*

Cultures: Proceedings of the Fifth International Congress of Anthropological and Ethnological Sciences. Philadelphia: University of Pennsylvania Press.

MERTON, ROBERT

1938 "Social Structure and Anomie," *American Sociological Review*, 3:672–682.

1949 "Manifest and Latent Functions," in *Social Theory and Social Structure*. New York: Free Press of Glencoe.

MÉTRAUX, ALFRED

1959 *Voodoo in Haiti*. Trans. by Hugo Charteris. New York: Oxford University Press.

MIDDLETON, JOHN

1955 "The Concept of Bewitching in Lugbara," *Africa*, 25:252–260.

MOONEY, JAMES

1896 *The Ghost Dance Religion and the Sioux Outbreak of 1890*. Fourteenth Annual Report of the Bureau of Ethnology, Part 2. Washington, D.C.: Government Printing Office.

MOORE, OMAR K.

1957 "Divination—A New Perspective," *American Anthropologist*, 59:69–74.

MÜLLER, F. MAX

1892 *Anthropological Religion*. London: Longmans Green.

MURRAY, MARGARET

1921 *The Witch Cult of Western Europe; A Study in Anthropology*. Oxford: Clarendon Press.

1937 *The God of the Witches*. Garden City, N.Y.: Anchor Books.

MURDOCK, GEORGE P.

1949 *Social Structure*. New York: Macmillan.

NADEL, S. F.

1946 "Study of Shamanism in the Nuba Mountains," *Journal of the Royal Anthropological Institute*, 76:25–37.

NAGEL, ERNEST

1952 "Problems of Concept and Theory Formation in the Social Sciences," in Maurice Natanson (ed.), *Philosophy of the Social Sciences*. New York: Random House.

NORBECK, EDWARD

1961 *Religion in Primitive Society*. New York: Harper & Row.

1963 "African Rituals of Conflict," *American Anthropologist*, 65:1254–1279.

NOTTINGHAM, ELIZABETH

1954 *Religion and Society*. New York: Random House.

OATES, WAYNE E.

1955 *Religious Factors in Mental Illness*. New York: Association Press.

OESTERREICH, T. K.

1930 *Possession*. New York: Smith.

PARKER, ARTHUR C.

1913 *The Code of Handsome Lake, The Seneca Prophet*. Albany: New York State Museum Bulletin, No. 163.

PARSONS, TALCOTT

n.d. *Religious Perspectives of College Teaching*. New Haven, Conn.: Edw. W. Hazen Foundation.

1944 "The Theoretical Development of the Sociology of Religion: A Chapter in the History of Modern Social Sciences," *Journal of the History of Ideas*, 5:176–190.

PERRY, WILLIAM JAMES

1923 *Children of the Sun; A Study in the Early History of Civilization*. London: Methuen, 1927 (2nd. ed., rev.).

PLATT, JOHN R.

n.d. *The Step to Man*, ms.

PORTMANN, ADOLF

1961 *Animals as Social Beings*. New York: Viking Press.

PROPP, V.

1958 *Morphology of the Folktale*. Philadelphia: American Folklore Society.

Radcliffe-Brown, A.
1933 *The Andaman Islanders.* Cambridge: Cambridge University Press.

Radin, Paul
1927 *Primitive Man as Philosopher.* New York: Dover.
1937 *Primitive Religion; Its Nature and Origin.* New York: Dover.
1956 *The Trickster: A Study in American Indian Mythology.* New York: Philosophical Library.

Raglan, Lord
1936 *The Hero: A Study in Tradition, Myth and Drama.* New York: Vintage Books, 1956.
1949 *The Origins of Religion.* London: Watts.

Rank, Otto
1914 *The Myth of the Birth of the Hero.* New York: Robert Brunner, 1952.

Redfield, Robert
1952 "The Primitive World View," *Proceedings of the American Philosophical Society,* 96:30–36.

Reik, Theodor
1931 *Ritual: Psycho-Analytic Studies.* London: Hogarth Press and Institute of Psycho-analysis.

Roheim, Geza
1943 *The Origin and Function of Culture.* New York: Nervous and Mental Disease Monographs, No. 69.

Sargant, William
1957 *Battle for the Mind.* Garden City, N.Y.: Doubleday.

Schaller, George B.
1963 *The Mountain Gorilla.* Chicago: University of Chicago Press.

Schmidt, Wilhelm
1931 *The Origin and Growth of Religion.* London: Methuen.

Schneider, Louis
1964 *Religion, Culture, and Society: A Reader in the Sociology of Religion.* New York: John Wiley; London: Sydney.

SCHREBER, DANIEL P.
1903 *Memoirs of My Nervous Illness*. Trans. and ed. by Ida Macalpine and Richard A. Hunter. London: Dawson.

SCHURMAN, J. G.
1888 *The Ethical Import of Darwinism*. New York: Scribner's.

SCHWARTZ, THEODORE
1962 *The Paliau Movement in the Admiralty Islands, 1946–1954*. New York: Anthropological Papers of the American Museum of Natural History, Vol. 49, Pt. 2.

SCHWEITZER, ALBERT
1906 *The Quest of the Historical Jesus, A Critical Study of its Progress from Reimarus to Wrede*. Trans. by W. Montgomery. New York: Macmillan, 1948.
1958 *The Psychiatric Study of Jesus*. Boston: Beacon Press.

SEARS, ROBERT
1943 *Survey of Objective Studies of Psychoanalytic Concepts*. New York: Social Science Research Council.

SELYE, HANS
1950 *The Physiology and Pathology of Exposure to Stress; A Treatise Based on the Concepts of the General-Adaptation-Syndrome and the Diseases of Adaptation*. Montreal: Acta.

SELYE, HANS, and FORTIER, C.
1950 "Adaptive Reactions to Stress," *Psychosomatic Medicine*, 12:149–157.

SIDMAN, MURRAY
1960 "Normal Sources of Pathological Behavior," *Science*, 132:61–68.

SIMMONS, LEO W.
1937 "Statistical Correlations in the Science of Society," in G. P. Murdock (ed.), *Studies in the Science of Society*. New Haven: Yale University Press.

SINGER, MILTON (ed.)
1959 *Traditional India: Structure and Change*. Phila-

delphia: Publications of the American Folklore Society, Bibliographical Series, Vol. X.

SKINNER, B. F.

1948 "Superstition in the Pigeon," *Journal of Experimental Psychology*, 38:168–172.

SKINNER, B. F., and MORSE, W. H.

1957 "A Second Type of 'Superstition' in the Pigeon," *American Journal of Psychology*, 70:308–311.

SLOTKIN, J. S.

1952 *Menomini Peyotism, a Study of Individual Variation in a Primary Group with a Homogeneous Culture.* Philadelphia: American Philosophical Society, 1952.

SPECK, FRANK G.

1935 *Naskapi: The Savage Hunters of the Labrador Peninsula.* Norman: University of Oklahoma Press.

1949 *Midwinter Rites of the Cayuga Long House.* Philadelphia: University of Pennsylvania Press.

SPENCE, LEWIS

1944 *The Outlines of Mythology.* New York: Fawcett Publications; London: Watts, 1944.

SPIRO, MELFORD

1952 "Ghosts, Ifaluk, and Teleological Functionalism," *American Anthropologist*, 54:497–503.

1964 (Ed.), *Symposium on New Approaches to the Study of Religion.* Seattle: University of Washington Press (for the American Ethnological Society).

SPIRO, MELFORD, and D'ANDRADE, ROY G.

1958 "A Cross-Cultural Study of Some Supernatural Beliefs," *American Anthropologist*, 60:456–466.

STEPHEN, LESLIE

1900 *The English Utilitarians.* London: Duckworth (3 vols.).

SWANSON, GUY E.

1960 *The Birth of the Gods: The Origin of Primitive Beliefs.* Ann Arbor: University of Michigan Press.

THRUPP, SYLVIA (ed.)
1962 *Millenial Dreams in Action.* The Hague: Mouton.

TITIEV, MISCHA
1960 "A Fresh Approach to the Problem of Magic and Religion," *Southwestern Journal of Anthropology,* 16:292–298.

TYLOR, EDWARD B.
1871 *Primitive Culture.* London: Murray.

UNDERHILL, EVELYN
1955 *Mysticism: A Study in the Nature and Development of Man's Spiritual Consciousness.* New York: Noonday Press.

VAN GENNEP, ARNOLD
1908 *The Rites of Passage.* With an introduction by Solon T. Kimball. Chicago: University of Chicago Press, 1960.

VOGET, FRED
1956 "The American Indian in Transition," *American Anthropologist,* 58:249–263.

VOGT, EVON Z.
1952 "Water Witching: An Interpretation of a Ritual Pattern in a Rural American Community," *Scientific Monthly,* 75:175–186.

WACH, JOACHIM
1944 *The Sociology of Religion.* Chicago: University of Chicago Press.
1951 *Types of Religious Experience.* Chicago: University of Chicago Press.
1958 *The Comparative Study of Religions.* Edited by Joseph M. Kitagawa. New York: Columbia University Press, 1961 (paper).

WALLACE, ANTHONY F. C.
1956 "Revitalization Movements," *American Anthropologist,* 58:264–281.
1958a "The Dekanawidah Myth Analyzed as the Record of a Revitalization Movement," *Ethnohistory,* 5:118–130.

1958b "Dreams and the Wishes of the Soul: A Type of Psychoanalytic Theory Among the Seventeenth Century Iroquois,"*American Anthropologist*, 60:234–248.

1959 "Cultural Determinants of Response to Hallucinatory Experience," A.M.A. *Archives of General Psychiatry*, 1:58–69.

1961a *Culture and Personality*. New York: Random House.

1961b *Religious Revitalization: A Function of Religion in Human History and Evolution* (pamphlet). Boston: Institute on Religion in an Age of Science.

WALLACE, ANTHONY F. C., and FOGELSON, RAY

1965 "The Identity Struggle," in Ivan Boszormenyi-Nagy and James Framo (eds.), *Intensive Family Therapy*. New York: Harper & Row.

WALLIS, WILSON D.

1943 *Messiahs: Their Role in Civilization*. Washington: American Council on Public Affairs.

WEBER, MAX

1904 *The Protestant Ethic and the Spirit of Capitalism*. London: Allen & Unwin, 1930.

WEBSTER, HUTTON

1908 *Primitive Secret Societies, A Study in Early Politics and Religion*. New York: Macmillan.

WEST, GEOFFREY

1938 *Charles Darwin, A Portrait*. New Haven: Yale University Press.

WHITING, BEATRICE

1950 *Paiute Sorcery*. New York: Viking Fund Publications in Anthropology, No. 15.

WHITING, JOHN W. M.

1961 "Socialization Process and Personality," in F. L. K. Hsu (ed.), *Psychological Anthropology*. Homewood, Ill.: Dorsey Press.

WHITING, JOHN W. M., and CHILD, IRVIN

1953 *Child Training and Personality: A Cross-Cultural Study*. New Haven and London: Yale University Press.

WHITING, JOHN W. M., KLUCKHOHN, RICHARD, and ANTHONY, ALBERT S.

1958 "The Function of Male Initiation Ceremonies at Puberty," in E. Maccoby, T. Newcomb, and E. Hartley (eds.), *Readings in Social Psychology*. New York: Holt.

WORSLEY, PETER

1957 *The Trumpet Shall Sound: A Study of Cargo Cults in Melanesia*. London: MacGibbon & Kee.

YOUNG, FRANK W.

1962 "The Function of Male Initiation Ceremonies: A Cross-Cultural Test of an Alternative Hypothesis," *American Journal of Sociology*, 67:379–396.

1965 *Initiation Ceremonies: A Cross-Cultural Study of Status Dramatization*. Indianapolis: Bobbs-Merrill.

Index

About the Author

ANTHONY F. C. WALLACE: Professor of Anthropology, the University of Pennsylvania; Medical Research Scientist, Eastern Pennsylvania Psychiatric Institute. A consultant to several government advisory commissions, Dr. Wallace has also served as a member of the Behavioral Sciences Division, National Research Council. Among his other books are *Teedyuscung, King of the Delawares* (1949) and *Culture and Personality* (1961). He is currently at work on a biography of Handsome Lake, visionary prophet of a revitalization movement among the Iroquois Indians of New York State in the early nineteenth century.

A Note on the Type

The text of this book is set in Electra, a typeface designed by W(illiam) A(ddison) Dwiggins for the Mergenthaler Linotype Company and first made available in 1935. Electra cannot be classified as either "modern" or "old style." It is not based on any historical model, and hence does not echo any particular period or style of type design. It avoids the extreme contrast between "thick" and "thin" elements that marks most modern faces, and is without eccentricities which catch the eye and interfere with reading. In general, Electra is a simple, readable typeface which attempts to give a feeling of fluidity, power, and speed.

W. A. DWIGGINS (1880–1956) was born in Martinsville, Ohio, and studied art in Chicago. In 1904 he moved to Hingham, Massachusetts, where he built a solid reputation as a designer of advertisements and as a calligrapher. He began an association with the Mergenthaler Linotype Company in 1929, and over the next twenty-seven years designed a number of book types, of which Metro, Electra, and Caledonia have been used very widely. In 1930 Dwiggins became interested in marionettes, and through the years made many important contributions to the art of puppetry and the design of marionettes.